The Light is always with us.

Also by Anderson Reed

*Lightseeds: A Compendium of Ancient and
Contemporary Crystal Knowledge* (with Wabun Wind)

Shouting at the Wolf

A Guide to Identifying and Warding Off Evil in Everyday Life

Anderson Reed

Library of the Mystic Arts
A Citadel Press Book
Published by Carol Publishing Group

Copyright © 1990 by Anderson Reed

A Citadel Press Book
Published by Carol Publishing Group

Editorial Offices
600 Madison Avenue
New York, NY 10022

Sales & Distribution Offices
120 Enterprise Avenue
Secaucus, NJ 07094

In Canada: Musson Book Company
A division of General Publishing Co. Limited
Don Mills, Ontario

Manufactured in the United States of America

Library of Congress Cataloging-in-Publication Data

Reed, Anderson, 1945–
    Shouting at the wolf : a guide to identifying and warding off evil
in everyday life / Anderson Reed.
        p.   cm.—(Library of the mystic arts)
    "A Citadel Press book."
    ISBN 0-8065-1170-2 : $11.95
    1. Good and evil. 2. Occultism. 3. New Age movement.   I. Title
II. Series.
BF1439.R44   1990   90-40166
133—dc20   CIP

For the *uwe kahunas*, the weeping priests of our ancient past, exiled long ago by materialism and conglomerate religion. These women and men were to the human kingdom what devic powers are to the stone, plant and animal kingdoms, and we need them desperately.

If we learn to honor the gift of their wisdom, they may come back to us. Let us pray they do before it is too late.

The events described here all happened, though I have telescoped some of the action for purposes of clear narration. The identities of people and places have, in some instances, been changed to protect the privacy of those involved.

Contents

PART I

The Broken Vow:
Evil and Human Evolution

Chapter 1

The Lost Way:
How the Circle Was Broken

Hope is the thing with feathers
That perches in the soul,
And sings the tune without the words
And never stops at all.

—"Hope Is The Thing With Feathers," Emily Dickinson

I am sitting at my desk staring at an appeal for money sent by a charity that seeks to heal the wounds we human beings have inflicted on the earth. In this letter, the world I live in is referred to as "the environment." The environment is in trouble. I am asked to send money to help repair what I and the other people on this planet have done to harm our host, the earth.

Environment, indeed. Everything that is wrong with the human race, its treatment of itself, its treatment of the earth, cannot be illustrated better than by the use of this term. All the great sweep of life, the delicately-made insects, the trees who outlive us by a hundred years and more, the awesome variety of furred and feathered creatures, the elementary powers and majestic stones, every living entity the Creator has manifested

3

here is merely "environment," a stage set, a backdrop for the activities of the human race! Environment!

Where better to find the clue that we long ago lost our way here than by looking to the terms *environment* and *weather?* The infinite variations of the sky, which used to offer human-kind information about planting, about the day's spritual mood—for Nature has moods, as we do—the flight of birds that told us, not merely where the birds were headed, but also why . . . changes in plant life . . . these flashes of the Creator are now mere background, secondary to human concerns, noticed only when they inconvenience us.

Our ancestors of all races listened to the winds, heard the voices of birds, read messages in the movement of the seasons. They felt the urgency of thunder, the blessing of lightning. They did not have to study aboriginal ways and investigate the rituals of "primitive" peoples, because our ancestors, unlike us, were not wallflowers at the dance of life. We did not, in times gone by, need to study shamanism from the intellectual point of view because the shaman's gift for moving beyond time, the medicine woman's ability to see the life around us as individuated parts of the sacred Whole, were the foundation and the guides of our lives. Knowing better than to let the mind lead the spirit, we would have found the notion of study-ing our connectedness with the all-life a ludicrous thing because it *is* ludicrous. It is normal to live with, and not dis-tinct from, the all-life. The idea of occasionally moving out of our isolation into contrived meetings with the spiritual forces in our world, so that we may temporarily join the swim of life, is madness. Such forays into what is real, taken as desperate attempts to heal our collective madness, is itself a symptom of insanity. The elements of living that many people now study as a sometime pursuit would have formed the basis of our lives—all of us, genders, races and religions, holding this foundation, and perhaps only this foundation, in common.

The dance of life continued, in the old days, without our having to be prodded to join in, without its being spoken about, because there was then no need to take special notice of what ought to come to our attention naturally.

Imagine a woman of the 5th century having to attend a workshop in order to learn how to read the morning sky, or a man wondering if the unusually early appearance of butterflies one summer had anything to tell him. If there was rain, it was given its due as a living entity, not slighted as mere "weather," as though the activities of the God-in-all exist only and exclusively as they affect human concerns. All of life had its existence apart from us, its own integrity-of-being, and this was known and respected.

Because we have electricity, the difference between night and day does not concern us very much. We wash our clothes in machines, so the nearby stream goes unnoticed unless it is polluted by an oil spill and we are inconvenienced by having to buy bottled water. We see our world only when it gets in our way. It's summer because it is uncomfortably hot, and winter because we must shovel snow. It's raining, so we cannot wear our open-toe shoes. It's fall, and we must be wary of bees.

And what are bees? The ancient Maya people, in attempting to represent, in their artwork, the ineffable, unrepresentable God, chose a bee to represent the Creator, for without bees, a great deal of our food and medicine would not exist. In our time, bees are enemies, to be sprayed or swatted if they approach us, invaders whose presence in our home is a threat.

Having banished from our lives nearly all of creation, we have placed ourselves in an adversarial relationship to the entire planet. What comes to our notice does so only because it inflicts itself on us, not because we welcome its company. When we can manage to avoid all notice of the life around us, we do, and consider ourselves fortunate: the life of water and air, of the trees and stones and animals has nothing to do with us except when it brings us trouble. To be touched by the life that shares this planet with us is to be inconvenienced, afflicted, attacked.

Since humankind became enamoured of its intellect and, in consequence, enslaved itself to its inventions, we have created machinery to separate us, little by little and then in great leaps, from contact with creation. Our cars move us around so fast that we don't see much of the world we drive through. We don't form relationships with the all-life, not even for a moment or two before we kill it. We don't know which trees were used to build our houses because someone builds them for us. We don't see alive the chicken we eat for dinner. We neither mine the gems we wear nor pick the flowers that decorate our homes. We don't carve our babies' cribs or make our parents' caskets. We buy our pets from stores. We fly high over the world in jets, seeing only the city we take off from, the city we land in, and geometric patterns of earth in between.

In losing daily contact with the energies that pervade and animate this realm, we have created for ourselves an unnatural relationship with the all-life, and we have already begun, as an evolutionary consequence, to lose our senses. We don't keep our psychic sense much beyond early childhood. We don't hear the words of the wind anymore, or the messages of the birds. We neither hear nor see the all-life because we have turned away from it and, in a very real way, also turned away from ourselves, because the force that animates and forms stones and water is the same force that animates and forms human beings. In losing touch with the life surrounding us, we have lost contact with the God-in-all and, therefore, with ourselves.

This turning away from the all-life, from creation as it evolves into destruction and then into creation again, has cut us off from the lessons of physical evolution. We have long for-gotten that we have teachers, teachers in volcanoes and lighten-ing, teachers in the sea and earth. Our teachers continue evolv-ing, but they cannot teach us what we are no longer present to learn.

We have tried to fill the awful void by focusing attention on ourselves, by chattering among ourselves because we no longer have anyone except ourselves to talk with. We cannot accom-modate quiet because we don't understand it, so we chatter. We chatter on the phone. We chatter by reading too much. We chatter by watching television. We chatter by creating and then slavishly following endless, sterile intellectual theories about

The Way Things Are. In falling in love with our theories, we have reached the point where we now believe that we are the world. Why not? Since we have learned to ignore the entire realm of creation, why shouldn't we believe we're alone here? But we are not the world, and at this juncture, considering the assault we have made on the air and water, the earth, plants and animals, even on the atmosphere surrounding the planet, we're lucky we are still permitted to live here at all. The grace of the all-life must be awesome indeed, for it has been patient with us, but how much longer can this patience last when, every day, we kill some aspect of life, every day, we try to obliterate whatever vestige of sense remains in our species.

Will the other inhabitants of the earth decide to get rid of us? The minerals, plants and animals can get along fine without us, as can the elementary powers. If humankind is the dependent species it is, our position at the top of the food chain is evidence of dependence rather than importance, then why should our companions here continue to put up with us? They don't need us; it is we who need them for our survival. We seem to be entirely unnecessary here.

But are we unnecessary? Is it possible that, despite appearances, the fourth kingdom has a role to play here? That while we seem not to have any gifts to give the other three kingdoms, there may be something as yet undiscovered about the human race? Do we have a purpose we are not aware of? Is there an even more intricate relationship among the life forms here than is apparent, and is the human race a viable, even a necessary, part of the all-life? If so, then how can we come to understand our place in the scheme of things?

The answer lies in what C.G. Jung named the collective unconscious. I believe that, however Jung meant it, the term "collective unconscious" is perfect to describe an essential, sacred, working component of the human race. This aspect is a living awareness, one that transcends language, belief and behavior, and which remains constant and *functioning* from one generation to another. This living awareness maintains itself without our conscious knowledge that it exists. Most important, it remains unchanged whether we scrutinize its contents or not.

Some people have interpreted this level of awareness as an aggregate of anachronistic information about our past rituals and beliefs, a pool from which we get strange dreams and current superstitions. The collective unconscious consists, they say, of disconnected, leftover threads from our ancient past and has importance only to mystics, anthropologists and ritualists. It is a kind of blurred archeological map of where we used to be.

Nothing could be more mistaken. The collective unconscious is not vestigial memory. It is our guiding power. This force contains the totality of memory of the human race—past and future memory. It contains, as well, the story of evolution on this realm, the evolution of human beings and all the other life here. It is not merely a record of the past but a vital and vitalizing power that reflects everything important to the history and progress of anything living on the earth.

And it is more: It is a sacred vow, a promise made by all human souls to participate as much as each can in the evolution of the species, and to respect the evolutionary needs of all our fellow journeyers here. This vow is meant to keep us aware of our purpose, our potential, and our obligations. The power of this reservoir propels us. The information within it, if we are attuned to it, prevents our veering from our collective path.

All the deepest feelings in humankind have their source in the reservoir of the collective unconscious. When we turn away from our common vow, we feel anguish. This anguish, and our inability to comprehend it with our waking consciousness, leads to bizarre behavior of every type.

As individuated parts of the Whole we are bound by the vow and tied to one another by it and by the commonality of remembering where we have been and where we are supposed to be headed. No one incarnating as a human being does so without making a full commitment to the sacred vow that informs and guides the human species. It is not possible to enter into human life as a casual journey; everyone entering into human life makes, before he is born here, a sacred, enlivening promise to join his energies with the fundamental purposes and obligations of humankind. Human incarnation is not simply an opportunity to learn, but rather an obligation to participate in humankind's condition, purpose, and responsibilities.

When many people diverge from the essential knowledge and guiding force of the collective unconscious, schisms are caused. The recognition of such a schism is what happened in the 1960's when a great number of people spontaneously forsook the values of those who had abandoned the vow. The same recognition of schism is what spurred people to create what is called the New Age. The deeply-felt and unavoidably painful realization that we have a destiny we are actually working *against* is a cry from the collective unconscious, a cry picked up by enough people that a change in attitude and perhaps even in behavior is affected. While there are shallow elements to the New Age, as there were to hippies and must surely have been to the Renaissance, the impulse that prompted each of these social phenomena came directly from the collective unconscious.

Any time a group of people attempt to renew our vows by moving away from social programming, it is a sign of the health and power of the collective reservoir. The greater the number of people who are willing to put up with ridicule and worse in order to facilitate that move away from false perceptions, the healthier for us all. The more a person permits himself to tune in on, and then be led by the calling of the vow, the stronger is that person's share of the collective reservoir.

It is in the reservoir, the energies surrounding the common vow, that the battle between our vow and the forces opposing it begins. There are grave symptoms of that battle in every waking consciousness today, and the effects of the battle are evident in all the scars that mar the face of the earth.

The closer we are to the all-life, the closer we are to our individual portion of the reservoir. The closer we remain to our reservoir, the more we are a part of the all-life.

The steps in early childhood that take us from sanity to insanity are taken in the moments we disassociate from the collective unconscious. The anxiety produced by our moving away from daily contact with the reservoir and our sacred vow is what makes us crazy.

Enlightenment, the mystic's term for total understanding, is nothing more—and nothing less—than complete immersion in the reservoir of the collective unconscious. From the reservoir, all is known and everything is possible. Without continual communion with it, we produce and then come to believe in falseness until falseness becomes a way of life, not just for one, but for everyone.

Because we have stepped away from our common road and have, particularly since the Industrial Revolution, refused to acknowledge our errors and our ignorance, we are ready now for overwhelming disaster to overtake us. We approach this brink as we enter the Christian year 1990, the Hebrew year 5750, the Chinese year 4688. The differences among tribe and between gender that we have not resolved will not be so strong as to prevent our common death.

We who could not make peace in life will nevertheless die all together, the issues that kept us apart all approaching the same end, at the same time.

The time is soon, unless we reunite with our reservoir of power and knowledge, establish again our connection with the all-life, dismiss our illusory picture of the hierarchy of earth life and abandon our delusional position at the top of it.

In the old days, when we danced with the life-forms we lived among, there were safeguards to keep people from the kind of spiritual harm we routinely inflict on ourselves today. Those safeguards were found in the all-life, as living entities, and were felt in the continual presence of discarnate spirits who influence us more immediately. As we began to disregard the guidance around us, we began to persecute the very people who might have helped us to see the disaster we were bringing on ourselves by breaking the sacred circle of creation. We persecuted the healers and mediums, the shamans and witches, the visionaries and mystics. In attacking the guardians of our moral boundaries, we created a rift between ourselves and our individual souls, and a rift between ourselves and our common vow. These rifts allowed us to engage in pogroms, wars, the theft of resources, and the hoarding of food and water as a means to killing one another.

If we had continued our dance of life, allowed ourselves to hear and see the all-life and to perceive our non-human companions here as our equals instead of our hostages, we might have healed the rifts between us and them. Peace would have prevailed because the peaceful resolution of differences is a part of our evolution. It is not evolution that has failed us, but we who have failed to keep to a master plan.

Prior to the great division between humankind and the all-life, when people did not assume that progress as a species meant shutting ourselves away from the other species, there were elders to remind us of our relationship to creation. When someone stepped away from what was natural, the elders told him what was kind, what was right, what worked and what didn't. It was the job of the elders to make sure the people were straight with the universe, their job to leave order in this world before they went on to the next.

In our time, we do not have elders; we have old people who do not know any more about living than we do and whose existence is increasingly burdensome to us and to them. They have, we say, outlived their "usefulness". In sane times, nobody old, nobody experienced, would have been viewed as useless. Instead of the wise counsel we once relied on from the elders, we now have an entire generation who don't fit into our lives, who have no purpose. This is a symptom of the increasing distance between us and our vow, our innate knowledge, and our integrity. For a people to turn on their children or their parents is a sign of extreme mental and psychic imbalance. In the deepest part of our being, we know this, and we hide from our shame by relegating our parents to ghastly institutions where they are humored or ignored until they die.

If we had continued our dance with the life around us and

stayed within—or at least reasonably conversant with—the laws of nature, we would not be executing our parents before they died natural deaths. Without the link between us and the elders, there is no longer anyone to tell us we're on the wrong road. Nobody argues against our shallow life, nobody talks about a better time, because nobody alive now remembers a better life. This is a dangerous point in the journey of the human race: there is nobody to tell us that we have strayed, and with the passing of our grandmothers and grandfathers, as we become old, we will inherit the elders' place merely by virtue of our age and not because we deserve respect. We won't truly be elders, because we don't know anything. We will be only the next generation of unappreciated, unheeded old people. This goes against the laws of creation.

We are at a pivotal point: We can continue devolving, or we can wind our way back to the sacred knowledge we once had by recovering the old ways, by reuniting with the life around us. In joining again with the all-life, we will begin a new journey. We can fight our way out of the vacuum in which we live. We can retrieve all that is ours by right—and by obligation. Reunion is not a choice any more. Reunion is our only hope.

We start the journey that beckons by giving up our notion of man as master. We begin by acknowledging our place as part of—and not the reason for—life on this planet.

The journey for everyone begins once the spirit pervading all of life has noticed you, and this can happen only when you have raised your level of awareness sufficiently to become noticeable to that spirit. Once you have been recognized and can feel that recognition, an exchange takes place. A partnership between you and the all-life is established. It is a glorious moment. It is also the end of your life as your family and society expected it would be.

Once on the path, there is no going all the way back to self-enclosure. You can weary of fighting for your freedom and run back to the prison society offers, but you cannot pretend to yourself, ever again, that you do not know what you know. You will never again be able to quite convince yourself that you haven't had a taste of what you were meant to become. You may live out your life as a fake, but you will never be entirely soul-dead again.

It is not hard to take the first step onto your path. Go outdoors and find a place that enlivens your spirit. When you're ready to do so, talk to the all-life manifesting around you, the birds and trees and the ground—the ground being very important. Tell it you did not realize how self-encapsulated you had become. Ask if you and the all-life can be friends. If you address yourself to a single being: a butterfly, a stream, a stone, everything alive around you will receive your message of apology and take hope from it.

After you have spoken, *do* something. Take food from your dinner and give it to the homeless cat who lives behind your apartment building. Buy warm clothing and give it to someone who lives on the street. Take the money you were planning to spend on a movie ticket and bring it to a pet store; pick out a couple of healthy-looking turtles or mice, animals that can learn the ways of the wild easily, and ransom them from their slavery. Take them to a place that has all the water they need, and where they can hide from humankind. Pray for their welfare.

If you spend your own money or give up a portion of your food, you are making a true sacrifice. Despite religious traditions of killing animals in "sacrifice" to gods, the taking of another being's life is not a sacrifice on your part. Sacrifice implies giving up something that belongs to *you,* going a bit hungry or making a hole in your savings, giving up time, or inconveniencing yourself for the good of another.

Having done something concrete to link your spirit with the spirit of the life around you, you will inevitably come to the attention of Spirit. I use this term as other occultists use it, to mean the guiding intelligence that oversees life. Spirit implies Creator, or God. It refers as well to the infinite power and propelling intelligence of every species. Trees have an overseeing Spirit, and that Spirit is a part of the Creator Spirit. Rocks, water, fire, human beings, birds, each has an overseeing Spirit, and the overseeing Spirit of each is a portion of God.

Having come to the attention of the pervading and guiding forces, you will find your spirit awakening as if from a long sleep. Once roused, that spirit will delight in your attention to it. And you will give your attention to it, more and more as time goes by, because the void of the false-you that made you be dead for so long recedes little by little in the face of the powerful spirit that is the real-you.

The linking of your human self to the all-life ignites the eternal flame that is the true you, and when you have taken this step you will begin to feel the fire of eternal life, the light of creation that birthed you, sustained you, and will never desert you. Not only won't it desert you, it won't even let you be: it will push and prod and nag you until you have stepped fully onto your path, and no matter what becomes of you, you will never be helpless again.

That's the good news.

The bad news is that once you've asserted yourself in the presence of Spirit, brought yourself out into the Light, you are going to be, at some time and in some way, attacked by spirits of darkness. It is inevitable. For every human being who enlivens the world by mating his consciousness with Spirit, there is a little less fear in the world. And fear is what keeps beings of the darkness alive and functioning.

The truth of the existence of evil was known to every culture of which we have records, in every era that preceded ours, and the stubbornness of our ignorance regarding this truth is a great mystery to me. Even considering the tremendous power we have handed over to our new priests, psychiatrists, it is hard for me to understand how something as potent and ubiquitous as evil is lied about. Occultists are not the only people who come under attack. Anyone who lives on this planet, especially one who has some power in his community or value to society, is going to be attacked by the darkness. I have heard stories from non-occultists time and again that verify the truth I was forced to learn the hard way, through grim experience, and which I was unprepared for because, in a revelatory symptom of mass insanity, we have elected to ignore the truth about evil. I suppose, given our decision to turn away from the all-life and concern ourselves with just ourselves, it was unavoidable that we should lie to ourselves about many things.

The denial of the existence of evil has caused incalculable harm. People have been told and have accepted as truth that evil originates within our own minds. This is a cruelly misleading extension of the absurd notion that we create reality, an absurdity that marks a nadir in species egoism. The lie that evil can work on us only if we believe in it has done more good for the forces of darkness than can be measured.

Our innards are not nearly as important as we love to think they are, and we control far less activity in this world than we like to believe. A little understanding of the various theories of psychology is helpful when based in spiritual understanding. But when psychology is separated from spirit, it is destructive because it leads us deeper and deeper into self-absorption and it does not, in recompense for the harm it causes, teach us anything valuable. Psychiatry has been turned loose on the population for much of this century, has been fully mainstream for thirty years, yet people are just as crazy as they were before its advent, and just as miserable for all the "knowledge" psychological theory has afforded us. Is it any wonder? When we began to feel the awful void inside us, individually and collectively, we apparently decided we could ease the void by studying it, investing in it, and by giving over our hopes to the modern keepers-of-the-void, psychiatrists. But looking to our empty insides for help makes as much sense as clutching at our legs in a windstorm.

There is of course something to be gained by looking at what makes us tick, but this very limited intellectual pursuit was never meant to be a lifetime search. The emphasis we have placed on psychology demonstrates just how desperate we are: instead of living a real life, we spend our lives searching for reasons why our lives are false. We look inside our minds, where there is only a very little to be found, ever turning inward, inward, until we go so far inward that we cannot see out anymore.

Every hour spent in self-absorption, scrutinizing the wrong self, every day spent brooding over our afflictions, is time during which we separate ourselves from the life around us, through which we might experience our real self. While ten hours thus spent may cause us no great harm, a hundred hours of separation are a hundred opportunities missed, opportunities to feel ourselves as a part of the God-in-all, to establish our flow with creation.

If we are ill, we must find a means to getting well. Giving undue attention to aberration cures nothing, and compounds the aberration by emphasizing it and perpetuating its importance.

Nothing inside your mind is going to save you. Only the de-isolation of your being can do that. Pondering your alienation won't make you less alienated. In truth, the separation we feel is the result *of* our separation, not the result of our feelings about it. Studying our aloneness and misery avails us nothing. It merely encourages more of the same. Worrying over our twistedness won't straighten us out.

Western sophisticates love to poke fun at primitive rituals, such as the belief of some head-hunting peoples that the power of an enemy can be appropriated by taking his skull. I wonder if, somewhere in New Guinea, there is an elderly warrior who recalls the old days of his tribe and who has the magical ability to see inside our cities. Does he know how many of us pay people to look into our heads, despite the fact that our society is demonstrably no better off for this scrutiny, and does he sigh and tell himself, "Those white people sure are strange, but who am I to interfere with their odd rituals?"

It would have been easier on me to have written this book as a dispassionate text, something painlessly theoretical, and to have left my own story out of it. I could have saved much agony of spirit by allowing myself that much privacy. But I knew, as I prepared this book, that I had an obligation to address my work to the lay reader as well as the practicing occultist and I felt that without my personal story, the lay reader might not have the frame of reference he needs: illustrations provided by personal revelation that illuminate the realities of spiritual warfare. The lay reader, as much as the occultist, needs to know the realities at work behind the scenes in everyone's life, for the perpetual battle between Light and darkness affects all of us.

Since my horrifying initiation into the truth of evil, and my experiences with the hidden, dark powers that invade this world and alter human life whenever they can, I have made an experiential study of exorcism, the nature of evil, and protection from evil's numerous manifestations. The fruits of my investigations have provided insight and aid for me and, many other people over the years. I believe that my understanding of evil and protection from it will be of use to the reader.

Please know that it is not my intention to promote fear, but to help the reader understand all of what operates in his world, to know what is and is not safe behavior. We must, while we still can, redress the wrong we have done to ourselves by lying about our common, daily, increasingly-powerful enemy.

Once when I was meditating about a particularly fierce attack, I wondered aloud whether perhaps the attacks I had endured were facilitated by my awareness of them. Was I, by noticing evil, allowing it to attack me? If I ignored it, would it leave me alone? A spirit voice—perhaps my own, perhaps not—told me, "You can never ignore something safely until first you are aware of it. Once you know it is there, once you protect yourself, *then* you can ignore it.

Identifying evil, what it is and how it enters human life, is the first step toward a sane life whether or not we routinely perform occult work. There are dangers in everyday life and dangers particular to occultism. It is not difficult to protect ourselves. If evil has already gained a foothold, we can get rid of it if we know how to find it and then how to remove it. If we examine our views of how people operate in this world and take a good look at our place as part of the all-life, if we set aside our erroneous assumptions, we may begin to live creatively instead of passively, safely instead of being victims

of what we do not know. In this world, what we do *not* know
is usually what does us in.

Our society's beliefs regarding evil are entirely wrong, and
we are as much in danger for denying ancient knowledge as
from we are the activities of evil itself.

Chapter 2

The Man Who Ate Rice: Personal Encounters with Evil

"You don't know much," said the Duchess, "and that's a fact."

—Lewis Carroll,
Alice's Adventures in Wonderland

Whether warding off an attack of black magic or simply keeping ourselves free of other people's negativity, the most suitable course we can follow is the course of reverence for the spirit, the spirit of ourselves and others. When we remember to honor ourselves, other people, and the all-life, we expand our consciousness with every moment of our lives.

The most effective means of warding off evil is to live a sane life. The foundations of a sane life are reverence and intuition. Intuition is an outgrowth of reverence. Even if we live earthbound lives and have no interest in metaphysics, we nevertheless need to develop our intuition. In this way we can insure the best life possible for ourselves and treat others with kindness and consideration. If we embark on a course of spiritual searching, it is imperative that we remain alert to everything that affects us, near and distant, small events and important ones. Everything that touches us makes its mark on our spiritual search.

With reverence for all that lives in this realm, we develop intuition. Intuition is not a closed faculty or a quirky gift that some people have and some don't, but a natural sense that all living creatures are born with. Intuition is a partnership between the one who feels it and the all-life that sends signals to *be* felt. Intuition is a flow of energy between Spirit—the birds, trees, stones, wind—and the alert being who receives that flow and understands the messages within it.

Every human being could be psychic, could divine and heal, could come to know intimately all of the invisible aspects of creation, could journey beyond mundane reality to all the realms of spirit, if every human being could retrieve his intuition. In Western society, we are taught to ignore our psychic sense, and so most of us lose touch with it in early childhood.

The reason Westerners view psychism as supernatural is that our society focuses on concrete reality that can be contacted through the five physical senses. This focus, materialism, shuts away most of what transpires between humankind and the rest of creation, and ignores the spiritual essence that informs and creates concrete reality. We are told that reality is confined to whatever can be measured in three dimensions or deduced through physics. Because of our society's prejudice for measurable reality and against formless reality, we are taught in childhood that the formless creatures we sense or even actually see are not "really" there. Anything that comes to our attention through psychic intuition is, we are told, a product of our imaginations. It is not "real." Anything that fails to meet the criteria social programming sets for reality is, we are taught, a creation of our own minds. This notion gives children a powerful boost toward isolation and selfishness, because it encourages a feeling of ownership about literally anything that does not fit social dictates regarding what is real and what is made up. If we sense the presence of an incorporeal being or intuit events at a distance, we are told that this sensing and intuitive knowing are born of our minds and are, therefore, a part of us. Our culture's way of ignoring formless realities in favor of three-dimensional ones is a choice our forebears made and we are stuck with.

Everything alive on this planet that has a physical form—stones, plants, animals and human beings—also has two formless components, the etheric and astral components. (Besides these, the human, stone, animal and plant kingdoms have mental components and emotional ones, which will be discussed later in this book.)

The etheric, or energy body, is energy that surrounds the stone, plant, animal or human being and feeds it throughout the life of the concrete form. People who have retrieved their psychic seeing can sometimes see the etheric energy that surrounds all concrete form. Everything alive has this etheric form, and the health of the form can be discerned by reading its etheric body. The astral body, or component, is the spiritual essence of the stone, plant, animal or human being. While the etheric body lives in this realm, right alongside the form it enlivens, the astral body has its existence elsewhere. The astral realm cannot be reached through physical means because that realm and everything in it is pure spiritual essence. This realm can be contacted when we are asleep or, if we have learned to do so, while journeying with our mind and spirit during full waking consciousness. The astral level of creation is the level of the soul. Everything alive, whether it has its existence in form or out of form, has a soul. You may be a short, green-eyed male human being with black hair and a timid, sensitive personality whose astral appearance is that of a large swimming creature with red wings, surrounded by fire. The astral body conveys our true nature. Its appearance does not necessarily conform to the laws of nature that exist on this planet.

Since everything in all four of the earth's kingdoms has an etheric and astral body, the fact of our inhabiting physical forms does not mean we are trapped in those bodies or limited to experiences those bodies can accommodate. In some societies, people are expected to attend first to their spiritual needs and only secondarily to their material ones. This is particularly true of native people in many countries, whereas transplanted people, like most Americans other than native Americans, lose touch with the urgency of spiritual life when they leave their homes and cut themselves off from their roots.

What can rescue us from the limitations of three-dimensional reality is an awareness of a great lack in our lives. This awareness may come about after we go through a period of feeling bereft without knowing why we feel this way. It may come about through a momentary connection with Spirit, an incident that startles us out of our absorption with mundane reality and propells us, for just an instant, into another way of looking at creation.

Perhaps, during a funeral, you found yourself staring at the highly-polished casket, your attention gripped by the dark wood. You gazed at the casket for a long while without knowing exactly why. A week later, while walking through a department store, you found yourself drawn to a piece of highly-polished dark furniture, and you stood staring at it for some moments without knowing why. Soon after the incident, a friend died. You may have put the two incidents together and found a framework. The sight of the furniture set off a psychic message. This was a bona fide psychic experience. Some people would call the juxtaposition of casket and furniture a "mere" coincidence, but it is a true coincidence in the most fundamental sense—two incidents coming together in your life *for a reason.*

The one who has this experience and fails to perceive the meaning in it is the one who left his psychic faculty behind in childhood. The one who allows the situation to speak to him is the pychic. The psychic and non-psychic have the same experiences; one allows everything he encounters to talk to him, while the other closes himself off from this communication. These two people live in the same world, and the world makes itself available to them in precisely the same way, but the psychic and non-psychic deal with their world differently.

Perhaps you were introduced to someone and, without having any idea why, instantly decided you wanted nothing to do with the stranger. Some time later, you learned that he had been arrested for a violent crime. Your feeling toward the stranger was an example of your psychic intuition at work. A psychic message registered in some part of your being, and whether or not you consciously understood your reluctance to be with the stranger, the uneasy feeling was, in itself, a psychic experience.

If we wish to reawaken our deeper faculties, we can connect with our deeper mind by the simple means of paying attention to everything we see, hear, smell, touch, or sense during the course of a day. Attention to changes in the sky, to birds, to the crackling of a fire, to our dreams and thought patterns will lead to our having hunches. Soon we will begin paying attention to those hunches. We may feel like embracing something without knowing why, or running from something without knowing why. That is our psychic mind speaking to us. Pay attention to that psychic mind and it will unfold itself as quickly as suits your ability to handle it.

When I was four years old, I had a dream that likely signalled the end of my natural psychic connection. In the dream I was outdoors by our house in New England, looking around at the world. There was a large, bloody hole in my forehead near the space between the eyebrows, in what occultists call the third eye. It is an important psychic center. People were running around frantically and someone cried, "She needs a doctor!," to which I replied firmly, "I do not—I need a lawyer."

The dream told me that something precious had been stolen from me, and this feeling of having been torn from my birthright stayed with me all through my childhood.

From about the time of that dream, I began to lose the ability to see incorporeal shapes and colors, to sense the spirits that, before the dream, I had seen often. I saw lots of formless things in the tiny pond behind our house. Well, really, it wasn't a pond. It was a swamp. Anyone but the realtor who sold us the house would have called it a swamp. It was a place of great activity, most of it taking place just beyond the realm of three-dimensional reality. I particularly remember a pink-orange spirit floating above the water who looked like a synthesis of a rabbit and a wolf. I remember a highlight of early childhood, a man who sometimes came through my bedroom wall. When he did not show up, life was only just bearable. When he came, life was worth living again. I believe he stopped coming to see me after the dream, or that I lost the ability to sense or see him. When we lose our close friends, as I lost mine then, it is like losing some of our own soul, because we lose the friend and also the gift of being able to talk with the great number of invisible beings around us. I wonder how many parents are puzzled when their children behave as though they are grieving, when no one knows what they are grieving over.

While I lost the ability to see and hear spirits, I did not entirely lose my ability to feel my psychic sense calling to me, for which I thank the gods. Contact with my intuition is probably what saved me from investing very heavily in social programming.

At about the age of seven I began to long for the connections to creation that I knew had been lost to me. I never said anything about this except to occasionally ask my mother, "Is it going to be midnight tonight?" When she said yes, a surge of hope flooded through my solar plexus into my heart. Midnight means no-time, and no-time meant that the window into the universe, now closed to me most of the time, would be open for a little while.

Occasionally, other people's dictates of reality conflicted with my inner knowledge. I flatly refused to believe the silly story that I could not become invisible or learn to fly. Once, I spent an entire afternoon trying to fly off the backyard picnic table. Why couldn't I do during the day what I knew I did in my sleep? Rather than allow myself to be vulnerable to other people's wrong-headed notions of what was and was not possible, I made the decision not to argue about flying and invisibility, and to keep the truth to myself.

As soon as I began to live on my own, at about the age of

nineteen, I found myself periodically moving as far from mundane reality as I could. For long periods I focused on the sky, actually and metaphorically. I knew moments of great transforming energy about which I understood nothing except that I was joining formless reality for bits of time, an hour, two hours, or more. As I realized how happy I was to be part of the energies that lie just beyond the realm of concrete reality, I began a long process of exploring the tools of the mystic—meditation, Tarot cards, astrology, seances. I leaned toward the school of occultism that bases everything important far beyond this world. It was many years before I saw how unwise it is to impute everything powerful to a far-away realm and forsake this world as undeserving of close attention. How much joy, charm and brilliance manifests here, and how few "serious" mystics ever see any of it!

Having learned that talking to people about esoteric matters furthers nothing, causes confusion, and steals energy from the process of seeking, I was disinclined to join groups and eschewed organizations of any kind in the interest of psychic purity and mental balance. Whether there was a helpful spirit watching over me to keep me solitary and safe, or whether this caution resulted from my own stubborn determination to do my searching my own way is a question for which I have no answer.

Talking with God and observing are the two major elements of every seeker's spiritual quest. After awhile, they become the foundation of his life. In time, they may become his whole life.

I offer here the story of my first personal encounter with evil. In doing so, I urge you to observe the ease with which evil invaded my life, and to note any similarities between my experiences and yours. If you are sure that you do not believe in the existence of evil, then bear in mind that, throughout the advent of evil into my life and even after its presence had produced physical changes in me, I did not believe in evil, either.

There came a time, after I had been on my own for about sixteen years, when I was ripe for the friendship of another occultist. Into this vacuum came a woman I will call Rose. Her experiences in the metaphysical disciplines were much like mine. Like me, she had worked as a psychic, medium, and spiritual explorer. However, her way of dealing with ordinary reality was alien to me. Like many who give up jobs in order to pursue their spiritual work full-time, she was always in debt, running from bill-collectors, hiding from the landlord, in a frenzy.

I was puzzled by her continual poverty. She was burdened by responsibility for her six-year-old daughter, Ellen. It seemed that Rose's husband Brian was not as distressed by their bills as Rose was. Either he didn't care or Rose was making things seem worse than they really were. I felt sorry for Rose in any case. She was forty-three and had the coping ability of a child. I lent her money. I gave her money. She always insisted that she would pay me back, but there was never more than the most feeble attempt at making good on that promise. I failed to understand the central point to Rose's life: she *needed* her life to be a mess because messes open entryways for spirits—all kinds of spirits.

She told me of dreams in which my deepest psychic dramas were played out. I was always most uncomfortable with these revelations because it seemed to me that the information she was ostensibly getting about me ought to be off-limits to anyone except me. She often told me she was necessary in my life. The self-aggrandizement in her when she told me "I could not do without" her did not flatter her. In truth I had gotten along fine without her for well over thirty years.

Trouble arose when I began to see how often I went out of my way for her and how rarely she reciprocated. I listened to her stories of woe, sympathized, offered insights. But she was unable to hear any of my troubles without becoming terribly anxious. I found it odd that my difficulties had such powerful negative effects on her.

A turning point in our relationship happened when Brian called to say that Rose, in Europe doing some psychic counselling, had fallen from a horse. After Brian and I talked, I began to pray for Rose. Suddenly a spirit entered the room and told me in no uncertain terms that I must not disturb Rose. He said there was something of utmost importance in the balance and that anything—even prayer—might upset that balance.

Brian called the next night to say that, except for a minor head wound, Rose was all right. I did not say so to Brian, but I was sure everything was not all right. Something bad had happened to Rose. My mind kept going back to a question I had about Lee, a young woman who sometimes worked with Rose and a small group of occultists, doing readings of many kinds, psychic and astrological and card readings. I barely knew Lee, but there was something in her manner toward me that put me off. Lee was about twenty-three, slender, with lovely features and dark brown, short hair. She was an all-American cheerleader type. She rarely had anything to say, even to her colleagues. I had no idea where she had met Rose or where she came from. I felt strongly that Lee had been the cause of Rose's fall, though I could not tell myself why.

When Rose came back, a week later, she was in fine physical condition but there was a strange remoteness about her in regard to her journey to Europe, as though she had participated in the trip but could not recall very much about it. Why was she disassociated from the trip, I wondered. Was this an effect of the head wound? When I asked Rose to tell me about the fall, she said that she and Lee had gone horseback riding by themselves, while the others shopped for souvenirs. Two young male stablehands had escorted Rose and Lee. While the women were riding, someone had apparently jabbed Rose's horse from behind, causing the fall. Rose said that one of the stablehands had done it, probably expecting the animal to break into a gallop and scare the inexperienced rider. She thought the young men probably did that sort of thing whenever they could get away with it. I was certain, however, that Lee had caused the accident.

While I did not understand the depth of Rose's troubles, I began to have the recurring thought that the Rose who had gone to Europe had never come home. The notion plagued me for months and would not go away.

In a brief time, Rose became irresponsible about keeping appointments. She kept me waiting a few times and, when I spoke to her about it, she blew up at me, saying that I was demanding, and refused to listen to what I had to say. She became cold and remote. The slightest thing set her off. She fought with her family and friends and became terribly self-righteous. Joking with her to ease her mood did not help, for her sense of humor had left her.

I decided I had to end the friendship: the difficulty of being around Rose caused me a good deal of pain. She did not wish to hear how I felt, and I did not care to be abused.

Oddly, I found that, once she was out of my life, she entered more and more into my thoughts and dreams. Did I miss her? Clearly the friendship was more burden than boon. Then why did I feel her presence in my house and why did she pop into my mind so often? There soon came a time when I began to feel sick to my stomach whenever I thought of Rose, and quickly following that development, I began to feel ill and exhausted a good deal of the time. Within five months of our last conversation, I had become ill and weak. In meditation and in sleep I began having strange, disturbing visions. One night, during a peaceful meditation, a huge, ferocious, drooling black dog intruded. I had dreams and visions of creatures who appeared only in the periphery of things, wanting not to be seen, skulking creatures trying not to be discovered. I dreamed of entering a woods and seeing, out of the corner of my eye, the hindquarters of a wolf as it slunk out of sight.

I had many dreams, visions, and unbidden thoughts of Lee. This puzzled me because we had never been friends and meant nothing to each other. I was puzzled by the frequency with which she came into my mind. Again and again, without my having any idea what it meant, I heard myself saying, "No one with a soul would have done such a thing." This referred to a minor incident in which Lee had come to my house to drop off some clothes Rose had borrowed for the trip to Europe. She had done the errand for Rose's sake, so that she and I would not have to meet. Rose and I, having parted with anger, had decided we were better off leaving each other alone.

There was an outstanding dream in which a spirit voice called me to stand before a sacred totem pole. He informed me that a terrible wrong had been done to me, and asked if I wished to retaliate. Having no idea what that wrong might be, I stood there awhile and considered the offer. At last I said, "I want to make it clear that I have done nothing to bring harm upon myself. That is what matters most. But there is already far too much pain in this world. I refuse to add to the burden of pain already existing, and so I refuse the offer of retaliation." The spirit voice then bade me leave the sacred totem pole, and as I did, I began to wake up. I thought of Rose, wondering if it was she who had harmed me. As I considered this, a spirit voice in my bedroom called out, "Are you sure it's Rose who has harmed you? Maybe it's Lee." Which was, I decided, ridiculous. Lee had no reason to harm me. We had never fought. Why would she bother me?

There were two vivid dreams that spring in which I saw coffins—mine. The first dream showed me a shroud trailing gracefully around the coffin. A spirit voice said, "It is very bad luck to see your own shroud before you die."

The second dream showed my coffin buried deep in the earth. I said to myself, "But I cannot claw my way out of the coffin and up through six feet of hard-packed earth. I'm not that strong. If I'm buried here, I'll never get out."

While I could not fully understand the dreams, I did not fail to perceive the warning in them.

Though I was ill most of the time, there were times when I felt the call of Spirit and did things by intuition, things I did not understand, but knew were important. When Spirit calls, fools ignore the summons at their peril. Several times that spring I was impelled to drive to places without knowing why. I made at least four trips to a shopping center many miles from my house, a place I never visited. What was especially odd was that I made these journeys at night, when the place was closed. I did not understand why I was making these trips, but

I knew better than to argue with Spirit.

I became weaker and weaker, and no doctor could help. Was I terribly anxious, they asked. No. They ran tests and came up with nothing. By summer, I had become so ill that, two hours after waking up in the morning, I needed a nap. I awoke on many mornings with a line of bites on both sides of my neck. Insects do not ordinarily bite in orderly lines, and the bites never itched. They were very painful. I joked to myself that they were vampire bites. I did not know then how much information comes our way through humor.

One summer morning during a nap I dreamed that Lee was standing on my doorstep, sneering at me. She said, "You know, I'm *not* coming in." She wanted in and was trying to goad me into inviting her. I replied, "You say this only because you think you can make me invite you in, but I tell you I will never do that. You are not coming into my house."

I woke right up, recognizing this as a classic vampire dream. Traditionally, vampires, supernatural creatures who get their substenence by draining blood from the living, cannot enter a house except by invitation. After the invitation has been extended, they may come and go at will, without permission. That first invitation is all they need.

I told myself I was having a nervous breakdown. For one thing, there was no such thing as vampires. More important, Lee was an inconsequential person in my life and there was no way that I was going to believe she was a vampire. Why would Lee bother to harm me when I hadn't even seen her in seven months?

But wait. I had seen her, and had forgotten the encounter. A few weeks past, I had dragged myself, exhausted and very ill, to a mall. While walking from the front entrance to a store, I felt someone staring at me. Looking up I saw, from a distance of at least a hundred feet, the face of a man superimposed on the head of a woman. The man was spirit. The woman was flesh. The woman was turned away from me. The man's face, floating over her head, was staring at me raptly, an expression of profound satisfaction on his face. As I turned away from him, wondering what there was about me that pleased him so, his woman host turned toward me. It was Lee. She did not see me, and I quickly left the mall.

One morning in late summer I awoke with the sensation of there being a large gold cross imbedded in my body, covering the entire heart area and all of the stomach. The object did not seem to have been sewn in, but had become a part of me.

I have always viewed the cross, an ancient symbol, as having far too many meanings to be claimed by any one group of thinkers. The simplest interpretation is that the vertical line means God's light touching the world and the horizontal line means God's light manifesting across the world. There are many other views of the meaning of the cross, and the symbol is neither Western nor Christian by right.

The crucifix, the representation of a human being either losing his life on the cross or gaining his higher power on it, is not the exclusive property of any single group either, being too profound and powerful a symbol to belong to only one philosophy or system.

Why had a gold cross become part of me? I had never worn a cross.

That day, I dragged myself to a pool of water and lay down, looking at the bright blue sky and wondering when—or if—I would ever be well again. Although this kind of thing does not usually happen to me outdoors when there are lots of people around, as there were that day, a spirit voice boomed down at me from the sky, "Don't you *get* it? You're under attack. Go home and light every candle in your house and I will explain."

I did not believe in psychic attack. By then I had put in seventeen very intense years as an occultist, and I assumed that if I had not seen black magic at work, there probably was no such thing. I supposed there were power-seekers who used their skills as a means to harm or steal from others, but I had never known any such people. And because I had grown up in Western culture, where we *know* there is no such thing as evil and further *know* that no such harm can befall us unless we believe in evil, I had not given the subject much consideration.

I dismissed the voice. But in that moment, something in the deepest level of my mind took over and made me obey the voice. I went home and walked through every room in the house, searching for candles, lighting each one and blowing them out, moving from the third floor to the second to the first. As I found the final candle, I reached out to light it and felt myself trying to move against a solid barrier. Pushing as hard as I could, I reached and reached until finally I was able to touch the flame to the candle. As the candle flared into light, the barrier disappeared. I felt enormous weights drop from me, and from the center of the universe a bolt of brilliant light flung itself through space and into my chest, straight through the heart. As my heart was washed, I began to feel alive for the first time in eight months. The light flowed through me, and I suddenly understood, with that most profound Knowing that will not be denied, that someone was using psychic attack to do me great harm. The attacker was Lee.

I sat down on the couch and, looking up at the brilliant sky, began to use every technique I had ever used for the testing of spirit messages. I stated aloud that there was no such thing as vampires, and that I refused to believe in psychic attack or black magic. A powerful voice boomed, "She eats of flesh that is not hers." By then, I knew the help I was receiving was beneficient help and not a trick, but I had to test it to its limits. I stated aloud again that the message was wrong. I did it once more. Each time I tried to push this information away, the truth of the situation was borne in on me until an ancient part of my spirit began to awaken and resonate to this terrible revelation.

As the afternoon wore on, I knew I had no more choice: I had to face the fact of black magic as an aspect of earth life, and as a danger—an emergency—in my life. From the afternoon of that terrible initiation, Spirit kept me working for a week and I had little time to speculate about the nature of possession, but I felt, as I moved about, doing what I felt impelled to do, that Lee herself was a pawn, and that she was possessed by something non-human, very ancient, and most powerful.

My first exorcism journey was to the shopping center I had, in bewilderment, visited several times that spring, at night. I travelled there with some water that I had blessed, and a white candle, wondering what I planned to do with them. There were shoppers milling about. Engaged in worldly concerns, they did not notice when I sprinkled blessed water in the corners of the shopping center. Nor did they notice when, after invoking the powers of Light into the candle, lighting it and quickly blowing the flame out, I planted the candle in some shrubbery near the center of the place.

I went to the precise center of the complex and, having no idea where I had learned any of this, established five crosses in the astral realm of the shopping center. I did this by giving some of my own energy to the creation of these crosses. There was of course no concrete physical evidence of the crosses because they existed in the soul, or astral, component of the place. That meant that anyone coming into contact with them would not see them with his physical eyes but would perceive them with his unconscious mind. If that person were psychic, he would know the crosses were there. If he was not psychic, he would sense them without realizing that he sensed them. This procedure is not the same thing as visualization. Visualization affects the visualizer and nothing else. The creation of an astral object, done by giving that object real energy, is an act of true creation. It causes a change in the astral realm, whereas visualization causes an alteration in the visualizer's waking mind. Visualization causes no changes in physical, etheric or astral realities.

These astral creations are sometimes called thought-forms because while they have an actual existence, they are made by thought-intention and are perceived by the unconscious mind or by psychic seeking. These forms cannot be contacted with the five physical senses. Having created the crosses, I invested each with flames of the Light power, knowing that these would last for a full day without being renewed. If I felt I had to renew the crosses and flames, I would have to recreate them all over again, as thought-forms usually do not last beyond twenty-four hours.

I assumed I was doing all of this because Rose and Lee and the other occultists were scheduled to visit the shopping center the next day, Friday. I consulted a calendar and found that this was so. A lot of malls and shopping centers in the mid-Atlantic region offer so-called psychic fairs, during which all manner of occult disciplines, from card readings to numerological and astrological readings to psychic and crystal-ball readings are offered, usually for a small fee. Clients include believers and scoffers. The believers are always on the lookout for a new card-reader or psychic, and these events allow them to sample several. If they are pleased with the reading, they may call on the reader at his house and get a longer session than the brief ones offered at the mall. Scoffers buy readings for the fun of it and, if a prediction happens to come true, well, that's even more fun.

The next afternoon, I drove to the shopping center again and parked. It was a stifling hot day, but something made me keep my windows rolled up. I silently prayed for everyone in the shopping center, Rose and her colleagues and the shoppers and store-keepers. I began to feel pressure against my car. The pressure grew worse until I simply had to get away from there. With final prayers and affirmations of the power of Light over dark, I drove away. As I pulled out of the parking lot, a tremendous power surrounded my car. I hesitated, wondering whether I ought to leave. Was I going because I had done my job, or was I going because something was forcing me out? It didn't matter; the pressure pushed me out of the lot and into the street. As I drove, the pressure increased until it was unbearable. I was rattled and gave thanks for the trips I'd made in the spring, for if I had been forced to make my way home along the winding back roads and then in intense traffic, I am not sure I would have made it safely. I could not concentrate on anything except the pressure that threatened to overwhelm me.

The feeling of pursuit and intense pressure came so close to obliterating my conscious mind that I truly do not know how I got home. I know there were three near-misses with other cars while I drove the first mile away from the shopping center, and then all of a sudden I was close to home without any memory of how I had gotten there.

Now that I was only a few miles from home, I relaxed. Looking up at a familiar roadsign, one I had passed hundreds of times, I turned left, as always. In a moment, I was utterly lost. The road twisted and turned and there were dead ends at the end of each road. There was no way out. I blundered from one dead end to another, reversing, then going forward, reversing, going forward, panicking for the first time. At last I found myself back at the spot where I had made the left-hand turn. The roadsign marking that turn was not the sign that had been there a few minutes before. The sign had been changed. But how?

Steadying myself, I drove home cautiously. I was beginning to realize that there was a powerful force around that shopping center. It had chased me away from the place and—this is what scared me the most—it had been able to follow me most of the way home, confusing me about a sign with which I had long been familiar.

That evening, I felt a strong urge to return to the shopping center. I sat in the parking lot and made more prayers and affirmations. The pressure against the car was just as bad this time, and there was a new feeling now, one of intense personal hatred. Up to then, the feelings had been of energy, pressure, intensity. Now there was a feeling of personality behind the pressure.

Leaving the shopping center, I was pursued by the same intense pressure that had pursued me that afternoon. Because it was nighttime, the drive was that much more difficult. I was again grateful to the force that had prompted the journeys of that spring.

As I felt the pressure let up a bit, and my tension subside along with it, a spirit voice spoke. "You will kill a child tonight." I felt I should not engage the spirit in conversation, but knew I must refute the declaration. "I refuse to accept that.

It will not happen," I said, and concentrated on driving and nothing else.

When I was about four miles from home, and a few yards from where I had made the wrong turn that afternoon, I was horrified as my car plunged directly into a group of teenagers walking along the road. They were on their way home from the school, just ahead, and not one of them was wearing light-colored clothing. As I screeched to a stop, I saw, amazed, that none of them was hurt. My car had not touched them. I hadn't plunged into them at all. My car was several yards away and none of the young people had even noticed me. Nothing had happened. There had been no accident.

Again, my perceptions had been altered by something outside myself, as had happened that afternoon with the roadsign.

I took a moment to collect myself before continuing on home, thinking, so much for this evening's work. Better rest up for tomorrow.

A little giddy, I was thinking what a good thing it was that I don't drink, because it might have been a four bourbon night, given the way the day had gone. Maybe, I thought, I ought to seriously consider taking up drinking. I didn't like the stuff. It tasted nasty. But escape would be so welcome, just for awhile, and I wondered . . .

There was a car behind me trying to drive up my tailpipe. Something about it seemed out of place. Were its lights too bright? Yes, but it was more than that. I felt not so much pursued as surrounded by it. I accelerated. It caught up to me. I went faster but it kept right up with me. The faster we went, the more it encircled me. Somehow, that car was wrapping me in its embrace.

"God," I cried out, "What the *hell is* that?" A spirit voice called to me, *"That* is the cross *you* have to bear."

Maybe not, I thought, whipping my car off to the left without using my turn signal. My pursuer shot past on my right, going too fast to make the turn. As it sailed by, I was swept by the desperate desire—almost a lust—to leap from my car, let my car roll down the hill all by itself while I rushed after the other car. For a split second I was conscious of nothing except getting my hands on that car. I wanted only to pick up the car and tear it and whatever was inside it into tiny shreds. Passion overtook me as I saw myself rip into that car and those people until there was nothing left. My face froze in a hideous grimace and my hands curled into claws.

It passed. The rage subsided. My pursuer had come so close to me that our energies had mixed. The rage I had felt was *their* passion to tear *me* apart. Was this how they felt when on the attack? Was this horror what I was up against?

As I was falling asleep that night, a power with the force of a speeding train slammed straight at my chest. I had experienced attacks like this for many years, and knew my only resort was to call out to God for help and fight with all my strength until the attack subsided. But this attacker did not let up. No matter how I fought, and I believe I have never fought anything so hard in all my life, the thing would not give up. Though I cried out for help again and again, nothing happened. The power slammed into my chest relentlessly and I grew dangerously weak. Suddenly I heard my mind tell the part of me that was fighting that my only chance was to fight the creature on the same terms it was using to fight me. With all the strength I had, I leaned my head forward—I could not move my body—and pushed my jaw out as far as it would go. I took hold of the thing's heart with my teeth, ripped the heart out, and spat it on the floor.

The force of the attack continued unabated for some moments, then leveled off. In a little while, the thing was gone.

I had been attacked in this way for long enough that I began to wonder why I had not taken the attacks seriously. Each was hard, each was terrifying, each was ferocious. I knew the attacks were real and not part of a dream because they always occurred before sleep, never during it.

I suppose I believed the assaults had something to do with our travels out of the body, that in leaving my body I sometimes stumbled into places where I was not welcome. I guess I knew there were immoral people somewhere Out There who

attacked occultists, but I never took these assaults seriously—
once they were over—or personally. I was convinced that practicing black magic was, well, silly, and could not involve me.
Looking back, I believe I told myself that each of these "mistakes" was the last. As I had no framework to put these
assaults into, I never gave the subject of black magic, in toto,
much thought.

The next day, once again taking action without knowing
what I was going to do or even where I was headed, I got into
the car and drove to Rose's house. I felt this was an errand of
utmost urgency, and knew whatever I had to do would be best
accomplished when Rose was not at home. Her work with the
occultists at the shopping center was still going on. The shopping center generally employed the occultists for a week at a
time, sometimes two weeks.

I took with me a silver crucifix and gold cross and a batch of
white paper towels. When I arrived at Rose's house, I drove
around it, circling it three times counterclockwise to unbind the
energy surrounding it and three times clockwise to bind it with
the Light. Hoping that Brian and Ellen were either away or
engrossed in something and would not see my car, I parked the
car at every angle I could manage that would allow me to face
the house from the four cardinal directions. I said prayers and
made magical protection signs over every door and window. I
paused awhile to think about my next step, and wondered why
the chimney was drawing my attention. It was a few minutes
before I remembered that, about a year before, when Rose and
I were still friends, I had been in the house on the day there
was a funeral for someone in Brian's family. I was shocked to
see that he and Rose had brought home several funeral
bouquets and placed them around the living room fireplace. I
had not known then why this upset me so, but as I sat there in
my car that night it suddenly came to me that cut flowers can
be programmed, or magnetized, with either positive or negative energy, and that those flowers had looked suspicious.
Picked flowers, still alive but quickly losing their life force, are
vulnerable. Once severed from their roots, they are separated

from the spirit force that oversees plant life. Still, they are not dead, and their energy can be appropriated for good or evil, as can the energy of human beings.

Someone had used the energy in those flowers to gain access to Rose and Brian's house.

Shortly after that visit, when I told Rose I wished she hadn't brought the flowers home, Rose said that she felt "something" around the house. She asked me to do a ritual of protection, and I had done so, paying particular attention to all the doors and windows. I realized, as I sat in the car that night, that I had not considered the chimney as an entrance point and had therefore neglected to place a protection on it. Whatever evil Lee was carrying had gotten into the house through the chimney and was, I saw, bent on harming six-year-old Ellen. I began to comprehend the scope of all this, and understood why I was at Rose and Brian's house. The power around Lee intended to extend its territory to include young Ellen.

When I was satisfied that I had done all I could, and that the energy around the house looked peaceful, I drove away. The operation had taken more than an hour, and during that time I had felt none of the pressure or threat I'd felt at the shopping center, but as soon as I left Rose's street for the main road, it began. I pursued me until I felt it would overcome me, and this time I had a very long drive ahead of me. I groped in my bag for the silver crucifix, keeping my eyes on the road, knowing better than to let the thing behind me get the upper hand by causing an accident. I placed the crucifix under my tongue. The silver made me salivate a lot, so I reached for a paper towel and spat into it. When the towel was full of spit, I tossed it out the window, appalled at myself. Was I now a litterbug, for heaven's sake? But I knew this was what I had to do. I kept the crucifix firmly under my tongue and used the next towel, throwing it out the window when it was wet. After I had gone through four paper towels and driven about ten miles, the pressure let up. In a flash I saw what had transpired. By being near the thing pursuing me, I had picked up some of its essence, its energy. That essence had exited my body through my saliva.

Its vibrations in the paper towel had naturally attracted it, thus lessening its ability to detect my vibrations. The being following me had been directed toward its own essence and therefore had lost the feel for mine.

This on-the-job training was enlightening, but I was frightened at the prospect of another assault on my heart. If the previous night's attack had been brought about by my exorcism of the shopping center, would tonight's attack not be far worse because I had detected the plan involving Ellen and created protection around her house?

I lay down to sleep and braced myself, praying for help. I waited, afraid to sleep. At last I was so tired that I drifted off to sleep.

I woke bolt upright. I had fallen asleep without being attacked. What was going on? I sat up, surrounded only by the peace of my house. "God?" I muttered, "Where are they?"

I was not, of course, expecting any kind of an answer, and was shocked when a firm but infinitely kind spirit voice replied, "They have been . . . dis-possessed."

I burst into tears, so grateful to feel the presence of a spirit who was on my side, for a change. The contrast between that voice and the energy it brought with it and all I had encountered for the past few days did me in. I sat there crying until, without the slightest warning, I was treated to a full-color wide-screen vision that took place on my bedroom wall. It revealed the entire story of my soul's existence from the beginning of my sojourn on this planet, so long ago that I cannot measure it in years, to the present. It showed me the future of my life here. It showed me everything I could possibly wish to see.

I suppose that vision was a necessity. It was time I began to know what I was doing in this life, for if I was to do more exorcisms—and I have since done many—I needed a broad view of what life in this world is *really* about, as opposed to what we *think* it's about. It may seem to the reader that the vision was a reward for some tough work, but I don't believe we get rewards, not if we're doing our jobs. What we get is to job and knowing to knowing, not from work to reward.

Rose called, as I'd thought she might. We had not spoken for about eight months. Tentatively, I told her some of what I knew about Lee. I knew I could not allow myself to care whether or not Rose believed me. This was my job, not hers, and I could not permit her views to hold any currency for me. I did want to warn her about my feeling that Ellen had been targetted by Lee's evil companion, though targetted for what, I did not know. Rose listened. She seemed to believe my story, what I told her of it. She said that Lee had indeed worked with her and the other occultists at the shopping center during that terrible week, and she said that Lee had been a disruptive influence on her colleagues.

Rose and I agreed that Lee was a deeply disturbed young woman whose spirit had been taken over by a much stronger being. Left to her own devices, Lee could not have caused as much trouble as she and her friend caused together. Surely Lee did not have the competency to harm people on a grand scale, nor would she have had the patience or strength to carry out an eight-month-long attack on me and make me so ill.

A few weeks after the exorcism, I went to Rose's house and was astounded to find Lee there. Why, I asked Rose, was she not more concerned about Lee's effect on her child and her home? For even if Lee had really been dis-possessed, as the spirit voice had declared, she might still be carrying a great deal of negative energy with her, to say nothing of a rotten attitude. Rose shook her head and admitted that she felt terribly sorry for Lee, who had been a lonely child, psychologically and possibly physically abused. Realizing by then that the psychological reasons underlying anyone's involvement with evil can be dealt with only after the evil has been expunged, I told Rose that she was playing with fire. The only way a vampire could return after being got rid of, I said, was through pity. The same is true of any type of evil. Feeling sorry for people who are engaged in wrong action does nobody any good.

I left the situation then. Sometimes I prayed for Lee, and I prayed continually for Rose, Ellen and Brian, but I knew that without the urging and direction of Spirit, I should not involve myself in Lee's life.

After that first exorcism, a spirit being occasionally visited me when I was alone in my house. I will not name him because I believe that to give him a name empowers him. He showed up without fanfare or warning, a spirit who came to appraise me. He appeared as a white man, nice-looking, with even features and dark hair. Sometimes he wore a white turban. I could not see the color of his eyes. The visions I had of him were always very vivid and clear, as though he had the energy to make himself more visible than spirits usually can.

The first time he came, he stared at me as though he had just been introduced to me, wished I did not exist, and intended to do something swift and emphatic about my existence. I said nothing to him and he did not speak. He measured me for a long time and then disappeared.

On nearly every visit after that first one, he appeared carrying a wooden bowl that contained some rice. While he watched me, he ate the rice. Sometimes he ate with chopsticks. Sometimes he used his fingers. There were never more than a few grains of rice in his bowl, and he never took his eyes from me as long as he was in my house. I understood that every visit was an assessment. I was never afraid of him, though I knew if I thought about him too much I might become very frightened indeed, because I had learned what he represented and I was coming to see that he had many subjects, ancient technique, and endless patience.

Sometimes he spoke, asking me if I was hiding from him, or whether I understood that I had no chance against him. I knew he wanted something from me, and that he could never have what he wanted, not because I am particularly brave, but because the connection he desired to make with me could not *be* made. I knew this, but he did not seem to understand it. In some way that does not translate well to earth-realm terms, I knew that I had transmuted some of my spirit into a vibration he could never reach. Once he challenged me to fight with him, and when I got tired of trying to explain that there was nothing in me for him, no part of me that he could use, I attempted to illustrate the point in the simplest language. I asked him to pretend that human beings in physical bodies are like cookie jars. I explained that you can smash the jar in your search for what you desire, and find there is nothing in your grasp except broken pieces. Some people's energy cannot be appropriated. It was not an elegant analogy, but he quit trying to make me fight with him.

Nevertheless, he kept coming back. I knew better than to encourage these visits, so I rarely talked to him and only once allowed a real conversation. He told me how much control he had in the world. He began to brag, which signalled to me that he was getting desperate, either about me or perhaps about people like me, people who simply will not give him what he wants from them. What he wants is fear.

He bragged that he had invented and had full control of a game then sweeping the young people, a fad game that appealed to the players' fear of being vanquished by a cleverness greater than their own, a game involving intricate plots and mythical beasts and dwellings. He bragged that he made great use of television, which was not news to me. What struck me foremost about him was not power, because he did not exude power, but that his mind was very limited. I wondered how someone with so little imagination had been able to function as well as he had, and for so long. I believe the answer lies, not in him, because he was not a very impressive being, but in the hopeless ones who served him and made their lives out of his purpose. Without his army, he was just another dissatisfied boaster with little talent and no mind worthy of comment.

Whether I came to his attention because of Lee or because he knew that I would become, for some time, a very busy exorcist, I do not know. He stopped coming to see me after a couple of months, and if I have seen him since, he has not looked as he did then. He has a wealth of disguises and many ways of approaching us other than through our waking perceptions.

Rose asked if I would come to her house on the day she and Brian and Ellen moved, and perform some rituals. She seemed uneasy. Perhaps, I thought, there was something in the house which she wanted to be certain would not follow her to the new place. As I arrived at the house and watched Rose and Brian's friends moving boxes and furniture down the walk to a waiting truck, I was shocked to see Rose appear, looking thinner and two inches shorter. I got out of my car and approached her, stopping when I saw that it was not Rose. It was Lee! In three months, she had gained a great deal of weight, developed heavy breasts and hips, and dyed her hair to look just like Rose's. Lee had gone from being a slender brunette to a chubby blonde. The transformation was shocking. I could hardly find the old Lee in the new.

While the moving was going on, I did my rituals without drawing the movers' attention, and took pains to avoid Lee. She seemed cheerful, joking with the others and laughing. Was she truly healed? As I was preparing to leave, I watched Lee walk across the street and speak to Holly, a friend of Brian's. As I had not spoken to Holly since I'd arrived, I waved at her and called, "Take care!" Lee thought I was talking to her, and she whirled around, her face tight, and snarled, "*You* take care. You take *good* care."

A few minutes later I went to my car. Lee was standing behind it. For the first time, I spoke to her. "Drive carefully." Again, her whole demeanor changed from pleasant to furious, and she growled at me, "*You* be careful. You be *very* careful."

Well, that girl wasn't doing anything to help herself. Had Spirit been mistaken in telling me she'd been "dis-possessed"? Then I recalled a vision I'd had a few days before, in which I had seen Lee standing on a landing in Rose's house, a large, imposing, evil spectre made of dark yellow mist right beside her. Lee had flung herself at him in a frenzy, begging and pleading with him to take her back.

I told myself that Spirit had not failed Lee. She had a desperate desire to remain with her dark friend, a desire greater than could be overcome by good intentions and intervention. People are allowed the full expression of their free will, always. It is the Law.

I agreed to attend a party at Rose's new house, though I wasn't sure it was a good idea to begin spending much time with Rose, who had once been so unreliable and might never be a faithful friend. As I dressed for the party, I considered taking along a tiny gold cross, thinking to help Lee by slipping it into her purse or perhaps dropping it through her car window. Would the sight of an obvious exorcist's symbol shock her? It might cause a reaction she would not be able to handle. As I thought this over, a spirit voice intruded loudly and unpleasantly, saying, "If you're going to give her a cross, be sure you give her the triple cross." I try to be very wary of spirit voices. Many of these voices are off-shoots of our imagination. Others are mischevous spirits. Some are downright evil. A very few are communications from our higher selves, or beneficent spirits. It takes, I have discovered, years and years of testing before we achieve any measure of discernment about voices, and for that reason all messages from voices are best discounted as phony, mistakes, or intentionally misleading until we have learned otherwise.

The triple cross message meant nothing to me anyway. I supposed it was a variation on the term double-cross.

Lee was there when I arrived at Rose and Brian's house. She looked even more remarkably like Rose. Most odd was the fact that Rose seemed to take the astonishing transformation as a compliment, which made no sense to me because Lee's appearance seemed a parody of Rose rather than a compliment. I said nothing to Rose about this, as I was learning when to back off.

I went upstairs to leave my coat in one of the bedrooms, and as I stood in the room alone, I had a clear vision of the party in progress downstairs. I saw Lee sitting in a chair, looking around. From the top of her head a periscope appeared and then a man appeared beneath the periscope. He was middle-aged and swarthy, with dark eyes and a cruel demeanor. He reconnoitered the room, then slid back down into Lee's head, the periscope following after him.

After making prayers for everyone in the house, including Lee and Ellen, who were downstairs together, I returned to the party. I did not feel Spirit urging me to work on Lee, so I made no attempt to give her the cross and I did not speak to her except to say hello and goodbye. I knew better than to do a job as dangerous as this might be without the help of Spirit.

I did speak to Ellen, hoping to find that she was back to her old self, but she was as rambuctious, selfish and rude as her association with Lee had made her. I wondered why Rose and Brian were not concerned about Ellen, but I had spoken with each of them in turn and would not bring the matter up again.

About a month after the party, Lee abruptly left town. I was glad, especially for Ellen's sake, and hoped Lee would find help in her new home.

I soon realized that I was uncomfortable in Rose's house and just as uncomfortable in her presence. She was developing a greed about life that put me off, and a self-adoration that was becoming hard to take. Very little of the spirituality that had once been in Rose's nature showed itself any more. Without a fight, without making an announcement, I left the friendship and went on to other things, hoping Rose would not call and ask where I was.

On a summer morning a few weeks after making the decision to disconnect from Rose, I awoke with a certainty that I must throw away everything I had received from her over the years. Without giving myself time to mourn the loss of these things, some of which were lovely statues, books and tapes, I searched the house for anything she had given me and wrapped them together in a large bag. It was especially hard to give up a lovely lithograph of mystical beasts and personages, but I told myself that all meant all, and I surrendered that along with everything else.

I prayed that any positive energy in the things I was throwing away might find other outlets, and then I separated myself from them by smudging the large bag and stating my intention not to be in contact with any of its contents. I threw the bag away.

Sometime that day I found my attention drawn to a large bronze crucifix, a Russian antique that Rose had lent me. She told me that I could not keep it forever because it was not hers to give away. It belonged to a friend, a collector of antiques. I had forgotten the crucifix when I was gathering together Rose's gifts. Getting it down from the wall, I cleaned it a little and, as I was drying it, I suddenly remembered the voice I had heard on the night of Rose's party: If you're going to give her a cross, be sure you give her the triple cross.

The Russian crucifix had three horizontal bars across the long vertical one—a triple cross.

I mailed the crucifix to Rose with a casual note suggesting she return the antique to its owner. The day Rose received the package, she called, sounding panicked. Had I felt there was anything bad about the crucifix? No, I told her, I had merely felt that, as I had kept it for some months, it was time to give it back. She seemed puzzled and more than a little upset by my refusal to keep the crucifix. We chatted about inconsequential matters and said goodbye. I never called her again.

For many months I had visions of Rose. She seemed to be searching for me. There were dreams about her, dreams that became increasingly pointed. She often tried to take things from me in these dreams.

After the dreams and visions made it clear that Rose was engaged in wrong action, there was a meeting between us that occurred as I wavered between sleep and consciousness. I found myself on a vast, flat plain. As I approached the sole figure visible on the plain, I saw that it was Rose . . . but it was not a Rose I had ever seen before. Her eyes blazed with a hot, passionate hatred I hoped never to see again. The savagery in her face was so shocking that it sent me reeling back into my body. As I came fully awake, I felt terrible. My leaving the plain, while a battle obviously waited, seemed cowardly. But I had not intended to leave. It was the shock of those incredible eyes that sent me hurtling back into my body. I wished I had been able to stay and deal with whatever had been meant to happen, but it was too late. I was awake.

Soon thereafter, I dreamed of flying to Rose's house and see-ing Ellen waiting for me, grinning. The grin made me uneasy. I said to her, "You're not *helping* me." She grinned wider, say-ing, "Of *course* not." Nothing in her face looked like a child.

With the visions and dreams, the out-of-body encounter and my increasing dread, came memories. I recalled a peculiar incident that had taken place on the day I helped Rose and Brian move. Rose and Lisa, one of her colleagues, had been talking to me about Ellen and her remarkable resemblance to Brian. Rose said she had never been able to find any of herself in Ellen, and I replied, turning to wink at Lisa, that there was a strong streak of her in the child. When Rose asked what I meant, I laughed and said, "When Ellen has the television turned up loud and you tell her to turn it down and she says she will, she leans forward and turns it *up* even more. When she has the devil in her, she looks just like you." A shocked response ran through the room, the kind of thing called a *fris-son* that takes place when someone makes a remark having implications he's not aware of, while others are. The incident left me wondering what I'd said that caused such a marked response in both Lisa and Rose.

Visions of the shopping center, the site of the first exorcism I had been called on to perform, came thick and fast. The place was wreathed in darkness, though I did not know why. One evening I fell into a deep sleep and found myself in the astral component of that shopping center, walking toward a store that looked very different from the way it had looked when I had last been there, many months ago. The entrance to the store took up one wall. On the other three walls were chains, meant for holding human bodies. In two of the three slots were living people. The third slot was empty; I knew it was meant for me.

In the middle of the store were Rose and five or six of her colleagues. I do not remember seeing Brian there. When they saw me, they were stunned and furious. Calling into myself enough Light for whatever lay ahead, I rushed the group and scattered them. They ran from the store. I went to the slots.

The victims were wrapped in cocoons of energy. I freed the
young woman on my left, though it wasn't easy. She kicked
out at me viciously in a blind rage. Apparently she had offered
herself to the group's purpose and did not want to be freed.
The other potential victim, also a young woman, was glad to
be set free.

My dream had revealed to me that my friends were black
magicians who killed people for their energy. I tested the
dream message by driving to the shopping center to see
whether the store would look as it had in the dream. It did, to
the last detail, with the exception of the holding slots.

I was so appalled by the implications that I claimed the store
and its etheric and astral counterparts for the Light. Unsuspecting people shopped there. Why should they have to brush up
against black magic? Why, for that matter, did anyone have to
put up with evil?

That night as I sat in bed, a motion outside the window
caught my eye. It was a bat, but not a creation of Nature. Its
cuspid teeth were the size of paring knives and its eyes blazed
the same passionate hatred I had seen in Rose's eyes during
our encounter on the plain. Someone was very angry with me
for taking its territory. But there was nothing that someone
could do about it. After hovering outside my window for a few
moments, the bat-creature left.

Musing about the third slot in the store, the one meant for
me, I recalled a conversation I'd had with Rose years ago,
when we were visiting in my kitchen. As I handed her a mug
of tea, I saw that she was very preoccupied. I left her to her
thoughts until she looked up at me, and then I teased, "Did I
tell you? I've found out how I am going to die."

She was quite startled, and immediately asked what I knew.
She was very serious and had no inkling that I was joking.
"Some day," I said, "I am going to hand you something and,
for the first time ever, you will say 'thank you.' This will cause
me to keel over dead from shock."

She went back to her interior monologue. But for a moment,
she had been surprised and, it seemed, deeply concerned that

perhaps I really had seen the manner of my death. Now I knew that she had intended to *become* the manner of my death.

The realization brought to mind another conversation, of three years earlier, during which I asked Rose why it was that with so many talented occulists in the world, she worked with such a dull group of people. None of them seemed terribly gifted, though Rose had been an accurate psychic, and I wondered why she was content in such lacklustre company. Before answering, Rose stared down at her hands for a long time. Finally she said, "Every one of those people has . . . has done something special."

Now I understood what special thing they had done. Some—perhaps not all—of the group Rose worked with had formed allegiance with a much larger organization, one whose members have assaulted this world for eons. The black magicians were marchers in the army of the being I have refused to give a name to, my erstwhile visitor and sometime foe, the man who ate rice and dared me to withstand his scrutiny.

In the nearly three years since I came to understand Rose, I have had only fleeting dream-state encounters with her. None of them encouraged me to believe that she might change her ways. Indeed, I have no way of knowing whether she can change.

I have seen Rose's hatred only once since I found out what she was engaged in. In this last dream encounter, I was seated at a large desk, writing, in an elaborate old house on a wide river. Sensing that something was taking place outside, I opened large French doors to find a barge right outside, two royal personages seated at the front, on opposite sides of the barge. Between them was Rose. Her eyes blazed the same hot savage hatred of the plains encounter. We stared at each other, and then I slowly closed the doors and returned to the desk. But it seemed to me that I had left something undone, something important, so I went to the French doors and opened them. The barge was gone. All I could see was the wide river. Sensing that Rose's presence did not matter to what I was about to do, I spoke aloud into the airwaves. I told Rose that her attempts on me were hurting only herself, that there was no longer any way she could harm me, nothing further she could do to me. I chose my words very carefully, telling her that she ought to change her ways without saying anything to indicate that I had any preference one way or the other. I did not plead with her to heal herself. I said nothing about wanting her to change. I knew I must not invest anything of myself, including feelings, in Rose. It would be dangerous to say, "I hope you change," because giving hope is giving energy, and I could not afford to give Rose anything, for what I gave would surely be used against me.

Having made my emphatic but impersonal declaration, I closed the doors and went back to my writing.

This book is my offering to anyone who has been assaulted by evil and needs help. It contains definitions of the various kinds of evil as well as techniques for warding off the many types of evil that afflict us. I have intended the book for the lay reader and the occultist as well, and have kept the particular needs of both in mind as I wrote it.

For every one of us who seeks the Light, there is a Rose. Ignore this most ancient of truths, as I did, at your peril. Learn ways of protecting and defending yourself and you will find, as I have found, that for every danger, there is a way to safety.

PART II

Dancing in the Dark:
Understanding Evil

Chapter 3

The Drum That Makes No Sound: What Is Evil?

"Now the iron tongue of midnight hath told twelve."

—*A Midsummer Night's Dream*, William Shakespeare

What Is Evil?

In searching through the known history of the human race, we find a single tendency—perhaps the one tendency we have long held in common—and that is an urge to make ourselves stand out, apart from and elevated above others, for purposes of exploitation and domination. To dominate a land mass or a species for ego-centric reasons, whether or not we abuse the resources of that land or species, sets us apart from the fundamental laws of creation.

Using our minds and physical strength to separate from the all-life has given rise to evil. Evil is energy out of sync with the creator. All the uses of power can be defined as energy-plus-intention. Evil, then, is the use of energy to achieve anything that runs counter to the welfare of all creation.

Evil, exploitive and unnatural, has been present on the earth since human beings began to differentiate themselves from the

55

all-life. By this point, we have nearly differentiated ourselves right out of existence. Evil grows stronger every day because we have refined our myopia so effectively that we do not believe what we wish not to know. If we tell ourselves that there is no contamination in the seas, the seas are fine. If we tell ourselves that there is no hole in the ozone layer, there is no hole in the ozone layer. If we tell ourselves that there is no evil, there is no evil.

We live in a stranglehold inflicted on ourselves by ourselves, unable to experience the world honestly enough that we might perceive what is right there in front of us. All of our woes have derived first from our having learned how to differentiate ourselves from the rest of creation, and then from our having fallen in love with ourselves *as* differentiated beings.

All we can make available to evil is our ego, by which I mean our mundane self-awareness, rather than our sentience. Evil could not work on us successfully if we did not experience ourselves as separated from creation.

The physical world exists through the operation of forces, the forces of elements and kingdoms, fire and water, stones and animals. A force is evolving energy. Air is a force, as is a tree, as is a human being. If someone feels kindly toward another person, his energy is channeled into emotion. His emotion may further evolve into action. That is a force. Everyone has energy, and energy is channeled through the body as physical activity, through the mind as thought, and through the emotions as feelings. Any thought, feeling, or movement of the body is a force. This is true of human beings, plants, animals, stones, the four elements and directions.

Evil, too, is a force. That is, it is channeled energy. Channeled energy, or force, is the product of essential energy, or life-force, and occurs through physical forms and without them. Evil has no physical reality, but it is still a force.

All of human evolution is a force phenomenon. Much of our evolution derives from nature's need to adapt our species to the world. Some of our evolution, however, derives directly from human behavior, and evil is a product of our past activities in regard to the rest of creation. Evil is energy that was cast off from humankind's energy when we first learned how to establish ourselves as spiritually apart from the all-life. Evil was an accidental creation. It has grown every time we have focused our energy on personal ego, national ego, racial ego or species ego. It can become, in certain circumstances, as personified as we are and it knows our ways because it feeds directly upon us. Indeed, it was born—or ripped from—the human race. It is like a child we never meant to conceive and did not know we'd given birth to, a portion of our energy gone wrong, an idea we once had and cannot bring back, a part of our life force that we lost long ago when we made the misstep of trying to evolve independently from the laws of creation. We cannot bring it back because it is not under our control, having become separated from our intentions and lost to our authority. We cannot destroy it, but we can learn to keep ourselves safe from it.

This energy, evil, has evolved just as we have, learning techniques of manipulation on the physical, mental and emotional levels of human experience. There is, at this time, a crucial difference between primary evil and the human race: Evil has never lost the techniques of magic, of energy transferrence, of impressing ideas on the living and the dead, while most of us have allowed ourselves to forget these ancient methods.

We are now at a terrible disadvantage in our encounters with evil because we need to understand how these things are done, and to recognize when they are being done to us. We must understand how others can influence us and know how to repell that interference.

There are three categories of evil, primary, secondary and accidental. The third category is not, strictly speaking, evil, but I will define it here along with the two actual evils in order to offer the broadest possible overview of the occult phenomenon we are dealing with.

Primary Evil

Primary evil is a force. It is energy focused by intention. This energy exists outside the laws of nature and therefore has no means of perpetuating itself, feeding itself, or moving from its place outside of this planet toward this planet. In order to keep itself extant, it needs to feed on something that is legitimate, something that does exist within the laws of nature. That something which feeds evil—unwittingly and knowingly—is human beings.

Evil, an energy force, can sometimes differentiate itself into personalities. These personalities are not human beings but they take on human characteristics because the energy of evil, as I have said, comes from the human race. Whenever evil personalities can manage to do so, they take energy from living and dead human beings. This allows them to maintain "life". An evil being can sustain itself and then go beyond mere sustenence to the acquisition of territory and influence simply by using a real human being, living or dead.

The relationship between primary evil and the human race is twofold: Individuated beings of primary evil need our energy in order to maintain themselves as personalities, and primary evil needs our cooperation in order to stick close to this planet. Without human energy and interaction, evil beings would lose first their individuation and then their energy. In other words, without us, they could not exist at all, in any realm. It is we who feed them and we who permit their proximity to the earth.

Evil works on the human race by taking advantage of our weaknesses, our illusions, and our desires. Evil works on us through subtle influence, moving close to us each time we fall into a state of emotional, mental or physical weakness. Evil feeds on our physical energy when we are tortured, and sometimes during ritual.

Primary evil can possess a human being without the victim knowing that he is possessed. Primary evil can take our energy without our having any inkling as to what is going on.

The more evil creatures there are, the better organized evil is. The more energy evil can take from human beings, the greater the opportunity for creating individuated evil creatures.

In other words, the more evil there is, the more there can be. The less there is, the less there will be. Primary evil is motivated by itself, not by anything outside it. Because it exists outside the laws of creation, it has no destiny—other than whatever it can make for itself. Because it was created by accident and did not come about through the laws of creation, it has no relationship to the plant, animal, or stone kingdoms, only to the kingdom from which it sprang, the human race.

There are human beings, alive and dead, who work in cooperation with the energy of primary evil, and these people are responsible for a portion of the phonemonon called secondary evil.

Secondary Evil

Human beings who disregard the laws of free will and arrogate other people's destinies for their own use are practicing secondary evil. These people are human, unlike primary evil, and their rights and responsibilities are the same that every human being has. They are bound by the laws of right action and responsible for any abrogation of others' rights. They are, therefore, responsible for their deeds and bound by the laws of karma to make reparation for any interference with others' will or energy.

Beings of secondary evil may be alive or dead, but they are always members of the human race and never stones, plants or animals. Sometimes these beings are in league with primary evil, and sometimes not. When a being of secondary evil is aiding primary evil with or without his knowledge, he is always engaged in furthering the needs of primary evil, foremost by giving some of his energy to primary evil and secondarily by taking actions that promote the requirements of primary evil. As long as he is engaged with primary evil, he is helping primary evil—*whether or not* he believes this to be the case. Sometimes a practitioner of secondary evil believes himself to be using primary evil to further his ambitions, but no human being can use primary evil without his energy supply being diminished, so he is being used by primary evil no matter what he believes.

Primary evil has, of course, no interest in the human race except as it provides food and opportunities for primary evil to stay close to this world. Primary evil will always maintain a partnership with secondary evil until the human being loses his usefulness. At that point, when he is no longer a conduit between primary evil and the human race, or when he has lost so much energy that he is not a good provider any longer, the energy of primary evil will absorb the final life essence of its human benefactor, at which point he will die.

Not all people practicing secondary evil are allied with primary evil. Some are occultists practicing black magic for the purpose of procuring energy or power. Some occultists assault other occultists for the fun of showing off their superior abilities. These games may end when a sorcerer feels he has established his superior position. They may end only when the occultist has killed his opponent, crippled him, or driven him mad.

Secondary evil, then, involves a real human being who may or may not be working with primary evil. When he is allied with primary evil, he may or may not be aware of this. The human being may be so deeply involved with primary evil as to be possessed, which means that his will is no longer his own. If he has been entirely taken over by primary evil, he has given permission for this transaction to take place because, while primary evil can influence us without permission, it cannot establish authority over our will and thus possess us until we give permission for this to happen. The trick involved here is that, while primary evil must ask permission to take over our will, it does not have to announce itself *as* evil. It can tell us that it is Jesus Christ, or our long-dead grandfather, or anything else that might encourage us to give up our will to it.

There are degrees of secondary evil. Any invasive magic practiced by one human being on another is, by reason of its being invasive, evil. The use of our power, will, energy, or any aspect of occult knowledge for the purpose of making another person do something that is not in his best interests is secondary evil. (The terms secondary and primary evil are meant to clarify human evil and non-human evil, and are not intended as value judgements. One is not worse than the other; the two evils are practiced by different entities.)

A human being engaged in evil can disengage himself from evil at any time. This is true of the black magician working alone and the one working in alliance with primary evil. The practice of evil does not imply eternity. No one is, by his nature, destined to practice black magic, and no one who has embarked on that road is obliged to stay on it. No one who has allowed primary evil to influence him or even to possess him is bound to continue his relationship with primary evil. All practitioners of secondary evil may step away from evil at any time.

Accidental Evil

This broadest of the three categories of evil involves woes of misdirection and mistaken purpose, as opposed to deliberate actions, invasion, and black magic. Accidental evil includes the phenomenon of ghosts, poltergeists, hauntings, much of so-called mental illness—including identity disorder, obsession, and battle stress syndrome—as well as types of possession that derive from error. Accidental evil will be addressed in the next chapter.

How Evil Thrives

Energy As Food for Evil

Before we can comprehend the activities of evil, we must look at energy and what it means. All of life is energy-on-the-move. Energy is not just what we do, but also what we think and feel. Intention is energy given direction. Desire is energy focused and magnified.

Because we are made of energy, we are affected by energy

in our proximity. If a thunderstorm approaches a town, that storm will affect everything in its path. Nothing alive is ever left out of the great circle of energy. Nothing alive is ever really on its own no matter what circumstances pertain at any given moment.

The only instance in which a being or a phenomenon of energy is set apart from the circle of life is when its nature or its intentions set it apart from the laws of creation. Since evil is an accidental off-shoot of humankind, energy cast off that took on existence of its own without having been created intentionally, and since it feeds itself wholly by means that do not fall within the laws of creation, evil is never part of the circle of life. It was not born naturally and its continuity of existence is based on stolen food. Its existence then is always outside the circle of life.

What does the circle of life look like, and what does it look like to stand outside it? All of creation has energy as its essential component. All physical forms in this world, stones, plants, animals and human beings, have energy at their foundation and energy as their common link. For this reason, there is a resonation of commonality between stone and human being, plant and bird. There is, as well, a resonation of commonality between all the members of the four form kingdoms and the elements. Air, water, fire and earth are forces of energy that exist without forms, whereas stones, plants, animals and human beings are forces-in-form made of the same energy of which the elements are made. All of the four elements and four kingdoms interact because they are made of the same essence.

Evil stands outside this circle. No stone, plant, animal or human being resonates to evil because there is no innate, rightfully-claimed energy in primary evil. For that reason, the elements do not resonate to evil, either. Therefore, evil cannot procure any food through the natural, daily interactions within the great circle of life. How, then, does it continue its existence?

Primary evil as a mass phenomenon is continually born and grows in the same way it was first manifested; it accrues from the accidental cooperation of the human race. As there were, eons ago, people who used their will to create separation and, in doing so, allowed evil to come into being, so there are such individuals and groups of people today. Evil as a phenomenon continues its existence by being perpetually, inadvertently created by the human race.

When evil differentiates into individual beings, how do these beings continue their existence? They do it by stealing the energy of human beings, either through torture or through prolonged attack—such as the attack I experienced at the hands of Lee.

Besides the taking of human energy through torture or assault, there are instances in which a human being freely offers his energy to evil. In such cases, the human being is seeking to join with a power he assumes is very great, and he hopes to receive, in return for his energy, favors of wisdom or power. This transaction never takes place, for once evil has drained a human being of his usefulness and his energy, it is done with him.

The only on-going transaction between primary evil and human beings involves a partnership between primary evil and people practicing secondary evil. A being of primary evil must have a contact on the earth if he is to continue getting the energy he needs to continue his existence, and if he is to stay close to human activity and seek out additional victims. This contact person is vitally important. He soon learns that if he does not bring victims to his master, through torturing people or establishing links through which the being of primary evil can assault a victim and take his life-force, the evil being will take his human contact for food. The human slave is motivated to find, in any way he can, human energy to feed his master for he knows that, if the supply of energy runs out, his own energy will be forfeit.

Primary evil may suck energy from a human being through mental torture. This accounts for a great many instances of so-called psychosis, in which a mentally-disturbed person is believed to be imagining things when in fact he is being attacked by primary evil for the purpose of taking energy. It is difficult for an imbalanced human being to hold onto his life force; the greater his imbalance, the easier it is for primary evil to steal his energy.

Primary evil often gets its energy from groups of people who have been tricked into believing that the sacrifice of their lives is an honor. Many incidents of group suicide for religious or patriotic purposes involve this phenomenon. Primary evil needs energy, finds a group of zealots, and influences the group to suicide by encouraging its members to believe what they already wish to believe—that their deaths will serve a grand purpose and aid in higher power. What their deaths actually serve is primary evil. These victims are merely dupes and are not practicing secondary evil. They believe they are serving a righteous cause. Their beliefs are mistaken.

Failing the acquiring of energy through compliance, there is torture. The life force that animates every human being can be appropriated without his consent if correct technique is used. While I do not wish to aid the workings of a deranged person by being too explicit, I have to offer a little information about torture in order to illustrate the dynamics of the torture-energy exchange. I will keep the technical aspects to a minimum for the sake of keeping hidden what ought to be hidden. Know, however, that a being of primary evil, as opposed to a deranged human being, is perfectly familiar with all this and cannot learn anything new from me.

In torturing someone, a balance must be maintained between engendering fear and keeping the victim in a susceptible condition of consciousness. Pain creates fear—fear of further pain. Fear is a kind of life force, an energy, and while you and I cannot use fear for anything, primary evil can take food from it.

The victim needs to be kept fearful but he must not be killed until his energy has been appropriated. If he dies before his life-force is taken from him, then it cannot be taken. His energy is not obtainable unless he voluntarily releases it. It cannot be wrenched from him. So the victim must be kept in enough pain—whether emotional or physical pain doesn't matter—to engender and maintain fear. But he must not be so badly hurt or frightened that he passes out from shock, blood-loss, or a heart attack. If he passes out, his fear diminishes. If he dies, his energy cannot be stolen.

The longer a victim can be kept aware and frightened, the greater the amount of fear he will manifest. If he can be brought to such a state of frenzy that he hysterically throws out his fear, then primary evil can grab that fear as he throws it out. Once that happens, the victim usually dies because he has invested nearly all of his life-force in fear. If he does not die, he becomes an ego-less, non-functioning creature without enough energy to sustain himself for very long.

With the death of the tortured man, primary evil has harvested some food for itself.

It is most often the case that people are taken to kidnapping and torture through enticement. Something cherished is promised, perhaps sexual favors, drugs, knowledge, or power. Once the human being who is working for primary evil has captured his victim, he can, with knowledge of occult/mundane anatomy, manipulate his victim's body in such a way as to keep him immobilized. It is possible, using this understanding of our physical and etheric bodies, to prevent someone from crying out or even knowing where he is.

Why Evil Provoked the Inquisition and "Witch" Trials

There have been times in history when primary evil received nourishment through wholly legal channels. The worst of these times in our recent history was the period of witch-hunts throughout Europe and North America, an era that included the Spanish Inquisition and the Salem witch trials among others. (I would prefer not to insult the Wicca religion by using the term "witch" as a synonym for evil-doer, but I must do so because the term has been a misnomer for such a long time that I cannot comment on historical matters without falling into the common usage of the term.)

The trials to which accused witches were put met the requirements for separating a human being from his essential energy—the separation making it possible for primary evil to take that energy. Long, drawn-out torture was the most effective way of taking energy from the living, but even brief trials such as the ducking stool yielded energy. The accused was strapped into a stool and lowered into water deep enough to cover her head. If water, believed to be the instrument of baptism, rejected the accused, it meant that she was guilty. If water accepted her—that is, if she remained immersed—it meant that she was innocent. The test nearly always took so long, however, that when they finally hauled the accused up, she was dead—her energy lost, in a frenzy of terror, to primary evil. Even the simple trials, then, were effective for taking human energy.

It is probable that most of the accusers, torturers and executioners involved in these trials believed they were serving God by helping rid the world of the devil. But in this world, belief and truth rarely cross paths. And mistaken belief does not excuse cruelty. Every one of the accusers, torturers and executioners who tormented their sisters and brothers during those hellish hundreds of years will, at some time, in some manner, have to make reparation for what they did. It is a time in our history for which the human race owes itself a major apology.

While it appeared, in all of the pogroms, that decent people were tracking down bad ones in order to save the world from evil, precisely the opposite happened. In the tortures and murders, primary evil was the instigator *because it was the beneficiary.* The men and women who were jailed, ostracized, tortured and murdered for being witches were not the evil ones; the evil ones were behind these persecutions. The Spanish Inquisition and all the other witch-hunts provided centuries of food for primary evil, keeping it energized, powerful, close to this realm and ubiquitous. Primary evil initiated and orchestrated the whole scenario, whether an isolated case of witchcraft in Scotland where one woman was burned alive or the many instances of mass burnings in Spain. Primary evil made use of humankind's belief that we can identify evil beings by physical characteristics. Evil used that wholly erroneous belief to provide itself with endless food, taking the energy of the accused witches while they were being tortured and murdered in particularly cruel ways. It was a banquet *for* evil, arranged *by* evil, and served up by the human race in a frenzy of fear and ignorance.

Slaves and Masters

Because there are so many partnerships between primary evil and human beings, some clarification about the slave-master relationship is necessary. The human being may be a willing slave, but he is not necessarily informed. He may have given himself up to his possessor for knowledge or power, or to be allied with a power greater than he has known. In order for the possessor to take possession, he must, in accordance with the universal law of free will, tell the human being that he wants to use him. But he does not have to announce himself as evil. He may identify himself as virtually anyone with whom the human being might desire contact. He may declare that he is God, the Buddha, the Virgin Mary, the earth god Pan, Allah, or an ancient god of the lost continent of Atlantis. He may announce himself as a humble monk who died young and wishes to help his fellow man by working through a living human being. Primary evil is capable of impersonating *anything* and *anyone*, and will use any of our desires and illusions in order to make allies of us.

The master-slave relationship between primary evil and human beings is where religions such as Christianity have gotten the idea of satan and satan-worshipper. In order for primary evil as a phenomenon—and especially for individuated beings of primary evil—to stay close to the earth, there must be alliances between primary evil and living human beings. The contact is vital.

Are beings of primary evil "satan"? Not exactly. Evil does not have a name, and religions have made a big mistake in personifying evil because the personification of energy or an idea makes that energy or idea vivid, thus bringing it closer to our realm than it needs to be. Any attempt to enliven a notion or a phenomenon must begin with energy. The giving of names creates energy.

Did human beings create evil? Absolutely not. Evil sprang from mistakes made by the human race, but its creation was accidental, so it cannot be said that mankind made evil. Further, evil achieved independence from its human source very quickly, and its existence is not intended to be entwined with the destiny of man.

In giving identities and characteristics to primary evil, we have been guilty of energizing it and attracting it to our world. The darkness that seeks our energy is best kept away from us, not drawn toward us by investing it with personality. Whether you call primary evil satan, the devil, Old Hob, or Mr. Smith, you are coloring it and thus enlivening it. By attributing characteristics to the phenomenon of evil, we create new false-hoods about it or perpetuate old ones. In this way, religions have done us no favor, because every religion holds to beliefs and superstitions about the dark force and there is, in these, a little truth and a lot of error.

Human slaves of primary evil often try to position them-selves as teachers or counselors, giving themselves access to the greatest possible number of potential victims. Sometimes the human slave, serving as a conduit between primary evil and the human race, is fully aware of his role. Sometimes he's been duped. Duplicity is the most-used factor in the interaction between evil and us. When we realize how many of our beliefs are based on illusion, we can see how easily we may be tricked. Our desires, fears and tendency to self-delusion make us vulnerable, and to the degree that we have invested in social programming, we are vulnerable on that front, too. Only the person who sees the world as it truly is can hope to be free of deception by forces outside him. Is there, anywhere in the world, such a person? Only the person who sees himself as he truly is can hope to be free of deception from inside himself. Is there, anywhere in the world, such a person?

While the life forms around us are real, and we are real, the way we perceive these forms and ourselves is often illusory. We are, from infancy, forced to live with certain givens that prejudice our seeing. If we are taught that we must fear dogs, we will grow up fearing dogs. The possibility that we will step aside from this assumption, even briefly, and get to know a dog on his terms—and ours—depends entirely on the strength of our share of the collective unconscious. If we have a strong feeling for seeing things as they really are, we will, at some point, feel an urge to set aside our prejudice about dogs, even if only for a little while. We will play with a dog, study his ways, and begin, with that first step, to cut loose from the precepts regarding dogs that we were raised with.

If we are taught that we are helpless without guidance and that nobody can ever achieve his own life view, that we must find a teacher to help us along our path, then we will seek out one teacher or guru after another. Often the teacher will be a carrier of evil, for, if your job is to find help and his is to create a link between primary evil and the human race, the two of you will come together as a natural consequence of your need for guidance and his need for a victim.

The master-slave relationship extends beyond the acquiring of food and influence, acquisitions made for primary or secondary evil, to the performing of tasks by slaves, alive or dead.

There is a long tradition of trying to force dead spirits to watch over our belongings. This is believed to be accomplished by killing someone in a manner that engenders great fear, and coercing the victim into believing that he will have a peaceful existence after death if he obeys you, and that if he disobeys you, he will be harmed.

This method of soul-kidnapping involves more than just torture-killing. It includes hypnosis as well, because the spirit of the dead man must believe what you tell him if he is going to follow your orders. This very tricky business backfires at least as often as it succeeds. For every compliant spirit who guards someone's altar, treasure chest, or territory, there is a spirit who panicked in the first stage of his death and entered the body of the killer. It is natural to seek safe haven in the arms of one's tormentor, as has been demonstrated many times in the torture chamber. The person inflicting pain is perceived, in stages, first as the enemy and then as saviour, because he is in the god-like position of being able to stop the pain. His approval, even his love, is sought by the tortured one because this love is all that can stop the suffering.

When someone kills a man or several men in order to rivet their spirits to a place and thus keep that place guarded, he is taking an awful chance. The spirit, if properly hypnotized, may obey orders and guard the tomb as instructed, but he may just as easily rush out of his agonized body—if he's been tortured—or his newly-dead body—if he was killed in a surprise attack—and leap straight into the body of his killer. It is one thing to take someone's energy, quite another to take his personality. Energy can be controlled; a personality usually cannot. It is far easier to manipulate a man's body than to take complete control of his mind.

A recent series of sacrificial murders at the border of Texas and Mexico illustrates how easily this method of soul-sacrifice can fail. Several men were tortured to death by a drug-dealing gang, the torturers hoping to receive protection for their drug business from the dead. Protection would derive, the gang hoped, from the spirits of the dead, who would guard the gang's assets and territory. Too, the gang hoped that evil would reward them for the gift of the dead men's souls. The killers were found out in a very brief time, however, and every facet of their operation was brought to light, from their worldly activity as drug sellers to their esoteric work as "satanic" torturers. The police had no trouble rounding them up, finding the remains of their victims, and eliciting confessions from the criminals. Absolutely *none* of the cult's beliefs about the power of soul-theft to protect them was borne out.

When the technique of killing someone in order to guard something works, it usually works by accident. If someone dies without warning, if he is young and strong and has no reason to think he might die soon, and if the shock of dying is powerful enough to disorient him, he may stay in or near the place of his death for a long time, maybe even hundreds of years. This is not due to the cleverness of his killer; he does not stay where he died because someone told him to, but because he is too confused not to stay there. This is the simple phenomenon of ghosts. If people do not have good deaths and journey out of this realm, they may stick around and bumble their way through a mockery of their former lives, moving without direction or purpose, their sole intention being to continue doing whatever they were doing right before they died. It is a very sad thing.

These ghosts are the reason why certain places feel scary to us. A graveyard, a house, a stretch of highway may repell us because there is energy there belonging to someone who died in that spot, perhaps last year, perhaps two hundred years ago. The energy is negative because the death was an unhappy one and the death-passage was aborted, leaving the spirit stranded where he doesn't belong.

The so-called curse of the mummy in an Egyptian tomb invaded by explorers was probably not a curse, which is intentionally-directed energy, but an aggregate of negative energy that accrued from the deaths of several people who were killed as tomb-slaves. When a functionary is told to guard a tomb and knows that his life is forfeit if the tomb is invaded, he will collect people, kill them in a ritual manner, and expect their spirits to guard the tomb. Some or all of the dead may do as they are told, but because they exist in a state of limbo, they are unhappy spirits and they produce negative energy. That negative energy is what really "guards" the tomb because it repells invaders. So when this method of soul-kidnapping works at all, it works because an atmosphere of unhappiness is established in the tomb by the presence of spirits in limbo, and not because the killer has hypnotized the spirits successfully.

The entire transaction is iffy because human beings are very difficult to manipulate in death. Sometimes the use of spirit slaves as guards works. Just as often—perhaps more often—it fails.

What Evil Looks Like

Evil does not give off bad vibes. This is the most important truth about primary and secondary evil, because it disabuses us of the mistaken notion that we can identify the presence of evil by reading our sensations and scrutinizing people for particular characteristics. The fact that evil is very difficult to spot should prevent our going on witch-hunts.

If there is no single perceptible characteristic of primary or secondary evil, then how can we know if someone is evil? The truth is that we cannot know an evil being except by the effects he has on others. Unless you are an exorcist with many years of experience with evil, there is no way you can identify it. The best we can do is to identify evil-*doings* when they affect us. We cannot expect to identify the doer.

Does this mean that, on the one hand there is evil working on this planet and that, on the other, there is no way of telling who is evil and who is not? That is precisely what it means.

True evil beings are impossible to spot because they have no single characteristic in common, and because their greatest need is to stay hidden. The evil beings I have seen have used some of their precious store of energy to draw people to them and then to soothe those people into believing that they were safe in the evil one's company. Evil beings can create an aura of peace around themselves and their homes. It is not a real peace, but a projection, done intentionally so as to encourage others to relax in their presence and trust them.

Other evil ones have no charisma at all. They may be so dull, so lifeless, as to be remarkable only for their drabness. This keeps them hidden.

I have never encountered an evil being who looked like the Christian idea of the devil. That depiction is a deliberate corruption of the pre-Christian god, Pan, an earth god, or earth spirit, who was said to look like a combination of human being and long-legged goat. Taking Pan's image and twisting it to personify evil was surely an attempt on the part of early church founders to make a case for Christians as the good guys and pagans as the bad guys.

I have rarely seen an evil being who looked like a tree or a stone or who bore any resemblance to an animal in its natural state. Primary evil may sometimes take on the guise of an animal because animals are closer than other life forms to human beings. For that reason, we tend to fear animals more easily than we would fear the power of plants or stones.

Primary evil takes the animal guise to which its activity is best suited. Since much evil activity takes place when people are sleeping, primary evil sometimes takes the form of a bat, cat, or owl, as these are nocturnal creatures. Because much magic is performed with the aid of water, and because water is a very powerful element, primary evil may sometimes take the guise of a toad or frog. Primary evil may take on the appearance of a wolf because wolves, when hungry enough, are frightened of very little except fire. Also, because the wolf and the dog are very closely related, primary evil may adopt a wolf-like appearance in order to move about on the earth without frightening domestic dogs. Dogs are often psychically sensitive and they sense the presence of evil very quickly. When they do, they howl and bark until the evil being goes away. There have been times, when I was under attack, when the dogs in my neighborhood set up a howl that went on until the attack subsided. A colleague whose work as an exorcist and counselor sometimes attracts attack has reported to me that several dogs in his vicinity howl when he is subjected to night-time attack.

Evil is not allied exclusively with any race, though surely all races are susceptible to evil. Evil is not allied exclusively with any religion or philosophy, though any of these may have evil working within them at any time. Religion is often a cover for evil. What safer disguise for evil than to present itself as a nun, a missionary? There is evil working among people who practice the old ways, so-called pagans, especially today with the revival of interest in ancient knowledge. There is evil among the disenfranchised. Herbalists and shamans and healers can be evil. Anyone can be evil, and no one and nothing is beyond evil's reach. Our naive attitude regarding particular religions and certain professions, such as counselors, those who give free meals to the homeless, and other apparently blameless endeavors, gets us into trouble all the time.

Because we in the West have been surrounded by Christianity for so long, we have developed notions that would link the activities of evil to Christian-related themes. Our social attitudes toward evil, nearly all of which are erroneous, lead us to mistakenly think that evil pays most of its attention to Christians. The underlying justification for this notion is the idea that since professed Christians are so much purer than the rest of the citizenry, evil is more eager to touch them than to bother with the rest of us. No group of people is inherently purer than others. Evil does not care more about Christians than about anyone else. Evil will seek out anyone potentially useful, wait to see in what ways he might be vulnerable to it, and then move in on him. That is how evil operates. The idea that evil beings put in time "punishing" anyone for following Jesus is ridiculous. Evil does not have energy to waste in punishing anyone.

Evil beings do not have a set of earth-realm rituals. They don't say masses backward or use inverted crosses in their work. They must understand the dynamics of all behavior in this realm in order to make inroads here, but they have no interest in our theories, rituals or religious beliefs except as those things afford them opportunities for invasion. If evil were as attentive to Christianity as our society believes it is, then evil would have to have grown from the church. But it didn't. It's much older than Christianity. The reason some people are confused about this is that the Bible offers an explanation for the existence of evil by stating that the Almighty gave this planet to a rebellious angel who had once been a Light-bearer. This assertion is not true. And the Biblical depiction of evil as a liar and deceiver is, while correct, much too limited to be of real use in understanding the nature and scope of evil.

Primary evil functions by making twofold use of our fear. When we are afraid, we are not as protected as we ought to be. Fear weakens the energy body, the formless and invisible energy that vivifies our physical form. Thus weakened, we lose our connection with the life around us that warns us of danger. We lose contact with our intuition and with the all-life that partners our intuition by informing it.

When we have been fearful for long enough to weaken our energy body, holes are made throughout that energy. An attentive being, waiting for his chance, can slip his energy through those holes and tie himself to us. Then he begins to suck on our energy. We become weaker and weaker. The weaker we are, the harder it is for our deeper self to either warn us that we're in trouble or guide us out of danger.

Another conduit to human energy is anger. When we are angry for a long period of time, we focus on our anger and begin to obsess over it. Obsession is dangerous because it leads to delusion. When we are focused on an issue beyond what is necessary, we must take energy from the healthy pursuits of our lives and invest it in this unhealthy pursuit. We create for ourselves what occultists call a thought-form, a mock-being born entirely of our energy. This being grows on the anger we give it.

There comes a time when the thought-form can float away from us. Its power is so great that it moves toward a person or situation that can provide it with even more anger than we have given it. After it moves away, we may process our anger and become healthy, but there is no way to recall the thought-form once it has left us. It floats like a balloon, moving toward energy that vibrates to the anger it is made of. If we are lucky, its energy will run out—and the thought-form will disappear—before it can become big enough to attach itself to a volatile situation such as a riot or a perpetually-angry family. If it cannot continue to feed itself, it will shrivel and disappear. If it finds nourishment, it will grow until it becomes big enough to find a home-base, such as a family where many angry people live together and generate anger on a daily basis. If our thought-form attaches itself to a home or prison or warzone it will continue to grow until it becomes powerful enough to feed other thought-forms, or to feed anger to already-angry people in its vicinity. In that way, we human beings create negativity that other people have to deal with, and we do it every day. If our thought-forms are small, it is we who must deal with them; if they are powerful, then others must live with them.

If we feel slighted and if we brood about this, the feeling of having been abused will create a rut in our consciousness and soon this rut will begin to attain a shape and color. If we feel that others have stolen our glory, the thought-form will look like an open wound, perhaps, or a tarnished medal. We may feel vengeful, in which case the thought-form will take on the appearance of a fierce beast. The form need not resemble anything found in nature. It may be a blob of colors with sparks shooting from it, a dark red hole, or a diseased tree. Its appearance derives from the quality of the feelings that birthed it.

Sometimes our thought-forms are appropriated by evil because the forms, being energy, are food. We tend to think of hurt and anger and the whole realm of negative feelings as a little less than real because they are unfortunate. But negative feelings are as real as positive ones. Because all emotion is energy, it follows that all emotion is food.

A major error we make in considering evil and how it operates is to assume that everything in the universe has moral boundaries. Evil has no morality. This is an important point, because sometimes when we are approached by evil, we are coerced into a relationship with it by being told that its way of looking at life is "different" from ours. It is, we are told, a kind of morality that is beyond the ken of the human race. This is nonsense. Evil has no morality whatever because morality assumes a knowledge and acknowledgement of right and wrong. To a being who is not even alive, and whose very existence depends on stealing energy, there is no such thing as right or wrong--there is only survival.

While I am usually loath to use animals for unhappy similes, it is simplest at this juncture to compare primary evil with cockroaches, though, of course, cockroaches are a legitimate part of nature. Cockroaches live through scavenging, often from human beings. So it is with primary evil. Without human energy, they would have no way to remain extant. Without our energy, they could not stay close to or live on this planet because there is nothing to draw them here except us. They have no claim to this realm. They are not part of the all-life.

Evil beings are like thought-forms, but they have grown so strong and so numerous that, unlike the ephemeral thought-form, they have managed to remain in existence for thousands, perhaps millions, of years. Because we know only a little about human history, we cannot know how long these unintended off-spring of ours have been in existence.

Are they united? Unlikely. Unity implies common caring, and there is no caring in these beings. But they are probably organized. It is easier to make an assault on your food if you divide up the labor involved in that assault. Too, it is far easier to keep an organized force going than to take your chances that, without others, you will be able to get your food and continue your existence.

What, besides food, do they want from us? Primary evil wants this planet. It has no place to be, and the search for food is endless when you have no legitimate claim to any energy, but must steal to stay extant. Primary evil has enough sense of intention to desire a place where food is in continual supply, and if they can connect enough of them to enough of us, there will be a permanent, assured transfusion going on between the human race and the phenomenon of evil.

Manifestations of Primary Evil

Because creatures of primary evil take their energy from us and because they were birthed by our mistakes, they are able to look like us. But there are two fundamental reasons why they are nothing like us. They do not exist within a cycle of birth, growth, death and rebirth, and they do not possess, unto themselves, any inherent energy, quality, or destiny.

Because they have no bona fide affiliation with any life form, they have no ties with any particular appearance. They tend, because we are the reason for their existence, to look human. If you encounter one of these beings in your dream state, it may be a female and then transform into a male. It may be short and then tall. It can change its physical appearance, its racial identity and its gender in a twinkling because, having none of these by right, it mocks all of them with equal ease.

While beings of primary evil can take on any appearance they wish, I have found the incidences of animal appearance to be rare and fleeting.

If you are traveling out of your body, asleep or awake, and you find yourself confronted with a being who changes its appearance often or quickly, you are dealing with either a mental projection created by a black magician, and therefore with secondary evil, or with a being of primary evil who is altering its appearance in order to find out what will appeal to you.

A friend reported to me an out-of-body encounter that took place while he was sleeping, and which he assumed was a nightmare, in which something chased him while changing from a female to a male to a small child and then to a female wearing curlers. This being was trying to find out what my friend would stop and talk to. Luckily for him, his intuition warned him away from the being at its initial appearance. He ran from it because he wanted nothing to do with it no matter how appealing its form. Had he allowed himself to be hooked by any of the chaser's false appearances, he might have had a nasty enlightenment that lasted for months and entered fully into his life. Instead, he had a frightening "dream" and got away from the being before the encounter could harm him.

Because primary evil is not part of the all-life, neither plant nor stone nor animal nor human, and because it is not an element, it has no gender.

Sex and Primary Evil

Some religious beliefs have steered us wrong by claiming that evil is urgently sexual, and that evil seeks sex with humankind because of its sex drive. That is wrong, for evil has no sexuality and its sole drive is to find food. Evil beings use our sexuality against us—as they use any aspect of us that makes us vulnerable—but they have no sex drive of their own because, having no gender, being non-biological, in fact unalive, there is no sex component in primary evil.

When people have believed, as they have throughout history, that beings of darkness engage our attention through sex, they have not been entirely wrong because evil will use any of our desires as a road into our lives. It is, then, a good idea to identify and work on healing any of your sexual difficulties, especially overattachment, because these can be used against you, particularly in your sleep state, when evil is most likely to approach you.

Primary Evil and Humor

It is interesting to me that our language contains such expressions as "satanic glee" and "devilish laughter." These are reflections of our ignorance regarding the dark force. In fact, no being of primary evil ever has a sense of humor. In an encounter with evil, there may be heavy-handed joking or words of sarcasm, but there is no real humor in these beings and no laughter. The idea of a dark creature laughing in triumph when it conquers us is a mistaken human creation. Primary evil has no sense of humor.

The two distinct differences between evil and us—absence of sexuality and humor—must not be used as "evidence" in witch-hunts. The fact that your friend Al has no sense of humor does not mean that Al is evil. Whatever the reason, human beings may lack humor and may be asexual; neither of these conditions means that a person is practicing evil or headed in that direction.

"Satan" Worship

How the Dead Become "Satan"

Dying is not the end of life, but a new beginning. That's how it is when we die successfully, journeying on to the realms beyond this one. When people die in fear or pain, die without warning, or die while still strongly attached to this realm, they may blunder around here for years, not knowing that they are dead and having no clear idea what to do with themselves. If they do not receive help from Spirit—and often they either do not get it or cannot understand it when help is offered—they make a whole new false life for themselves in the shadow world of the dead, mocking the real life they have left, going without guidance and nourishment. Sometimes they learn to cause trouble among the living as a substitute for having any real existence of their own. Having no ability to journey on, sometimes having no understanding of their state, these ghosts may learn to abuse the living as a focus for their unhappiness. If they know they have died, they may use the living as a target for their rage at being dead.

Often, when a person dies and cannot make peace with his new circumstances, he may grab the body of someone near him, someone of mere physical proximity or someone who loves him. He will live through that body for as long as he can get away with it, as is described in the next chapter on accidental evil. Though he doesn't fully comprehend that his action is wrong, he has a vague feeling that something isn't right. A sense of unease leads him to action—any kind of action—instead of reflection. He does not want to face being dead or acknowledge that he is abusing someone's body, so he looks for means of replicating the life he once had and feels ought to belong to him still. If he was musical, he will force his unwilling, unknowing host to find music for him. If he has an appetite for alcohol or drugs, he will force his host to find these for him.

If the unhappy dead man cannot find a host whom he can possess, he will search for anyone living who might further his desires for the life he abruptly or painfully left. He cannot possess these people, but he torments them with his cravings and urges them to behaviors that imitate his.

It is these unhappy shadow-beings, the rebellious, angry dead, who cause much of the trouble wrongly attributed to evil. In order to make a place for themselves, they approach the miserable, the left-out, the confused, the mentally-disturbed, the bereft. They seek out anyone who might be manipulated. They will find anyone who indulges in dangerous occultism such as the Ouija board. They will find disenfranchised, confused young people who, drifting and without dreams of their own, are open to direction by a spirit force. If the young person takes drugs or alcohol and the dead spirit desires this, a bond is quickly formed.

The miserable spirit does not necessarily intend to cause harm. He's just trying to find a place where he can live a reasonable facsimile of his former life. Often, these beings are not aware of what they are doing because they behave wholly on impulse. They are running from the fact of death, and they run toward the familiar. Most dead people cannot be blamed for inhabiting a limbo state. Often, their deaths have been so cruel or confusing that they do not know they have died and so are unable to journey through the death passage.

There comes a time, however, when the spirit is able to see a bit more clearly than he could in his newly-dead condition, and if he sees that he is influencing or beleaguering another and chooses to continue doing so, he is doing wrong. At this point, he is responsible for his behavior, though hardly responsible for how he got where he is. At this crucial juncture, he should have the decency to leave the living alone. If he doesn't, if he allows his regrets and desires to take over, then he has taken a step down a dark path.

He may become a manipulator. Many dead people do. They may have known power and influence when they were alive, and fear that their new circumstances won't be as joyous as their lives were. They may have been indoctrinated by religion and fearful of the death journey because it may lead them to hell. They may simply be afraid of the unknown. They may be so strongly attached to life in this realm that they cannot imagine leaving here and stubbornly refuse to do so.

If they wish to stay here, there are always, sadly, people who will interact with them. Amateur occultists deal with them all the time in seances and over the Ouija board, believing that they are Freud or Einstein, or whoever the naive beginner desires to talk with. Having learned that a man is crying out to talk with his dead wife, the spirit may pretend to be that woman. Having felt the longings of an incautious occultist who desires a spirit guide, the spirit—who is unable to deal successfully with his *own* existence, let alone help another—will gladly take on the role of "spirit guide" and lead the unsuspecting occultist a merry dance indeed.

When a low-level spirit, a miserable dead person, makes itself available to one person, trouble ensues. When that spirit makes itself available to a group, enormous troubles grow out of the group's desires and the manipulations of the unhappy spirit. The potent combination easily leads to a group psychosis in which suggestible people are enflamed by one another's passions in the same way that a mob gets out of control. A little prodding from the spirit, who can push his urgings on people by tapping into their energies, and who need be neither seen nor heard in order to be powerfully influential, may move people to action. When a group of people are running on high energy, even hysteria, they need an outlet. The outlet has to be something that will whip them into greater and greater frenzy, not something calming. What whips people into a frenzy best of all is making other people mad. The group needs to find a cause that will enflame others, as they are enflamed.

Sometimes there is a political or ethnic climate that affords the chance to make people mad by attacking a cherished ideal or slurring a race. Whatever the ostensible reason for making noise, the *true* reason is the desire to be noticed and to empower oneself by getting other people all het up.

At this time in our society, it is sometimes difficult to find issues that will make people mad. We're jaded. We're used to assassination and drugs and children being killed by their own parents. It was inevitable that people on the look-out for a cause that would enrage their fellows would sooner or later find "satan." When we passed the point of being shocked by sexual behavior, fratricide, and disobedience to the laws of nature and man, we were ready to be shocked by the devil. When our aimless young people and our disaffected older ones could not find any other way to gain attention, devil-worship made us sit up and take notice of them once again.

Young People As Worshippers of "Satan"

A great deal of media attention has been focused lately on the involvement of young people in so-called satanic cults. The news is filled with reports of young people killing themselves in pacts with the devil, torturing and killing others, desecrating graves, and talking openly about their supposed link with evil.

These young people are certainly disturbed by something, but there is no chance that they are being used by primary evil. Primary evil needs above all else to comport itself in such a way as to go without notice. Its slaves cannot minister to its needs if they attract attention. Why would beings whose fundamental requirement is anonymity bother with unstable, erratic, possibly addicted adolescents? Kids call attention to themselves with outrageous talk and outrageous behavior. Those who use drugs or drink may be so unreliable as to be completely uncontrollable. They have no sense of safety, or else they wouldn't be talking about their association with the devil, let alone flaunting it.

These young people are being disturbed by forces of confusion and anger manifested by dead spirits who are trapped in a limbo state. Members of these "satanic" cults are being abused and misled by miserable ghosts, not by primary evil, which has no use for them.

Absolutely none of the "satanic" symbols used by people who overturn gravestones or paint "satanic" graffitti on walls has anything to do with primary evil. *666* and the names "devil" and "satan" are all Western, Judeo-Christian creations.

"Satan" and "devil" are our names, not those of evil. Whatever symbols or names belong to the force of primary evil will
not be revealed to explosive, troublesome people who could
not possibly be of any use to primary evil because they know
nothing of hiding, nothing of stealth.

Where, then, did these so-called satanic cults get their
"information" about the darkness if they did not get it from
primary evil? They got it from us.

Cults are founded out of dissatisfaction, anger, and aimless-
ness and are surely fueled—either during their formation or
soon thereafter—by floating, dead, low-level spirits seeking to
stir up trouble. But the reality of unhappy dead people does not
excuse us from the contributions that we have made to this
mess. Our young people first heard horror tales from their
parents, as bedtime stories. They grew up on gory, inexcusably
sadistic movies because their parents allowed it. When they
read at all, they read creepy stories about the dark side of the
occult without being offered any tutoring in its positive aspects.

And after sixteen years of our allowing this influence, we
are shocked when our teenage daughter comes home wearing a
T-shirt with *666* emblazoned on it. We're stunned when our
son is arrested for helping kidnap a neighborhood boy, a blood
sacrifice to satan. Where did our children learn all this horror?
They learned it from us. We permitted it as continual entertainment from the time we gave them their first "cute l'il devil"
Halloween costume until we rented the umpteenth blood-and-
gore movie for the family VCR. Yet when all this comes
together as a reality we must face, we believe we have something to be outraged about.

Who do we suppose raised our children? What effect did we
expect our lifetime programming of evil-as-titillation would
have on our kids? Or didn't we think about it? We didn't think
about it.

Blood Sacrifice for "Satan"

When satan-worshippers kill themselves with the intention of giving over their souls to evil, they run a terrible risk of being taken, after death, into situations they cannot control. Primary evil, steering clear of them while they lived, welcomes the gift of their energy once they are dead. Primary evil always needs energy, and the energy of someone who thinks he is giving himself to a personification of evil is as useful to primary evil as it would be if there really was a "satan" waiting on the other side to grab his soul.

It is imperative that the family and friends of someone who has killed himself as a gift to the devil pray for him, create rituals as suit them, and get any kind of spiritual aid they can for the departed one. The spiritual energy the dead one receives—prayer and ritual being directed energy—may make the difference between his being absorbed by evil and his having enough strength to get past the evil beings who will try to trap him. Without the help of the prayers of the living, without ritual aid, only his own power can save him. If he died under the influence of alcohol or other drugs, or was terribly confused before his death, his death passage will be difficult and may not end successfully.

Blood-Offerings

Followers of the darkness are not the only ones who offer blood in exchange for favors, their own blood or someone else's. Making death offerings to the Almighty is a nearly quotidian event in the Old Testament and in other records of ancient cultures. The spirit of rain was given human sacrifices, as was the spirit of the sun, or of grain.

Some cultures offered up the warriors they had captured in battle as thanks for victory. Before a battle, some of one's own tribe might be killed, their lives offered as gifts in hope that victory would be granted by whichever god-force oversaw the fighting.

Not all blood-letting is meant to be fatal. In some cultures it was, and still is, a means of personal transmutation to cut oneself and let the blood flow into the earth, mingling with the earth's vast power. In offering some of the only physical entity we can truly claim as our own, our bodies, we are asking the gods to recognize our sincerity and reward it with wisdom, power, or both. Sometimes, bits of flesh cut from a person by a spiritual leader or by the giver himself are offered in supplication for one's own benefit or the benefit of another person.

The initial popularity of Jesus was surely due, in part, to what was two thousand years ago an astounding concept, that someone could offer his life and suffering for the good of all, *for all time.* The idea that further sacrifices would be rendered unnecessary by that one sacrifice must have been profoundly revolutionary.

Possession

A being, living or dead, can be taken over by another being, his will, mind, spirit, energy, emotions and, if he is alive, his body controlled by someone other than himself. A possessor need not be alive in order to possess someone. He need not be human, either. A possessing entity needs only to have consciousness and the ability to form intention.

While there are many instances of accidental possession, which will be addressed in the next chapter, and of benign possession, which will be addressed later in this section, most types of possession are malignant.

Malignant Possession

Possession with intention to usurp the will of another is malicious possession. There are four types of this kind of possession:

- possession of the living by the living
- possession of the living by the dead

- possession of the dead by the living
- possession of the dead by the dead

Aside from benign possession, any instance of possession will derive from one or more of the three basic categories of evil: primary, secondary and accidental. Someone may be possessed by both primary and secondary evil.

A possessing being may be innocent of malicious intent. He may have died, and in a panic over being dead, joined his energies to a living body. He acts through hysteria and means no harm. Accidental possession is not evil.

Malicious possession is the work of a being who understands that what he is doing is wrong. He possesses someone in order to work his will through the possessed one. Primary evil, which is not human and has no physical form, will always try to possess human beings in order to feed from the victim's energy and remain close to this world.

Secondary evil, performed by human beings, causes possession when it takes control of either a living or a dead human being. Possession occurs when someone's will is taken over. The possessed being need not be alive and have a body in order to be possessed. The reason for possession by secondary evil is a desire to steal talents or energy, or a desire to maintain or extend the territory of one's influence.

Perhaps a being of secondary evil has died and does not wish to give up his earthly work. He must then take over the will of a living being and try to live his life through his victim. This happens a great deal. One who has been practicing black magic is interested first and last of all in power—his power. He has spent years building a power-base for himself in this world and he cannot take his worldly influence with him into death. He can take his own personal supply of power with him, but he cannot take his earthly connections, his money, his fame, or whatever followers he may have. In death, if he travels beyond this realm, as is right, he must leave behind everything he has acquired. A being practicing magic must be fully absorbed in his work for it to be effective. The practice of magic—evil or

Light—is not a part-time job. The condition of total absorption in a magician's work leaves no room for a so-called normal life, and when such a person dies, it leaves no room for the fact of mere death. Someone who has been circumventing the laws of the universe in order to make black magic does not willingly bow to natural law and step gracefully off-stage when he dies. He will try to find a slave, someone who can take on the master magician, and provide the physical form and earthly contact necessary for the continuation of the evil magician's life.

The slave is eager. Usually he has known the master for a long time and he may have been preparing for this role for years. He may be the dead one's student or associate and therefore feel honored to give over his will and resources to help his master maintain his influence in the realm of the living.

Beings of secondary evil sometimes possess the living as a means of extending their authority and power. A man may need workers and because he can possess more than one person at a time, he may build his own army through possession. He may possess the dead while he is still alive, thus empowering himself in the realm of the dead while he remains in the realm of the living. These dead slaves perform tasks in the living world, and influence the living and the dead, comprising a work force the possessor can use while he is living and continue to use once he is dead.

At some time in our lives, we all come up against someone so persuasive it's hard to refuse them. They may be physically threatening, express themselves in a powerful manner, or be so charismatic that we are swept away by the force of their personality. It is hard for us to keep a grip on our own desires in the face of theirs because, in comparison with them, we feel so puny.

These experiences do not befall us often. When they do, we should be grateful because these encounters allow us the opportunity to investigate just what it is about the other being that seems so wonderful, and to ask ourselves why we feel so insignificant by comparison.

If the other makes no effort to control our behavior or beliefs, fine. If he seeks to tell us what we should think or how we ought to live our lives, we are in danger and should make tracks away from him as fast as we can. Many cult situations provide examples of the living possessing the living. Malice does not exist in every instance, but malicious intent is not all that matters here. Anyone who coerces another person by mental assault, physical restraint or emotional attack is working outside the boundaries of right action. He may believe he's engaged in manipulation for our own good, or for a cause so great that its importance excuses his actions, but no cause is *ever* so great that it matters more than our free will. Free will is a fundamental law of life, not an occasional privilege.

A possessed person may try to escape possession by leaving his body and traveling out of this realm, as though he were dead. If he does so, he frees himself of the possessor who now has only the physical form his victim has left behind. Given a choice between leaving our bodies—which we will do in any case when we die—or remaining with our bodies and, thereby, remaining in thrall to the possessor, the wise choice is to leave. In leaving, the victim has a chance to strengthen his weakened will and to heal the aspect of his being that allowed him to be taken over. There is always a possibility that the possessor will try to follow the fleeing victim through the realms of the dead, but if he does, the escaping man has access to spiritual aid. He needs only to call out for it and he will get help. If he stays in his body, however, hoping to get free of the possessing entity while holding onto his body, he may find his will so badly smothered by his attacker that he is unable to cry out for help. In that case, he takes a very real chance, not only that he will lose whatever will he still has, but also that when he eventually does die, there will not be very much of his mind and spirit left. When faced with a powerful possessor, it is better to flee one's body and survive than allow oneself to be entirely overpowered, body, mind, and spirit.

When a master-slave relationship of longstanding is involved, however, the master may not let his slave off by allowing him to flee his body. He may pursue his slave and drag him back to the realm of the living, where the half-dead human being will exist in a twilight state for as long as it suits his master, possibly for many years. A possessor does not automatically lose power over his victim when the victim leaves his body, because the connection between possessor and victim is not made through the body but through the spirit and the mind.

Crimes Caused by Possession

When we hear of a crime involving extraordinary passion, passion beyond the normal range of expression—such as someone being stabbed a hundred times or dismembering a body in a state of extreme rage—we are usually hearing of a crime committed by two people, the possessed and his possessor. When we hear of a crime that the perpetuator cannot remember or seems disassociated from, we are often hearing about a case of possession. The reason a man may stab another to death is plain human fury; stabbing him a hundred times is the work of an alien spirit working through the killer.

When a killer or rapist cannot remember a crime, that may be because he did not commit the crime; the being possessing him committed it and the accused was out of his body during the crime's commission.

While I hesitate to identify any red flags of possession, there is one signal that occurs so frequently that it should be mentioned—with the caveat that, in tracking evil, there is no sign that always announces the presence of evil. This common characteristic of possession is the presence of a voice that does not seem to be coming from the person using it. The voice will sound disembodied, as if it lives outside the body of the speaker, yet activates the vocal cords. In cases of possession that is exactly what's taking place; the possessing entity activates and has full use of the body of the possessed, but the possessor does not, strictly speaking, live in his victim's body because, in one physical form, there is not room for two spirits.

Criminals who perform the same acts repeatedly are often—though surely not always—possessed by a being who desires the behavior inherent in the crime. Many rapists are possessed by angry dead human beings. Others are possessed by primary evil which, though having no sexual urges of its own, uses the invasion and shock of rape in order to make a powerful connection with the victim. Any means of traumatizing a human being is a potentially useful way to possession. Some rape victims are possessed by their rapists or by the possessor who controls the rapist. Traumatic attack, whether rape, a mugging or a beating, may be an attempt by primary or secondary evil to take over the will of the victim.

Any assault on our psychic balance, even an attempt to frighten us that does not include physical contact, may be a possessive ploy by primary evil. It may be an assault by secondary evil, particularly if we find it difficult to get the experience out of our minds. It is possible that a practitioner of black magic is working on us through mental assault, and if we find ourselves beginning to obsess over an incident, this could indicate mental attack. If the situation that captures our attention so powerfully was preceded by a physical assault, then we may very well be the focus of an evil manipulation.

Crimes with a distinct military theme perpetuated by someone with a mania for military clothing and/or ritual are not usually instances of possession by primary or secondary evil. These crimes involve possession of the accidental kind, possibly possession by someone who died in battle. These sad situations will be addressed in the chapter on accidental evil.

An individual who commits acts of mental, emotional or physical violence, and then does not seem to remember his actions, may, in fact, be under the influence of a would-be possessor. He may be in a vulnerable state, and unable to protect himself, allow another's influence to take over his will for just a moment. If he regains his strength, the would-be possessor will probably give up on him and leave him alone. His temporary victim will remember little or none of what he did while under the influence of his attacker, and his friends will see only that he behaved, for just a moment, in an uncharacteristic manner. These attempted possessions occur most often when we are depressed, angry, influenced by alcohol or other drugs, or when we have recently undergone a devastating loss or change in circumstances.

How Possession Occurs

The first requisite to possession is lack of faith in oneself and lack of strong, positive feeling for one's life. Looking outward for satisfaction, looking to authority figures to tell us how to live, or perpetual unhappiness with ourselves makes us susceptible to possession.

After we become vulnerable, we open ourselves to possession through electroshock "therapy", heavy addiction to consciousness-altering substances, and anything else that causes our etheric, energy body to weaken or separate from our physical form. Electroshock, alcohol and other drugs, extreme physical assault from surgery, or even a series of accidents such as car crashes, weaken our etheric energy more than anything except prolonged torture.

Electroshock "therapy" so badly weakens a person's etheric energy that it produces, for years after the treatment, an etheric thinness that is to one's energy what hemophelia is to one's blood. If possession is in the offing, we have little strength to fight it off. The fight against would-be possession usually takes place without our being aware that the battle is going on. This does not mean that our physical bodies are not engaged in the fight; possession may seem a spiritual subject, but it manifests in the flesh as long as we are living.

Drug and alcohol use, over time, produce the same etheric thinness. They also separate us from our deepest knowing, and without intuition, we often do not know that danger is near.

The effect of anesthesia on the etheric body is greater than the effects of it on our physical body. A healthy person can heal his etheric energy after one operation, or one accident involving surgery such as a bad fracture. But healing takes time, and when we are subjected to anesthesia more than once every few years, our etheric body thins as rapidly as it does when we drink alcohol to excess.

Bad Company

People have always tended to gather in groups for comfort, psychic warmth, and the exchange of information. Comradery is a natural human need. Unfortunately, it often leads to disaster, for it is most often within groups that an evil being, primary or secondary, will see his chance and take it. This is especially true of groups dedicated to causes, such as groups of spiritual seekers or patriots. Religious mania, ethnic grievances and political ferver all tend to excite people beyond what is healthful. When frenzy is actively sought, an essential component of the group's work, then danger is present for all. Any time a group of excited, driven people get together, there is a good chance that at least one member of the group is already possessed. His possessor may be responsible, in fact, for the frenzy the group routinely experiences. He may have brought everyone present into the fold by exerting his influence on each of them separately so that he could work his evil on them collectively.

Anyone attending group encounters as a regular occurrence offers himself to the possessing spirit who is *really* behind the group's activities. If there is no possessing spirit behind the group when it first comes together, there is a good chance that after the group has maintained itself for awhile, a potential possessor will enter the picture.

If we are engaged in group work of any nature, the most important issue for us must always be how *we* feel about the issues under scrutiny, what *we* wish to do about them, and not how others feel. Our attention must always be on our own psychic balance, not on achieving others' approval. We must never sublimate ourselves to the purpose of a group, no matter how exalted its ambitions may seem.

Isolation

The counterpart to excessive group contact is excessive isolation. It may appear, at first glance, that a person who surrounds himself with only his own company is likely to spot the intrusion of an alien thought or urge because he is so used to himself. It does not happen that way, however. When we spend too much time apart from other living things, especially human beings, we lose the ability to distinguish between our own consciousness and an invasive presence. When our thoughts become our sole companion, we will of necessity expand the subjects of our thoughts, making us vulnerable to others' ideas, or we will compress our consciousness to such a degree that we create a vacuum within our minds. Soon, the energies floating through our minds are not our own energies but intrusions which we cannot identify as intrusions. We have forgotten what outside influence feels like, and cannot sense outside impulses or ideas as foreign.

Demons

We can be influenced—but not actually possessed—by partial beings who are not individuals but simple energy cast off from human desires. When people have a great lust for something, whether that something is sex, a drug, the thrill of watching a fire or of watching someone being hurt, the desire creates more of itself because excessive desire is self-pertuating. All excessive desire is innately explosive. It is the tendency of powerful desire to perpetuate itself beyond what its human creator can handle. Some of the desire leaves his control and splits away from his consciousness, as does a powerful thought-form.

If there is nobody around who shares a like desire, then the floating off-shoot will dissipate until it no longer exists. But anyone who feels a similar desire will attract the off-shoot, which will attach itself to the desire he already has. Thus, the receiver of that off-shoot finds himself suddenly feeling far more inflamed by desire than he was, and the additional desire may well be more than he is capable of handling.

This is how a person can progress from low level involvement to obsession. Whether the object of his desire is alcohol or horror films, the results are the same. Each time he indulges a desire of dubious value, he chances attracting a portion of floating desire that matches the desire he has generated. If there is an off-shoot near him, it will be drawn to him as metal to a magnet. When that happens, he may lose all control, having been overwhelmed by a passion bigger than he.

These off-shoots are demons, not whole beings, but highly-charged energy—dangerous energy. The reason they have long been considered beings, and are called demons, is that an aggregate of these off-shoots can be controlled by an evil being. One entity may hold sway over several of these semi-beings, these energies, because he has just enough of the desires these off-shoots are made of that he is able to attract them, but he is not so powerfully inflamed by this desire that he is controlled by it.

An evil being who can command these energies without being controlled by them is a master of energy-manipulation. It takes considerable expertise to attract and use them. To disperse them among the living or the dead, for purposes of enslaving those who are touched by these off-shoots, takes great understanding of the ways of humankind and the dynamics of energy. This is why people have long believed that demons were the product of a personified evil being such as the devil. Only a being of consciousness and power, and one with knowledge of the occult secrets of life, can move desire-energy around with intent. It is the purpose behind the movement, and not the off-shoots themselves, that give demons the false appearance of being whole beings. They are not individuals. They are merely energy. They must be directed by a sentient being. Otherwise they would move about without direction and most of them would dissipate before they connected—accidentally—with human desire.

Demons, then, are not created by evil. Primary evil cannot

create; it can only appropriate. Demons—semi-beings—are purely the creation of excessive desire on the part of human beings. If this energy is taken by evil, then it can be directed by evil. But it was birthed by human energy.

Benign Possession

The use of someone's body by another is not by definition an evil phenomenon. Many cultures function positively with possession. Spirits help, in everything from spiritual rituals to such mundane activities as the search for food and water, by entering the energy field of human beings and using their bodies to speak, dance, and heal. In some cultures, notably in Africa and South America, these spirits choose their human helpers and urge them to cooperate by speaking to them in visions and dreams. Sometimes these spirit contacts follow a serious illness, and sometimes they come without warning. In some cultures, people are trained for years before the spirit gods use them as their priests. Sometimes, a spirit will enter someone's body without any prior indication that it means to use the human being in this way.

This type of possession is assumed to be a cooperative partnership between the discarnate spirit and its living human friend, and since no abrogation of free will is apparently involved, these incidents of possession do not fall within the types of possession discussed in this chapter. They are not malicious possession and they do not involve primary, secondary or accidental evil.

This kind of possession is sometimes called mediumship, but it is only one type of mediumship. Not all mediums are possessed.

Sorcery

Sometimes a person with knowledge of energy-as-power will use his understanding as a means to acquiring other people's power. In doing so, he acquires the other's energy and learns how to manipulate it. Such practice is usually called sorcery. Sorcery, or black magic, can be practiced through virtually any of the esoteric disciplines: healing, magic, shamanism, witchcraft, ceremonial work and divination. But a sorcerer need not be an occultist at all. Sorcery is routinely performed within religions and is, to some degree, part of the founding of all organized religion.

In order to create a broad social base for a new theology, it is imperative that the founders incorporate into their religion as much of the prevailing philosophy and spirituality as they can. They do this by appropriating the beliefs of existing religions even while denouncing those religions. A new religion can best compete with an established one by appropriating it. The taking of existing practices *and* the denouncing of them are both means of appropriation.

Individuals follow this formula when seeking power not rightfully theirs. Knowing that someone has the ability to see future events, the power-seeker who does not have this ability and desires it will try to steal it, intact, from the one who has it. He does this by wrapping his energy around the being he means to steal from. Having touched base with the potential victim and encircled him with his energy, the thief then sends out messages meant to confuse the other. He hopes that there will be so much confusion in his victim's mind that his victim will lose his grip on his energy. When that happens, the attacker can make psychic contact with his victim's essential energy. If he can make his victim weak enough while building his own psychic strength, he will, he hopes, wrench away the talent he wishes to obtain.

It would be easier for everyone if all talents were of the profound variety, but some coveted abilities are shallow and, like bundles of clothing, they can be snatched away.

Kindness, for example, or a deep resonance with art could not be stolen because these are not attributes but qualities. Psychism is not a quality, nor is tap-dancing. These skills can be stolen; qualities cannot be stolen. Skills are not part of our deepest selves, which is why we can lose a skill we had in childhood. Anything that is not a part of our deepest selves can be stolen by another person as easily as it can be tossed away by us.

Sometimes when people have learned the arts of healing, they may amuse themselves by figuring out the techniques of killing. In coming to understand what keeps the soul connected to the body, what keeps the body vivified, and what keeps the spirit attuned to the earth, a being of power may decide to experiment with what he has learned by disconnecting someone from his body as a kind of learning exercise. After all, he tells himself, if he can put someone's spirit back into the body it's been dislodged from, why not see if he can dislodge it?

And if he can dislodge it, then why not appropriate some of that spirit for himself? Someone else's energy added to his own would make him a powerful magician indeed. Besides that, he would have proven his superior esoteric ability by stealing someone else's energy.

All practitioners of the occult run the risk of becoming bad occultists instead of good ones, of practicing evil magic instead of Light magic. It is impossible to learn anything major without being able to infer both good and evil from that learning. After someone has spent many years looking into the causes underlying the laws of life, he may become inured to the issue of right-and-wrong. Having invested a great deal of his life in searching out *reasons-why,* he may not care any more about *should.* It is human nature to become overinvolved in the mechanics of things. When the nuts and bolts of science, politics, or metaphysics have taken our full attention for so long that we become enamored of the dynamics themselves, it is easy to fix our minds on the "how's" of life and foresake the "why's" entirely.

Remorse and Redemption

Many of us treasure the sentiment that a bad person can be turned around by a good example, or by the timely intervention of an angelic being whose mission is to set the bad one straight and show him light from darkness. This is a lovely thought but it hardly ever comes to pass. People with a predelication for manipulating and harming others merely increase their inclinations from one lifetime to the next. The increase of negative activity makes them disinclined to expose themselves to good works and, ultimately, to good people. After they have formed a hard shell around themselves and lost any capacity for empathy, they are very hard to reach. If they've been selfish and heedless of others for many lifetimes, it is unlikely that they will have made any good friends who would desire to help them.

The likelihood of such an encased, self-absorbed power-seeker stumbling into an afternoon showing of *Heidi* and being converted by Shirley Temple is very small. We like to think that bad is unattractive and unsatisfying and, therefore, that people engaged in wrong action will become so miserable that a spontaneous conversion might take place within them one day, as in fairy tales. The truth is that the longer someone engages in wrong action, the harder it is for him to feel anything for right action.

Memory is a powerful dictator. If someone has spent lifetime after lifetime perfecting methods for abusing his own gifts and other people, he will continue along this dark path until and unless a force intervenes to show him that there is something better than destruction, black magic and evil.

The Ethics of Seeking Powerful Knowledge

Some people seek to know for the pleasure inherent in knowing. Others seek knowledge for gain. Not everyone who wishes to gain money or status or power does so because he is cruel or insensitive. A great deal of what is considered right or wrong regarding metaphysical knowledge is cultural. For some, power is clean only when it is offered to them by the universe. For others, any power that is lying around unused is fair game. The difference between those two views is a cultural difference. It is not our business, I think, to dictate to cultures outside ours what is proper and what isn't.

We do, however, have to define limits for ourselves as we go along. For some seekers of power, the rules change as power is accrued. This is fundamentally dishonest, for what is right within our deepest being is right according to our connection with and understanding of the collective unconscious. That is, we know right and can identify and define it for ourselves before we are born. To change the rules of right and wrong as we explore and pursue power is to lie to ourselves—the most vicious kind of lie there is.

In coming to know power, there are people who betray themselves by altering the rules as they understand them. Such people, whether or not they are occultists, are often empowered by the spirit world. The spirit realm is linked to this one because of need. The spirit realm needs human cooperation. Without us, its power is limited. With us, it can affect change beyond what we human beings alone can affect. Spirits aid this realm all the time and in every aspect of earthly life. (In this discussion of the spirit realm, I am excluding the realm of evil, which exists apart from the realm of good spirits.)

It often happens that a spirit chooses as its helper a human being with a strong urge toward some manner of occultism, healing work, psychism or shamanism. The spirit, who may not make itself known to the human being with whom he is working, gives aid to that person in many ways. He may bolster his human friend's intuitive faculty, give him additional energy, or guide him. I do not refer here to channeling, which I will address in Part III, but to spirit aid.

The spirit helper and human being may, after years, reach an impasse because the human being begins moving in a direction dangerously close to black magic. He may do this with malicious intent or because he wishes to explore all of the occult, the good and the bad elements of it. The human being has free will. He is not a slave of the spirit. The spirit may try to show him all that is wrong with the direction the human being has taken. If that doesn't work, then the spirit is bound by the laws of right action to stop helping his human friend.

This is a crucial and dangerous place for the human seeker. He may not even know that he has a spirit helper, but he certainly feels it when the powerful aid he's had for years suddenly withdraws. When this happens he may cast about for a substitute for the help he misses. While casting about, he may find something ugly. He may be approached at this crossroad by a being of primary evil, a being of secondary evil, or an unfortunate opportunity to learn methods of working that run counter to righteousness.

A person who has taken on the esoteric arts as his life's work and is accustomed to substantial assistance will feel helpless when, for the first time in years, he is all alone. He will flounder. He may lose his ability to discriminate. He may accept *any* help offered. Having already turned to questionable practices—this decision being what caused his spirit friend to leave him—he may not hold himself to the high standards on which he once insisted. He may, within a short time, place himself in deep trouble.

He can learn that he is in trouble by asking himself what, precisely, he wishes to gain from his work. If he asks this question periodically and answers it with complete honesty, he will see his errors, the wrong turns, the unsavory practices, the associates with whom he is not quite in tune. He will be able to remove himself from wrong action and go back to where he was before he made that first wrong turn.

But if he does not ask himself, periodically and forthrightly, what he hopes to gain from his work, he may continue down the wrong path for years.

The single question we must ask ourselves, paying scrupulous attention to the thoroughness of our answers, is what do we want from the occult endeavors we're engaged in. Without asking that question, there is nothing to prevent our turning down the wrong path.

It is manifestly part of human experience that our tastes, views and desires change as we grow. As this is fundamental to human life, so it is fundamental to the life of the metaphysician. The only way to know, from hour to hour and year to year, what our true motives are in pursuing metaphysics, is to ask ourselves what we are doing in this arena and what we hope to gain from our search. Attention to that question and its answer may, during difficult times, times of change, be the one thing that keeps us straight.

Black Magic

Taking or attempting to take anything that does not belong to us by using the occult disciplines is black magic. From the theft of another's energy or talent to the invading of his physical or psychic space to intruding on another's will, all of these are black magic *whether or not* they are perceived as such by the perpetrator. Stepping outside our own boundaries with the intention of doing to others what we would not wish done to ourselves is black magic. The intention to do harm is unnecessary to the performance of black magic; merely to intrude, even if we do not consider our intrusion harmful, is to perform black magic.

Any endeavor that necessitates psychic stealth is black magic. This includes spying on another by using our psychic ability to see. When we operate on a level outside three-dimensional reality, we must at all times remind ourselves to stay within our own boundaries and not to stray. Attempting to coerce another by the use of psychic suggestion is intrusive. For the reader whose familiarity with and deft handling of the occult arts has led him to use those arts for the "good" of others when those others might find their ministrations invasive, these strictures may seem unfair. But it is the very ones who have practiced their esoteric skills for a long while who are most apt to step over their boundary lines into someone else's territory—especially for that person's "good".

Killing someone through occult manipulation is obvious black magic. But no practitioner begins his immoral work on a major scale. The wrongful use of our abilities starts with small actions, as the embezzler who begins by stealing pocket change.

Every action we take in our lives is like a note struck on a drum, the drum being the whole living universe. When we touch another being with respect for his rights, we honor our own spirit as we honor his. Each thought, each action creates a vibration to which everything resonates, as sound resonates. The resonating of our personal sounds enlivens, not only the physical world, but all of creation. The sounds we make come back to us in time.

In moving beyond the laws of right action, we manifest a vacuum for ourselves, and within that vacuum, we create no reverberating sounds. Enough theft, enough destruction, and we become like broken drums, unable either to give or to receive the vibrations of creation.

We can keep ourselves safe from primary evil by paying close attention to our motivation and expectation in every endeavor. We can keep ourselves free of interference by practitioners of secondary evil if we follow a path of caution and righteousness.

No one except ourselves can keep us safe. The understanding that we bring to our lives is our protector; there is no other. Everything we choose *not* to know about the dynamics of human existence poses a threat to our well-being. Each time we endeavor to understand ourselves and how we relate to the all-life, we create a zone of safety on our life path.

All of us, at some time, find ourselves confronted by accidental evil. The following chapter offers a broad view of the incidents of accidental evil. Part III contains methodology for steering clear of all kinds of evil.

Chapter 4

Things That Go Bump in the Night: Accidental Evil

"Hell is time arrested within and refusing
to join in the movement of the wind and stars."

—*The Seed and the Sower*, Laurens Van Der Post

Accidental evil is the term I use to identify a wide range of human woes, nearly all of which derive from botched deaths. Accidental evil refers to situations born of human ignorance, misdirection and misunderstanding. Accidental evil is not created through malice, but any of the miseries of accidental evil can result in situations as horrifying as those born of outright malicious intent.

Before we can sort out the various kinds of accidental evil, we must consider the primary impulse behind all of life— movement. Everything alive is continually and perpetually moving. Even dead things move, changing from fur or flesh to soil, from leaf to compost. Energy, the essence of life, seeks always to grow and move. When energy is stifled and cannot move in a healthy manner, it will continue moving anyway—

104

moving within itself in an unhealthy way, growing backward, so to speak. No matter how rigid the circumstances of its being, energy will not simply stop moving.

Growth with free movement is good. Growth where free movement is impeded causes physical, mental or emotional illness. Blocked energy is sickness-producing to a living form, causes aberration in a mind, and prompts bizarre and useless emotional expression.

All incidents of accidental evil spring from blocked energy or stifled movement. Every unnatural occurrence in the evolution of humankind—including the advent of primary and secondary evil—sprang from energy misappropriated, misdirected or misused.

The ills of accidental evil are especially tragic because most are preventable. Many, from the phenomenon of ghosts to incidents of mental illness, could be resolved if only we in the Western world had not forsaken ancient knowledge. Many preventions and cures for miseries of accidental evil are found in the healing traditions of pre-Christian cultures.

If we are able to travel outside Time and beyond three-dimensional Space, we afford ourselves a spectacularly informing overview of living. No single lifetime is isolated from prior existence. Our souls vibrate to the *whole* of our experience, not simply to the current lifetime. The fact that most westerners operate within a single time frame means that most of them are aware of only a small portion of the totality of their being.

Every lifetime in form, as a tree or a bird or a human being, every experience outside of form, as a spirit (a discarnate being) has an impact on the existence that follows it. These incarnations and discarnate experiences form, in toto, an intricately-woven design, the pattern for which is unique to each being. It is we who create the design: the greater our access to the whole pattern, the greater our chance for mental, emotional and physical health. The less we understand about the truths underlying our lives, the harder it is to create vibrant, powerful lives for ourselves.

The Death Passage

Every turn in our lives, every change in circumstances, offers the opportunity to grow or to shrivel. The most powerful transition in human life is death. Some people have easy deaths and others do not. The difference between the person who completes his death journey successfully and the one who gets snagged in a bad death situation often is just plain luck.

Viewed from a short-sighted, worldly perspective, death is an ending. But death is a far more powerful change than that: it's a new start on a new kind of existence. Dying looks easy to the living because it appears to be the end of action, a wholly passive surrendering. We think of dying, not as a participation, but as the abnegation of all responsibility. But there is nothing passive about dying. Dying takes *work*. It requires perspective and vision. Most of all, it demands preparation.

Because most of us die without knowing how to do it well, we die as participants in a lottery; some will have a successful death journey—by luck and luck alone—and others will blunder into untenable situations that may entrap them for hundreds of years.

Reports from the dead, received through mediums and recorded in many cultures, indicate that successful death journeys are by no means assured. Many myths and beliefs about dying offer detailed views of challenges that stand between dying and safe arrival in the realm of the dead.

Our culture conditions us to loathe and fear death, but not to prepare for it. This is a very peculiar attitude toward an unavoidable confrontation: nobody gets off this planet alive, yet we make no preparation for the death journey. It is axiomatic in Western culture to "deal" with death as though it did not exist. This most egregious of all the denials we engage in causes a great many of the woes of accidental evil, woes that affect the dead and the living, every day.

Our greatest obstacle to good death is ourselves, our ability to affect an intelligent attitude toward death, even, in some instances, to acknowledge death when it comes. Everything we do *not* know about death contributes to death-illnesses, such as ghosts and certain kinds of possession. From our acceptance of death and willingness to cooperate with our deaths as full participants, everything else proceeds. If this were not so, there would not be as many hauntings, lost souls, or incidents of possession on this planet as there are, as tradition tells us there have always been.

Building the Bridge from Here to There

Ladders and bridges, which figure in our everyday metaphors, are what move us from one level of existence to another. When we die, we must build a bridge of energy to take us safely out of here. We do this by holding intention within our being.

In order to build this bridge of intention, we must gather all of our energy. The first gathering is of our physical and etheric energy, the second is of our psychic energy.

As we leave our bodies, we should look around and be sure that all of our energy comes with us. If we have been ill for some time, or if we are very old, our energy will not be as strongly attached to our bodies as it would be if we died young or died abruptly, as in an accident.

It takes, generally, three days for our energy to leave our bodies. For that reason, nobody should be buried or cremated until he has been dead for a full three days. Many cultures acknowledge this three-day period. Healings can be affected when soneome has been "dead" for less than three days. Sometimes people come awake in morgues within the three-day period because they have enough energy in their bodies that their spirit can reenter the body.

The Biblical story of Jesus raising Lazarus from the dead is presented as a miracle because, it is implied, Lazarus had been dead for longer than three days. To "raise" someone from the dead within three days is not a miracle because the human body does not give up all of its energy until it has been dead for that long. The exceptions to this are bodies weakened by prolonged battles with illness and those worn out by old age.

As we leave our bodies, we will find in most instances that the body's tendency is to give up its energy. It will not be difficult to gather up what is ours. But if we die in stages, such as being in a car crash and then brought in terminal condition to a hospital, we must take our energy from the body as it lies in the hospital and return to the scene of the accident, absorbing as much of our energy as might still be there.

If we become aware that we have died only after we have left our bodies, then we must go to where our bodies are, in the funeral parlor or hospital, and absorb energy from the body. We must then go to *any of the places* where our dying or dead forms have been—a hospital, a morgue, the actual place of death, and scan the body for energy, taking back all of what is ours.

After absorbing our energy, we should ask Spirit for help in making a good, strong death passage. If we call out to Spirit for aid, we will receive it. Our attention should be focused on the death passage and we should not, in that crucial time, allow the grieving of relatives and friends to draw us back here. There will be plenty of time later on for our loved ones to grieve and if we wish to help them with prayer, we can do so after we have successfully concluded our death journey. There is no good reason to stop the death journey in mid-flight.

It is during the death passage that we encounter what may be a major obstacle to freedom—the battle with ourselves over the truth of being dead. Many people refuse to accept their deaths and stubbornly refuse to move on when their time comes. This can create great difficulties for them, and for the living, as will be described later.

In order to create a strong bridge of intention and move out of this realm, we must, having gathered all of our energy, make a conscious, emphatic determination to release all of our worldly attachments. It is all right to love people here, or to love this realm, but love should not be a binding or impeding thing. When the fact of our death is upon us, it does no one any good to regret the truth and wish we could stay. If we wish to stay, then at least some of our consciousness *will* stay, and that is what creates ghosts. As long as we maintain a grip on any aspect of this realm—another person, a situation, or a place—then, while we will be able to take some of ourself out of here, a portion of our consciousness will remain behind.

It isn't only people we're attached to. We may be unwilling to let go of worldly success, or to forget a battle-in-progress. We may not have considered what it would be like, some day, to do without our brothers and sisters, not only because we love them but because they have always been part of our lives. Habit, as much as emotional longing, can hold us here after death.

Anger can hold us here too, particularly the kind we consider justifiable anger. Anger and regret, as much as dependence, can separate some of our energy from the bridge of intention we must build in order to leave here with our spirit intact.

The Free State

Having gathered our energy and released our attachments, we need then to create for ourselves a state of hope and happy anticipation of the journey we are about to begin.

It is natural that we view our lives here as the whole show, though of course it is really only a brief interval in our total existence. It would help our death passage if we could, when we are alive, remember that this life will end one day, and that there is a universe of new experiences waiting for us. Change is hard for human beings; we tend to root ourselves where we are happy, or at least in familiar circumstances. It would do so much good in our current life, and in the death to come, if we would consider from time to time that the existence we have now is only our *current* life, and that this life will inevitably be followed by new experiences. If we could manage some awareness of this life *as* temporary, it would help us, while we are living here, not to concern ourselves with trivia, or with things we cannot change. If we stopped to consider, periodically, the fact of death and the inevitability of change, we would do much to prepare ourselves for a good death journey.

Unnecessary Reincarnation

The issue of attachment is more important to our after-death destiny than any other single issue. It is attachment, to agreeable circumstances and unpleasant ones, that returns us to new lifetimes here far more often than is meant. Reincarnation as human beings is not meant to happen hundreds of times. It is not a master plan that brings us back here again and again, but our emotional overattachment to unresolved issues and desire.

Perpetual rebirth in this realm creates far more problems than these incarnations can solve. For every single issue we come back here in order to resolve, we take a chance on creating several more issues that will, in future incarnations, have to be resolved. It is a fool's game, and the best way to step out of this endless cycle is to affect one good death for ourselves, a death during which we truly and *absolutely* release the attachments, happy and unhappy ones, that might bring us back.

We can not, of course, make such a potent declaration of releasing unless we have made strides in this direction during our lives. It would help this process immeasurably if we could, during the course of life and on a daily basis, distance ourselves from passionate feelings, because these bind instead of free us. It takes work and vision and discipline to become free. It does not happen through outside agents. We must do this work ourselves. If we can manage this distancing, we will lose nothing in soul growth because distancing does not mean shriveling. Emotion, empathy and compassion are not the problem. Excess of feeling, positive and negative, is the danger. We can love and still be free once we learn how to sense the difference between neurotic, clutching love and honorable love: love that enriches instead of restraining.

We've all heard the expression, "dead and gone." Many of us, after death, are dead but not gone. Failure to clean out the psyche, with the help of our deeper, all-knowing consciousness, keeps us hovering dangerously close to this realm, all too ready to jump into another, probably unncessary, incarnation.

The decision to return here for another life should be made with full access to the collective unconscious. The decision should never be made in response to the life we have just left. When we come back to this realm, we should do so as a deliberate, thoughtful choice, not a knee-jerk reaction. We should not return because we are drawn back here by issues left undigested by the life we have finished.

Kind and Unkind Grieving

It is not an act of love to grieve excessively or overlong for a departed one. We can help our loved ones best by doing two things: by making certain that a dead person is neither cremated nor buried until he has been dead for a full three days, and by honoring him and his departure with just enough ceremony to satisfy our need to grieve and his need to leave. We must never give a dead person such a passionate, energizing ritual that his spirit is inclined to give back some of its energy into his body. That would be disastrous. We must not set up such a howl over his passing that his spirit is attracted back here where he does not belong. To do so is a major discourtesy. It is not our departed friend's job to comfort us. He needs to get on with his journey, and there is no excuse for our doing anything to halt his progress.

The funeral ritual should be one of goodbye, not an expression of our regret over his passing. Too much mourning may encourage a spirit to try to reconnect with us. We owe it to any departing spirit to give him a send-off; we must not invite him to return. Whenever we send excessive messages of grief into the airwaves, we are tugging at a departing spirit at the very moment he is trying to get out of here.

Varieties Of Accidental Evil

Ghosts

When someone refuses to leave the stage after the final curtain, he may stay around this realm if he likes. He may create an illusory world and life for himself, based on the life he has known and refuses to give up, and based, in part, on the desires he cannot let go of. He can create a world made of the realities he has lived and the fantasies he has engaged in, dreams that went unsatisfied during his life.

Because he does not have a real life and because the existence he creates adheres to his desires rather than actual reality, he may fall out of sync with changes taking place in this world. He may stay here for hundreds of years, riveting his attention to a single place or event. Once he has mated enough of his energy to a place, perhaps to a house where he once lived and was happy—or was miserable—he can stay right where he is for as long as the place continues to absorb his attention and, thus, his energy. Unless a force outside him, such as spiritual aid from a healer (dead or alive) manages to remove him from that place, he can stay there as long as he is so inclined.

Ghosts are impelled to remain in this realm for one of three reasons. They may not know they are dead and be so terrified of the revelation of their deaths as to rush from one place to another, from one activity to another, as a desperate means of remaining ignorant of their condition. They may be so thoroughly embroiled in emotional issues that they are unwilling or even unable to let go of the situation and permit themselves to be dead. The power of emotion is far greater in some people than in others, and when it occurs in ghosts, may be so potent that it overwhelms any possible awareness of death. The third element in the creation of ghosts is desire, whether for a physical substance such as alcohol or food, or a need to discharge emotion or to acquire recognition. There are people who, in life, were so timid or frightened that they did not allow themselves to fully express their personalities. Having been half-dead for all of their lives, they seek a vibrant expression of themselves after death.

Any or all three of these conditions is a death-illness, a charged and unhealthy situation preventing the death journey. Any impediment to a successful death journey may create a death-illness.

Accidental Possession

When someone dies abruptly and, to his way of seeing, inappropriately, neither old nor ill and of no mind to die, he may attach himself to a living person because he simply does not know what else to do. If he does not know that he is dead, he will at least sense the absence of the body he's used to. But instead of telling himself that the absence of his body means that he is dead, he covers up the truth by using another's body and trying to make that body accommodate him as well as his own body did. Fear of death is a condition of terror that some people just cannot handle, so they seek refuge. Refuge is found in a friend or family member, or perhaps a colleague—anyone who has an empathetic connection with the dead man. Anyone who grieves strongly for the dead one can become his target.

When a dead spirit takes over the body of another person, he is challenging the rightful owner to a battle of possession. The living one is, after all, just as strongly attached to his body as the dead man was to his own. The living host may sense that something is very wrong and, through sheer will, cast off the intruder. It is not necessary that the victim be fully aware of what is happening to him, nor is it necessary that he discern the presence of his departed friend. The deeper mind, our portion of the collective unconscious, knows when something as out-of-place as a possession is occurring and sounds an alarm. If our will is powerful enough, we can cast off the possessing entity before it entrenches itself in our lives.

If the dead spirit loses his host, he will look for another. Often, he finds another very easily. People are sometimes possessed by the spirit of a long-dead ancestor. The possessor may be able to find a host in every generation of his family for several generations until he is finally forced to leave or his family becomes strong enough to get rid of him. Many situations involving family "insanity" are the appearance from generation to generation of a spirit who possesses his descendents.

How can a spirit continue to possess others for so long? In spirit reality, there is no such thing as time. Time is an earth-realm construct and does not have real meaning away from the world of the living. A spirit who is possessing a living being has lost more than just his physical form. He has also lost the consideration of time. To a spirit there is no time, so the changing appearance of this world—the movement of seasons or the evolving of towns into cities, of horse-drawn buggies into cars—does not impart a sense of passing time to the spirit. He notes the changes he sees but he does not care about these because they do not affect him. He does not react to the events resulting from time because, to him, there is no time, there is only event-unfolding. He will have an urge to do something, and there will come a point when that urge is satisfied. But he does not say to himself, "It took me five years to achieve that," because for him there are no years, there is only the forward thrust that comes from urge and desire. Beyond wanting, there is very little *to* a possessing spirit of this type.

Accident and Intention

Accidental possession derives from death-illnesses—unwillingness to acknowledge death, or desire and overwhelming emotion. The "accident" here is the unfortunate circumstances that the dead man is simply too weak to overcome, and for which he does not receive aid.

But the spirit's abduction of another person, or the attempt to do so, is not an accident. It is an intentional step, and while the ghost is not responsible for the mess he made of his death, he is responsible for possession. Even when born of sheer terror, possession is nevertheless an act of invasion. This kind of possession, and the death that prompted it, is not the awesome, negative act conducted by primary or secondary evil. An accidentally-possessing entity is not evil. He is a lost soul doing a bad thing, but he is not reprehensible. He is ill.

Susceptibility to Possession by Accidental Evil

The etheric body and its strength or weakness is important to all three kinds of possession: primary, secondary and accidental. In the first two kinds of evil, however, the disposition of one's will is also very important. A potential host to primary or secondary evil must have a leaning toward passivity or a desire to join forces with his possessor, for it is impossible to be taken over by true evil unless, on some level of our being, we have agreed to the partnership.

It is different with accidental evil. Anyone, even a strong-willed person, can be assaulted and overcome by accidental evil because the death-illnesses that create accidental possession are very human maladies, such as fear, excessive desire, or overattachment. Because we human beings are all encumbered, to some degree, by these difficult aspects of human life, it is easy for accidental evil to approach us by mating its illnesses to our own.

If there is a powerful empathetic connection between the dead spirit and his host, possession is facilitated by that bond.

Fascination with the occult is a vulnerability nobody can afford unless that fascination is informed, tempered, and disciplined with *knowledge* of the occult. I have seen several instances of accidental evil among occultists. In these instances, the host was passionately involved in occultism but lacked any real education and the requisite sense of caution. Fortunately, many of these instances of possession pass quickly because the host, having allowed possession by what he thought was a brilliant spirit (or assumed to be an aspect of his own soul), soon tired of the possessor once he learned that his friend had nothing substantial to offer.

Factors such as boredom and the absence of satisfying spiritual contact render one vulnerable to possession. The spirit may seem to be an entity of great intensity. There is an urgency, an immediacy to the possessor that overwhelms us. We assume the spirit's intensity indicates a powerful nature. In truth, it indicates desperation. The would-be possessor is in an hysterical condition because he must find a living human being through whom to continue his existence. If we have never felt such urgency as we do from him, we may open our will to him.

Habits, too, make us vulnerable, particularly habits that overexcite us. If we are used to drinking alcohol or taking drugs, if we are used to sadomasochistic sex, if we are continually imbalanced, we can easily be approached by a dead spirit. We don't notice his desire to participate in our habits or to keep us mentally imbalanced because his presence feels like part of our own being. If our tastes or habitual behavior frequently cause us blackouts and we are targetted by a dead spirit, he can align himself with us while we are unconscious.

Cultural Attitudes Toward Accidental Possession

The wide variety of taboos regarding death and dead people indicate that many cultures, ancient and current, know how hard the death journey can be and realize the dangers the living are exposed to during and immediately following a death.

In some cultures the possibility of possession by the dead is considered so important that healers/exorcists are trained to deal with possession when it occurs. Only a trained professional is likely to meet with success when he tries to coax a possessing spirit out of someone's body. When he does succeed in getting the spirit out of the host, he often (according to published and verbal reports) attributes his success to the intervention of spirits whom the dead one trusts, perhaps relatives of the spirit's deceased relatives.

Even after the dead spirit leaves the host, there may be trouble. The spirit may panic all over again once he's left the body and finds himself in a disembodied state. He may reenter the body he has just left, or he may attempt to take over the body of the exorcist or anyone else in the vicinity.

Getting a spirit out of someone's body is only a partial exorcism. Getting him to leave the earth realm and journey on is the full solution. This requires great powers of persuasion and it requires help from Spirit.

Battle Stress Syndrome and Possession

Many cases of aberrant behavior by men and women who have fought in wars or spent any time in the military or lived near battle sites are incorrectly diagnosed as stress-related when they are actually consequences of possession.

A soldier's energies may be excited to the point of hysteria because he knows he may be killed at any moment. If he is killed, he may panic and enter the body of the first accommodating living person he can find. The most suitable being is usually a nearby soldier because his energies are excited to a high pitch by the battle. The soldier does not have the discernment he needs to know that something is invading him. He's too frantic, frightened, or merely nervous to be paying attention to his intuition. In the height of battle, it is easy for a newly-dead man to join his energies to the energies of his buddy. This happens often.

The living warrior goes home after the war and finds himself doing things not in keeping with his personality. Because he has been involved in a war, his loved ones and therapist attribute his changed behavior to stress. It is *not* stress. It is the daily influence of another person, living right alongside the warrior's body. The beleaguered man does not know he's playing host to his dead buddy. If the dead man is disinclined to leave, either because he isn't fully aware that he is dead, or because he feels cheated by his death and is determined not to be dead, then the host may be his host until the host himself dies.

Battle-related accidental possessions are especially frightening because the intruding spirit can implant all of his war-ravaged memories within his host. The possessed human will muse over battle scenes—even those he did not participate in.

Eventually the spirit's tormented remembrance will overtake his host's consciousness. The victim will become obsessed.

I believe that many instances of hostage-taking and killing on the part of veterans are due to this phenomenon. The restless, angry, spirit of the dead man lives alongside the increasingly restless, angry spirit of his host. The veteran's tension grows so great that his need for relief is as overwhelming as the spirit's. The possessed veteran with or without premeditation, takes hostages in his house or goes to a schoolyard and grabs some children. If he is lucky, he will stop with the taking of hostages. If not, he will kill.

Talking to a therapist about stress will do almost nothing for a beleaguered host-veteran. He does not need merely to discharge mental energy but to be rid of the possessing spirit. Without the help of a healer/exorcist, the veteran will continue to feel restless and angry and obsess over battle scenes. His therapist and loved ones will assume that his fascination with war derives from his personal experiences. But they do not; they are created in the veteran's spirit by the possessor's obsession with his death during war. The explosive combination of pressured veteran and hysterical possessor leads to many disasters which our culture wrongly attributes to veteran's battle stress.

This tragedy could be dealt with if our society understood this common occurence and knew how to deal with it. The fact that many dead people refuse to accept their new status—or simply do not know of it—is the reason why some cultures have elaborate rituals relating to dead bodies and the home and relatives of the dead. Prayers for a good death journey are necessary when a loved one dies. Prayers for our protection are imperative for the living when someone close to us dies. Closeness is a matter of empathy. It is also sometimes geographical. We can be assaulted by a would-be possessor just because we happened to be near him when he died, not necessarily because we love him or are related to him. Prayers for our protection are particularly important when a death has occurred abruptly, through accident or murder. Without the conscious knowledge that death was on the horizon, it can be difficult for a recently-dead spirit even to know he *is* dead, let alone function calmly enough to make a good death journey.

Drift-Beings

There is a danger of our being accosted by primary evil as we enter our death transition. Primary evil, always on the look-out for energy, lies in wait for the dying. It tries, through fear or shock, to wrench energy from the traveler. Because some people die suddenly and are therefore in a state of shock as they enter death, it is not difficult for a being of primary evil, lying in ambush, to separate the recently-dead spirit from some of his energy.

I had occasion to observe this challenge from primary evil when a young friend who had died in an accident came to see me a few days after his death. (I am a medium and dead people often come to see me because they know I will see and hear them, as many other people do not.) I told my friend to return to the place where he was killed, and then to the funeral parlor where his body was being readied for cremation. I instructed him to reclaim any energy that still lingered at the site of the accident, and then take back all the remaining energy from his body. I asked him if he felt revulsion about being cremated. He said he didn't, so I told him to look his body over before it went into the crematorium and gather any remaining energy.

Several hours after this conversation, I was getting ready to sleep when a particularly nasty-sounding spirit shouted at me, "You goddamned *bitch*. I had a tasty morsel right under my nose and you snatched it away, you bitch!"

I call these entities drift-beings: non-individuated parcels of primary evil whose sole intent is to find food. They are semi-beings, scavengers who survive by taking scraps of energy from the dying as they pass through the threshold between the realm of the living and the death passage. Drift-beings, unlike individuated beings of primary evil, lack sufficient consciousness to keep themselves thriving. They take the little bits they can get, which is not much, and have a minimal existence. Nevertheless, they are an annoyance to the spirit trying to get out of this realm. In instances of suicide, they can be more than mere annoyance.

Suicide

I am not concerned here with the moral issues involved in suicide, issues that must be resolved by each person according to his lights, but with the occult/practical implications of suicide deaths.

When we kill ourselves, whether as a coup-de-grâce because we are terminally ill and suffering, or for mental or emotional reasons, we lose energy. We lose it because, in the act of turning on our body, we become disoriented—and this is all a drift-being needs. He will move in on us as we pass out of our bodies and enter the threshold, where he awaits the dying. Because we are not in control of our emotions, he takes some of our energy before we know we are being attacked. If we are not at war with ourselves over the suicide, feeling justified without feeling resentful or angry, there's not much for us to lose by this encounter because we will sense attack when it comes. We sail on, knowing we meant to be dead. As long as remorse does not set in, our intention to leave this realm will propel us onward. The drift-being will try to snatch what he can, but as long as we are at peace with our deaths, we will not lose anything we cannot afford to lose.

The usual suicide, however, is fraught with charged emotion and despair. Focused on the negative aspects of his life, he has a hard time maintaining any control at all during his death passage. Control is made possible through self-awareness, and if we have reached a state of such extreme imbalance as to have killed ourselves, our awareness is muddled.

For this reason, suicides tend to leak energy, like dropping coins out of a hole in a purse. This makes a suicide more vulnerable to energy-theft than are other journeyers through death's threshold.

If we are angry or in thrall to any overpowering emotion, if we fear that our suicide will render us a non-being or send us to hell, then we may be in trouble. We cannot move beyond the threshold between realms, the place where the drift-beings are. Since we have neither the strength nor, possibly, the intention to move through that threshold, we may stay within reach of the drift-beings long enough to lose a great deal of energy.

There is, in every suicide, even the one who feels at peace after his death, some element of counter-desire, some portion of consciousness that does not want to die. This is true no matter how horrible our lives have been. The very fact that we have to turn against our bodies in order to die is evidence that our souls are not ready to depart. If they were, we would die naturally.

The part of our consciousness that does not desire death wars with the part that wants it. While the two portions battle it out, our journey stalls at the threshold of death. Only once we have made peace with the actuality of our being dead can our spirit move past the threshold.

If a suicide feels that he should not have killed himself, he can nevertheless make peace with his death by choosing acknowledgement over regret. If he indulges regret, he will remain at the threshold and the mercy of the drift-beings.

It is imperative that everyone left behind after a suicide make no angry judgements about the departed one. Our regrets will add to his regrets. Our anger will reverberate within him, for suicides are always exquisitely sensitive. Our negative feelings will make his death passage more difficult than it already is.

Only after someone has made a safe transition—this can take from a few days to a few years—is it safe for us to vent our anger over the suicide. Though it is difficult, we must release—not repress—our hostile feelings as a matter of courtesy to the dead. Suicide makes for a very touchy journey, and the suicide needs all the help he can get. It is asking a great deal of the living to request that they set aside their "right" to anger over his death, and that they do all they can to mitigate their grief, but the rights of the suicide supersede the rights of the living because the dead who journey in an imbalanced condition are in great danger of becoming lost souls. They may return to this realm and possess someone. They may lose their way and take hundreds of years to complete their death passage. They may, if disturbed beyond what they can handle, remain at the threshold and be absorbed entirely by primary evil.

Accidental Death and Hauntings

When a life is terminated abruptly by an agency outside the dead one's free will and if, despite this, the deceased has a successful death passage, there is still the chance that he may have left behind some of his consciousness. This consciousness is what is discerned when we say we feel a ghost around us. There are, as has been discussed in this chapter, whole people who become ghosts. But partial consciousness is the cause of most hauntings, not the presence of a whole personality.

There are exceptions. Whole beings may attach themselves to a place where they were executed or died in a terrifying accident or murder, but in the main, what we experience as hauntings are portions rather than the whole of a dead person's energy.

If a woman has been raped and murdered and has been able to leave this realm with all of her energy intact, she may elect not to take the terror of her death with her. In that case, though she leaves, the ordeal imprints itself on the atmosphere surrounding the scene or attaches itself to the earth where the ordeal took place. Many deaths create history: the victim leaves but his death-ordeal remains at the scene of the horror. Often, when a dreadful death is known, people will say that the reason its location feels haunted is that the woman who died there three hundred years ago is still there. Usually, that's not so. She is gone. But the fear her death engendered in her, the passion of the one(s) who tormented and killed her, and all the other negative energies generated by the experience have remained at the death site. These energies imprint themselves on the airwaves at the site in much the way pictures and sounds imprint themselves on video or audio tape. Because they are powerfully-imprinted by the passion of the experience, they will not go away by themselves. Mild energies, positive and negative, dissipate in time; powerful ones do not.

Something purposeful must be done to those energies by an exorcist or other healer, if they are to be removed. Left alone, they will continue to interact among themselves and thereby generate enough power to remain where they are. If people carrying negative energies act these out at the site, having been attracted by the dolor of the haunting which matches their own feelings, the site will increase in negative power. It often happens that a place of negative feeling will attract negativity from the living again and again. In this way, sites of negative passion become empowered and energized because their existence inclines similar energies toward them. Once a place has endured an assault from negative emotion of a powerful kind, it can, through attracting similar actions, become a sinkhole of negativity and be very difficult to heal.

Negative energies, like positive ones, can imprint themselves on the airwaves or the earth or to any concrete form. It is very difficult for any energy to remain long in moving water because, next to fire, water is the fastest transmuting force on this planet. Fire and water are elements of quick transmutation. Air and earth transmute slowly. Sometimes the energies attached to or imprinted on air or earth are so powerful that they simply cannot be transmuted by the element holding them.

Powerful negative energy may remain in the ground despite the building and demolition of one structure after another. A strong stamp of sadness or anger will remain on that ground though the place hosts a church, a school, a house, and then a parking garage. The coming and going of many people over a long period of time will have some mitigating effect on that energy, on the ground and in the air, but will not remove it entirely. Only intention and skill can remove extremely powerful energy once it has been set.

Slave Ghosts

One way in which a dead person who has not achieved a full death passage can be abused is through slavery, and this is not unheard of in any part of the world.

Some years ago I met a young man who told me about his five-year-old daughter's playmate, a little girl dead over two hundred years, who "lived" in the man's old farmhouse. When I expressed outrage at him for allowing his young daughter to play with a ghost, the fellow explained with deep solemnity that he had been unable to find good daycare for the child and felt, at any rate, that his daughter was better off at home than playing with strangers! The most pitiful thing was that he and his wife were glad for the help the poor little ghost gave them, including her kindness in piling extra blankets on their bed during very cold nights.

When I asked him how he knew the ghost was a little girl, he said, first, that his daughter could see the ghost and had described her, and then that he had chanced upon the girl's tombstone behind his farmhouse. He had been able to read the tombstone and knew her name, which meant, of course, that he could call her by name, thus binding her to his family by familiarity.

I was so appalled that I begged him to let me do something for the ghost. Nothing doing. He wanted his child's playmate and his unpaid household help to remain right where she was.

Years ago, when I lived across the street from an auto body shop, I looked out the window one night to see a group of men, perhaps ten of them, standing in the lot where the damaged cars were parked. The men wandered among the cars, looking inside each one. They walked with jerky, robotlike movements. This puzzled me until I realized that the men were dead. They were enslaved spirits, moving like an army of marionettes, doubtless brought together by a master for purposes of labor. I think they were searching the wrecked cars for energy left behind by those occupants who were traumatized or killed in car crashes.

Zombies

I mentioned earlier that every dead person needs a full three days before cremation or burial to assure that all his energy exits the body. As a rule, people's spirits do not pop out of their bodies like toast from a toaster. Energy leaves a dead body gradually.

It sometimes happens that a person who does not know he is dead can leave his body, without knowing he has done so, and continue "living" with absolute certainty that he is alive. This certainty and the energy he invests in his "life" makes him vibrant enough that he can become visible to the living. That is why people who are not used to being mediumistic sometimes see ghosts in their homes, or wandering through graveyards. A ghost who does not realize he is dead can become angry over being ignored by the living, and he may chase a car as it moves through the graveyard or run after someone on the street, wondering why he is being ignored and becoming increasingly angry at this treatment. As his anger increases, he becomes more visible.

The body of a dead person can be used for slavery without the spirit of the dead one having any connection to his body. Bodies are useful for labor, and as vehicles for getting around among the living. A being of primary evil can use his living human slave to procure a body for him from a graveyard or morgue. His consciousness can enter that body and he can then use it as long as he has enough energy to keep the body from disintegrating.

This phenomenon, which results in partially-decomposed bodies being animated by primary evil, are a reality often reflected as fiction in books and films. The creation of a zombie can be accomplished with or without the use of drugs.

Most unfortunately, there are times when a dead body is obtained while some of the owner's spirit is still connected to his body. These beings, spirits who are trapped in their own bodies and enslaved, are zombies.

The life of a zombie is not a long one because the body being used belongs to the energy animating it, and this energy, though it can be enslaved for a time, will eventually be compelled to join the spirit that left it. The energy inside the body is like a tiny stream and will soon flow toward the larger pool of energy to which it vibrates.

For obvious reasons, a cremated body cannot be turned into a zombie. The zombie phenomenon is a good reason for keeping the rule dictating a three-day waiting period between death and burial. The more energy left inside a buried body, the greater the chance that evil will dig up the body and use it. Bodies left in mortuaries are less likely to be stolen because there are people around them who would note their disappearance. Buried bodies are not missed as long as the graves that held them are left in the condition expected of new graves.

If physical labor is desired, must the controlling power use a zombie? No. Ghost labor will do for many tasks because concrete objects can be a moved without the use of physical force. The power of the mind, directed toward moving an object, can accomplish it. Moving an object from one place to another without touching it physically is called teleportation. The object moved is called an apport. A book can sail across a room without any visible moving force and a ring can disappear into thin air. A spirit can move objects. Under the direction of a powerful being, hypnotized spirits can be used as slave labor, as was the case in the auto body shop across from my house.

Zombies are not always slaves, not always being abused by something outside themselves. A dead person who has not fully disconnected from his body can give some energy to that body on a continual basis and move himself around. There isn't enough of him in the body that we could say he has had a miraculous recovery. He is not recovered. Enough of him is outside the body that he is truly dead. But enough remains inside the body that he can animate it. This occurence happens most often when people die in solitude, far from anyone who might bury them. I believe it happens most often in mountainous areas because great masses of rock contain and give off so much vitalizing force that a person can feed from that force and compensate, with it, for the portion of his energy that has left his body. He can maintain himself without, strictly speaking, being alive.

Poltergeists

There is a phenomenon of ghostlike energy that arrives in a house without warning, causes disruption, then leaves abruptly. The force behind this is not a ghost. Ghosts and ghost-energy tend to remain, unless exorcised, right where they are. A poltergeist is a temporary force created by two aspects of living human beings, and usually by two separate people. Poltergeists are erratically-moving energy. Sometimes they move solid objects around and sometimes they destroy objects.

Poltergeist energy is born of a combination of dislocated mental intention and overabundance of psychic energy. The phenomenon has nothing to do with either dead people or evil. It is not under anyone's direction, and is not caused by malicious intent.

When someone has an overabundance of energy, which happens during puberty and sometimes during menopause and menstruation, the energy cannot be contained by that person's physical form because the body cannot use all of it. What the body can't use, it casts off. Sometimes this extra energy accidentally combines with the strong thoughts of another nearby person. The combination of directed thought and floating energy creates a force which affects objects and/or manifests as powerful atmosphere. This is purely an energy phenomenon.

When young people—for this situation occurs most often in a house where there are children going through puberty—have more energy than their bodies need, and when someone in that house has a good deal of unprocessed emotionally-charged thought, a potent force is made of the two.

Suppose there is a young man with excess energy born of puberty. He lives with a dissatisfied mother whose life disappoints her. She does not intend to create disruption, but her emotions are so strong that they begin to take on a particular direction. What was once an infrequent thought of unhappiness becomes a continual awareness of misery. Her bitter thoughts come together with the cast-off, unchanneled energy of her son. The young man's energy gives power to the mother's thoughts, and her thoughts give direction to his cast-off energy. The young man's energy, directed by the mother's thoughts, becomes a power. Dishes break. A table moves across the room. There may be a feeling of electricity in the atmosphere.

There is no ghost in the house. The activity and charged atmosphere are caused by thoughts, which are the guiding element, fueled by energy that floats without anchor because it has been rejected by the young body that does not need it.

As soon as the young person has stopped generating excess energy, the phenomenon will cease, even if the mother is still unhappy. If it should happen that the miserable mother begins to feel better, then the phenomenon will end as her dissatisfaction ends, even if the pubescent one is still generating too much energy. In order for the poltergeist to take place, both elements must be present, the drifting energy and the guiding emotions.

It is not necessary that the two elements come from two beings. It is possible for one person to generate both elements of the poltergeist, but this does not happen as often as when there are two participants.

The reason that this activating force is present during puberty or menopause or menstruation is that during these times our bodies undergo changes in energy levels beyond those experienced when we are ill or simply aging or growing taller.

During puberty, we receive energy from our astral body, or soul. Part of our consciousness that belongs to us but is not inside our body during childhood enters the body as we go through puberty. Before puberty, this energy is connected to us but does not have as powerful an influence on us as do the aspects of our consciousness that live within our bodies all through childhood. The entrance into the body of soul energy at the same time our bodies are being filled with hormones creates an excess of energy.

When a menstruating woman is involved in the poltergeist occurence as the source of energy rather than the controlling mind, it is because her menstruation cycle gives her body more energy than it can handle comfortably. Her involvement in a poltergeist phenomenon may also be due to a cyclical state of overexcitement. Some women are excitable during their menstruation time and some are not.

In no case is the poltergeist situation anything to be frightened about. It is not caused by evil of any type. It is temporary and will pass.

Solving Problems of Accidental Evil

Because troubles caused by misdirection or death-illnesses make themselves apparent more easily than situations of primary or secondary evil, they are more likely to receive help of some kind. If the help comes from someone who doesn't know anything about accidental possession, or about ghosts or poltergeists, the healer may make the situation worse. If the healer is a mental health professional who works with drugs, he will worsen the situation for all participants and may also muddy all the symptoms so badly that only a healer with vast experience will be able to sort things out. Bumbling interference by ignorant practitioners is the greatest danger in healing victims of accidental evil.

The single most positive aspect of these situations is that proper rectification makes all of the participants happy. The possessing spirit or disturbed ghost, when handled gently and according to correct procedure, is content to go on his way. The possessed host is glad to be rid of his unwanted guest and the ghost-troubled family will be only too thrilled to see the situation healed.

In all cases of accidental evil, the difficulty we face is not in the handling of these situations by competent professionals, but in finding those professionals. When they emigrated to America, some of our forebears made the awful mistake of leaving behind not only the poverty and prejudice they meant to escape but also the old ways and old knowledge—methods used for thousands of years. Their descendents are in the position now of having to retrieve the old, well-tested knowledge from the past. Retrieving takes a lot of searching and a lot of time.

If you believe you have a situation on your hands that involves possession, *do not attempt to handle it alone.* You may cause more trouble than you can possibly anticipate. Possessing spirits are not dealt with effectively through talk, and you can not expect that tossing out a prayer to a diety who may or may not exist will have any effect on the situation. When confronting a dead person who does not know he is dead, the worst thing you can do is to tell him he's dead. *Dead* and *death* are powerfully unhappy words among the living; imagine the ghastly effect they have on people who really *are* dead and cannot face the fact. Only a naive or cruel person would try that kind of shock therapy on a confused, miserable spirit.

Matters of haunting and possession, especially those rare cases of possession involving multiple personalities, must not be intruded upon by an amateur. Your job is to find good help. This is not an easy task. The best beginning is to use a technique for contacting Spirit, or God, one from this book or one that you have tested and feel suits you. Tell the universe that you need help and why.

Then, make discrete inquiries of a trustworthy friend, pastor, or the person in town with a reputation for good spiritual work. Ask if he knows of an exorcist. Be certain that the exorcist you approach is not someone who learned healing or exorcism in a weekend workshop, but someone with actual, viable experience.

It may be necessary to approach someone from a culture unlike your own. There are people in the United States who honor and still practice the old ways. Some of them practice very powerful good magic. Some practice vile magic. You are on your own in discerning which is which. Some African, native North and South American people have knowledge of accidental evil. They will call it by another name, by the way, as the term "accidental evil" is my term and not a traditional one.

If you are able to find help, talk to the exorcist or healer for a good long time and see what you feel about him. Once you and he have made contact, his reputation should cease to matter to you. Your intuition about him is *all* you need consider. He may be known in town or famous worldwide but that tells you nothing about his competence. It may mean only that his followers are gullible, or that he has an efficient public relations team behind him. Try to let go of any intellectual perceptions and ask yourself what is your gut feeling about him. Don't let yourself be overwhelmed by his title or appearance. The fact that someone has a lot of strange items draped about his neck does not mean he's gifted. Just because he has an unpronounceable name or a background you cannot begin to understand doesn't mean he is connected to the kind of help you need. Be judicious in choosing help and refuse to allow yourself to be rushed into anything. Do not permit yourself to be overcome by another's personality or strong opinions. The problem is yours and nobody can tell you what road to take in solving it.

If you know you are dealing with a situation that involves only energy, such as sad feelings around a house, and you're sure that you are not up against an actual personality such as a case of possession, then you are safe in using any or all of the removal techniques described later in this book. Start with the simple ones and, if you feel a need to go beyond those, use the more complex ones. In any endeavor involving the occult or spiritual troubles, the simple ways are always the best ways.

Misalignment and Insanity

Our being comprises several aspects, sometimes referred to as bodies: the physical form; the energy or etheric body that surrounds, enlivens and informs the physical body; mental and emotional bodies; and the astral or soul body that guides, teaches, protects and inspires us in our sleeping and waking states. Sometimes the astral body is called the higher self.

Our etheric body can be thinned, weakened, or torn. It can shift away from the physical body—but not by much, for without the enlivening etheric body, the physical form would die.

The mental and emotional bodies, sensitive to the information and energy we send them, can be knocked out of alignment with our astral body. There can be misalignment between the astral body and our physical and etheric bodies, too. Misalignment between any of our components and the astral body happens when, for example, we are dealt a shock or when we undergo major surgery. Anesthesia is hard on the physical and etheric components of our being.

The astral body itself is sturdy, but its connection to our etheric energy and to our physical, mental and emotional bodies must be maintained. It can happen to any of us, at some time, that our astral body is misaligned; this means that our ability to communicate with it and its ability to reach us is thrown off, not that damage is done to the astral body itself. Weak contact between our minds and emotions and the astral body can be caused by indulgence in overly passionate emotion. When emotional turmoil leads to obsession, the disturbance can create rifts in our waking and sleeping connection with the astral us. Alcohol, so-called recreational drugs and therapeutic drugs when taken in amounts greater than our physical, emotional, mental or etheric components can handle will cause misalignment between those component parts of us and our astral self. Either the astral body will not be able to contact us at all, or its contact will be unclear. Our intuition will be stifled and the flow between our waking mind and our deeper, all-knowing mind will be impeded.

In any of the above-mentioned instances, the astral body is

not itself weakened. That can occur only through the most intense assault on it—which implies intentional attack—or a great shock delivered to our other component aspects.

Everyone experiences a mild form of misalignment when he takes a path that fails to inspire him spiritually, or to feed the spiritual nature he has already developed. Once we see how bored, angry or dispirited we have become and make the necessary adjustments, our astral body returns to direct alignment with the rest of us.

The usual problem in misalignment, then, is in the connection between our astral body and our physical, etheric, emotional or mental elements. The astral body itself is assailed only rarely and under extremely powerful circumstances.

It sometimes happens that our mental body entrenches itself in a place out of sync with our current lifetime. The mental body can anchor itself in a past or a future incarnation, and in this or any other realm. It can entrench itself in someone else's life, too.

When our mental body has joined itself to the past, the future, to a lifetime belonging to ourselves or another, we can become so deeply entrenched there that our current circumstances lose all interest for us. Our energies are inclined to follow our physical needs first, because the primary need for all of us is to remain inside our body, and this requires keeping our body healthy. But after the needs of our physical form, the emotional body is our greatest energy-draw. As we become more and more attracted to the time and place in which our emotional body has anchored itself, our mental energies soon follow. Once our energies have entered that other situation, we lose contact with current reality.

This phenomenon explains why there are people in mental institutions who believe they are Napoleon, Cleopatra or Jesus. The man who believes he is Napoleon is not "crazy," not making things up or creating a fantasy. His mental body has become so closely allied with Napoleon's life and possibly also with his personality that, in real sense, he *is* Napoleon. He becomes Napoleon by having vivid, immediate access to the energies swirling around Napoleon, to the energies and thoughts Napoleon generated, and to the circumstances of Napoleon's life.

The man who believes he is Napoleon, or who lives in a realm nobody on earth has ever heard of, or who thinks he is a marcher in Caesar's army is not making invalid claims. His trouble is that he has successfully tuned into another time and place, and because he has tuned into a reality—not a fantasy— he is imprisoned by that reality because it *is* a reality. He is an undisciplined, out-of-control medium. He needs the help of a competent occultist, one who understands all the components of our being and can travel outside of time and three-dimensional space, as shamans do.

Instead of help, he may receive the condemnatory assault of ignorant practitioners of mental health, who compound his troubles by torturing him with electroshock and/or potent drugs. Enough of these wicked assaults and the man may become so damaged that there is no chance of healing him.

The fundamental cause of tragedy in these situations is not the patient's mental illness, but the stubbornness of his psychotherapists. Some schooling in the old techniques of dealing with mental aberrations, some education in shamanism and mediumship, would enable our society's healers to guide the sick person's mental body out of the place it's ensconced in. Understanding the ways in which occultists move across time would help therapists to comprehend the true nature of mental illness and teach them how to deal with it.

The fact that cultures outside mainstream Western society have been available to our healers and that we, as a culture, have rejected outside help, is evidence that our mental health professionals don't really care to help their patients. A "crazy" person is, in truth, merely a conduit between doctors and their theories. "Insane" people, who are in fact always either misaligned or possessed, could be helped if our so-called healers would simply allow those who understand the dynamics of misalignment and possession to impart their knowledge.

Mental   and   emotional   attachment   to   inappropriate circumstances causes misalignment. Possession by any of the three kinds of evil, including accidental evil can, over time, lead the possessed being into times and places with which the possessor is associated. In this way, a possessed person can be both possessed and misaligned. If he is possessed for many years, there is a strong probability that he will endure misalignment as well as possession. His will and etheric body having been weakened by possession, it is almost inevitable that his emotional and/or mental bodies will fall out of alignment with his current life and into circumstances that absorb the attention of his possessor.

If our psychotherapists educate themselves in the disciplines of shamanism and mediumship, they will learn to identify instances of possession and misalignment, to guide the afflicted away from their troubles by gently separating possessor and possessed, and realigning component bodies.

Memory and Neurosis

Time is a concept. Time-constraints and time-structures are not so much actual as humankind's consensual agreement to believe they are actual. It is very easy to move outside of time. It is also easy—sometimes unavoidably so—to allow a compelling situation from another time to drag our consciousness out of the now and into that other time. We often carry around with us situations that pertain to a past existence. It is possible to be aware of, and afflicted by, situations that pertain to a future experience, but these are rare because future events do not carry the emotional weight of past ones.

Past-life involvements that still hold our emotional attention may give us current tendencies. These memories may be of something wonderful or terrible; as long as they carry emotional weight, they will affect us. The experiences that live in present-life consciousness are usually our own, but they may, when extreme emotion is involved, be someone else's memories. It is not necessary, in that instance, that we have any involvement in our current life with the person whose other-life traumas are affecting us. The memory is what holds our emotional energy, not the other person and not our relationship to that person.

The fundamental misunderstanding our society must deal with has to do with what memory really is. Memory is not actually a mental or emotional attachment to events happening outside the now. Memory is a situation living *within* the now, regardless of when it first transpired. Memory is not a record of something over and done with, but a currently-felt, currently-perceived reality that we have brought into the present though it did not have its advent in the present. Memory is not a trauma that is "over" but one that we have continued into current existence because, for us, it is not over at all.

In mild situations, this phenomenon leads us to feel strongly about certain kinds of love affairs, or to champion causes that have a counterpart in the circumstances with which we are currently living. It may as easily evince itself as a feeling of revulsion for something as an attraction.

In order to deal successfully with strong feelings deriving from other-life situations, we must understand that our notion of memory as a record of events-past is erroneous. As long as a feeling, a fear, a thought, or any state of being which comes to us from another lifetime has any impact on the present, then we are dealing with misalignment. The other-life situation is a living and informing aspect of our current existence *and is as reality-based* as any other aspect of our lives. Until we come to a resolution of the other-life trauma and make peace with the energies we have invested in it, it will play a role in this lifetime because it is not really "past" until we have resolved it and let it go.

We create the same troubles for ourselves by leaving childhood memories to wander around in our psyches. Thus, when someone tells his therapist that he is plagued by the "memory" of his parents' divorce, which happened when he was four years old, a mistaken notion is at work. The divorce is not a memory but an actuality in the patient's current life, a fully alive situation that informs the existence he is currently living. The patient does not *believe* the event is happening; it *is* happening.

Anything that constrains, informs, colors or helps direct the life we are living in this day is wholly real. In that sense, there is no such thing as memory. There is only still-happening and no-longer-happening.

Much misery could be alleviated and many of our difficulties resolved for good if we understood the truth that time is more concept than actuality, and that we bridge time far more often than we realize, in our sleeping and waking states, whether or not we have any desire to do so.

The relationship among our component bodies must be balanced. When any of these moves out of its synchronistic relationship with the others, we have troubles. Our emotional and mental components are most likely to move toward, or away from, any aspect of our lives to which they have a strong reaction. This moving away needs to be recognized for what it is before it can be dealt with successfully. If any aspect of us moves too far away from the rest of our being, the misalignment can badly warp our contact with the astral body. This leads to major difficulties.

Also, the miseries caused through possession by any of the various types of evil must be understood completely if we are to heal "insane" people, or those on the way to becoming "insane."

Besides a full, knowledgeable understanding of misalignment and possession, it is imperative that we as a society cease to ignore the inevitability of our deaths and stop cringing in the face of the death-change. The death journey is the most important transition we make. We must learn to prepare for it so that we can do it well. Most death-illnesses could be prevented if we were taught preparation for death, and were fully cooperative when the time came for us to die. Every death-illness takes a great toll on two victims, the one whose death has not been a successful one, and the one who is beleaguered by a ghost, a lost soul, a possessor. Death-illnesses multiply easily because each trapped spirit spreads his illness among the living. Too, he often creates difficulties for other souls in limbo. It does not have to be this way. We achieve nothing by fearing our deaths—before the fact or when we face them.

Beginning today, we can avail ourselves of many methods for staying straight with ourselves and for keeping the horrors of evil at bay. Taking complete charge of our consciousness and our lives is not an overwhelming proposition, and one need not become a full-time occultist in order to gain insights into the hidden dynamics behind life in this realm. There are many ways to clarity of purpose and many ways to sane living. Suggestions to help the occultist and the lay reader to find and follow their personal paths are offered in Part II of this book.

PART III

Shouting at the Wolf:
Confronting Evil

Chapter 5

Singing a Song of Our Own:
Living Sanely in the Presence of Evil

To be in hell is to drift;
to be in heaven is to steer.

—George Bernard Shaw

The best defense against psychic attack and the influences of negative energies, intentional and accidental ones, is a sane, self-determined life. The greatest favor you can do yourself, whether you are a practicing occultist or have no interest in mysticism, is to maintain yourself in a state of hopefulness, joyous expectation and good cheer. No technique can do for you what your own good will can do, and nothing I have to say will help as much as your willingness to avail yourself of the powerful wisdom you carry within you, every day, in your share of the collective unconscious. Know yourself. Honor yourself. Honor the glorious life that surrounds you—all of it. From the partnership between you and the sacred powers of this world, everything you can ever need will come to you when you need it.

The life and energies of every woman and man is of potential use to evil, primary and secondary. Everyone, no matter

141

his path in life, is vulnerable to the tragedies of accidental evil, as a victim of others' errors or a creator of his own errors. Occultists are no more likely to be ensnared by evil than anyone else is. All of us must learn how to live sane lives.

How can we create a truly sane life? What is sanity? Let us start with what sanity is not. Sanity is not blindly accepting anyone else's version of reality or anyone's view of how we ought to live. Sanity is not catering solely to our ego, nor is it the shutting off of any aspect of our being: the emotions, body, mind, spirit, or our portion of the collective unconscious.

Sanity is the acceptance of our *own* experiences and perceptions in the face of "proof" from other people and social institutions that our views are "wrong" because they do not match the views held by others. One of the most insidious elements of life in our society is the assumption that our lives are meant to validate social programming. On that single point rests an enormous amount of what we do; that single element of life causes us to shut ourselves away from the true-us. It has this effect on us in every aspect of life. Our culture engages historians, sociologists, psychiatrists and the media to do what we believe must be done: to impose upon us a common view of reality. The reason for this imposing of socially-approved views of life is fear: As a culture we are afraid that unless we can force the majority of us to comply with particular givens, everything we have achieved and everything we believe we understand will unravel. The truth is that without the continual reinforcement of commonly-held cultural views of "reality," most of our beliefs and some of our ways of living *would* unravel.

The Shattered Mirror

The reason there can never be an honestly-come-by common view of reality is that the interaction between each human being and the rest of creation is unique and cannot be duplicated or perhaps even understood by another person. Pretend that the world is reflected in a huge mirror. Then let us imagine that when human beings first arrived here, that huge mirror reflecting all of life broke into millions and millions of pieces. Ever since then, everyone has picked up a tiny shard of the mirror, held it up to reflect the world, and told himself, "This is what the world looks like." But the tiny reflection each of us can see tells us only what can be revealed in our miniscule shard. Nothing of what others can see is available to us.

In fairness, we need to understand that there can never be a common view of reality because each of us is capable of seeing only so much and no more. If we cannot make peace with this fact, then we will have to learn tolerance and accommodation because a commonly-held world view is not a possibility, not now and not ever.

To understand why this is so, we must realize that all human races did not arrive on this planet at the same time, or for the same purpose. All are here for reasons unique to them, and all seek their lives here in ways appropriate to them and only to them. We are not all the same; this must be respected.

Our need to evolve peaceably is part of the energizing and informing world-view of the collective unconscious, but we will accomplish this evolution in various ways. There is, then, no such thing as humankind's common goal; our goals are many. The best we can do is to mind our own business and allow others to mind theirs.

When we first began minding other people's business, we were motivated by envy. We envied others their resources or the size of their dwellings or the large herds of animals they possessed. Since then, people have been fighting perpetually over Who Gets What. Who Gets What is the galvanizing force behind most human activity. This force produces warfare on a physical and a psychic level.

Warfare, since man first envied his neighbor, has been so pervasive that it is commonly accepted as a natural part of life until and unless someone points out the possibility that it is neither natural nor desirable, let alone inevitable.

That is an example of how easily led, how easily

programmed we all are. Unless someone opposes a prevailing activity, most of us jump into that activity with both feet.

War is a hideous example of mindless conformity, and by its hideousness, it stands out. Less dramatic, but equally destructive, are the endeavors that we make every day, to homogenize our individuality within the common culture. These endeavors run from conglomerate religion to social mores to modish ideas about how our bodies should be treated—ideas embraced by lay people who have no means of finding out whether or not the ideas will benefit them. As soon as a modish idea is replaced by another modish idea, also misunderstood, it too is embraced by many people. Why do we need to be told what is good for us? It cannot be that the information we get from institutions of health parroted by the media is demonstrably correct, because the opposite is so often true. Countless ideas accepted by the masses are later proved wrong and debunked. If our informant's record for good ideas is as poor as it is and has always been, then why do we follow it? Can it be that we have forgotten how to listen to ourselves?

That is the answer, of course. If we can begin to listen to our desires, pay attention to what our body tells us it thrives on, know our emotional territory, and open our spirits to the lessons available to us from the three non-human kingdoms of the earth, from the elementary powers and the powers of the six sacred directions, then we will soon find new, sane ways of living. We will learn the wisdom of self-direction, instead of looking to other people to tell us what to do.

That is sanity. Self-propelling and self-directing create real lives for us. Following others creates death-in-life.

Physical Energy and Psychic Energy

Everything we can see is form made alive by energy within and surrounding it. The aspects of earth life we do not see, the directions and elements and other such non-dimensional realities are also made of energy. Rain is energy. Fire is energy. Fire and rain change the composition of things. That is physical reality. Psychic energy changes the composition of things, too. We simply do not see this phenomenon while it is transpiring.

No aspect of three-dimensional reality is impervious to energy outside it, and the emotions and thoughts of human beings are as influential in the world as are fire and rain. Human emotions and thoughts can change things as effectively as bombs, or a gift of flowers. This is particularly true where emotion and thought are carefully directed and controlled. It is easy to comprehend the reality and impact of psychic attack, the assault of one being's energy on another being, when we remember that people throw themselves, heart and soul, into war on enemy clans or war on other races. The same phenomenon takes place on the psychic battlefield as takes place on the plains of war; the only difference between psychic warfare and Dunkirk is the physical, *visible* aspect of warfare.

The human race is made up of passionate thought and passionate emotion, which it makes concrete in a variety of physical ways. And throughout history, as we have been able to dig it up and understand it, people have been aware of the realms of spirit beyond three-dimensional reality, and maintained contact with it. Until the last couple of hundred years, even our own society was aware of the laws of spirit and the ramifications of our conduct toward it.

Since we have turned away from creation and the daily confluence of our lives with the all-life, we have begun talking only to one another and, naturally, have found ourselves lacking. Instead of realizing that we need more than just ourselves if we are to *live* instead of merely survive from day to day, we have hardened the shell around ourselves. There is, in the great scheme of things, a reason why we live among other life-forms and not alone. We have forgotten most of the other life-forms. Between forgetting the all-life and our unnatural and unwarranted elevation of the human kingdom, we have lost our ability to discern what is good for us and what is not because we have only other human beings, living in the same vacuum we live in, with whom to compare experiences.

In this enclosed state, we have learned to worship, or at the very least to be hypnotized by our own inventions. We give to these inventions the degree of attention and reverence we once gave to the whole living world. What we once held sacred was reflected in the sky, the trees, the hills and oceans, the wealth of animals, rocks and flowers. We have shut these reflections of the Almighty and its Power away and have put in their place our own inventions because everyone needs something to revere. Reverence is a deep human need.

Our inventions are technology, psychiatry and physics. It is to these that we now direct our attention and awe, and to these we look for guidance in all levels of life.

Technology

Let us look at what our worship of our intellect and these three inventions has wrought. Technology has made our lives easier on a physical level. Because all changes in one aspect of life must be balanced by changes in another, the ease in our physical life has evoked a burden in our mental states. We have time to fiddle with ourselves that we did not have when there were no washers, microwave ovens or cars. In making this extra time for ourselves, we have made it possible to get up in the morning and simply *be* all day instead of worrying about all the things we have to *do*. Besides our jobs, we need not bother very much with activity. But has a restful way of living been the result of our inventions? Quite the opposite. In the time we might be spending sitting, doing nothing at all, possibly opening our spirit to the world we live in, we rush around filling our time with the kind of trivial *doing* that may become our *un*doing—partying, shopping when there's not a thing we need, flinging ourselves into excessive drinking or excessive physical fitness, placing demands on our bodies that make no real sense. If we drink too much, we destroy our physical form. If we run too hard, we also destroy our physical form. The motive for the first is escape. Might the motive for the second also be escape?

What are we running *from?* Is it ourselves and the emptiness of our own company, our incessant chatter, our desperate need to make ourselves believe we are *living* when in fact we are running on an endlessly-turning, computerized, state-of-the-art treadmill?

Our invention of technology has yielded time, but we dare not spend that time relating to the real world. Why not? Are we afraid of what we might learn if we stopped running and stopped talking for an hour and listened to what the all-life had to say?

Psychiatry

We invented psychiatry. Any tool intended to help the mind or body, if well-meant, can be a boon as long as we remember that it is a tool and not an entity to be worshipped. When psychology was new, it opened up some closets and gave us a different way of looking at how we become what we are. That was useful, possibly important. Then, after psychiatry entered mainstream western life, a terrible shift occurred. A tool became a weapon. One no longer had the option of using the techniques of psychological theories on himself if that was right for him. Suddenly the tools of psychiatry were being used *on* us instead of *for* us, and we no longer had any choice about it—or anything to say about its validity. Today, nobody seems to have much to say about its veracity. Psychiatry has become a worshipped authority, as the Bible is a worshipped authority. Anyone who questions psychiatry's effectiveness or the authenticity of its tenets is forced to defend himself against charges of heresy. In many parts of the world, the Bible is accepted as the word of God: one is not permitted to question its origin. So, too, in many parts of the world psychiatry is accepted as the work of God.

Perception and Sanity

Our road to mistaken perception and mistaken belief always leads from the passionate love we give, to illusion. Our personal desires create illusions that, for the most part, belong to us alone. Another's desires create his illusions, and so on. But there comes a day when the illusion of one person becomes, first the property, and then the prison, of many. From this evolution-of-illusion we get politics, religion, fads and all manner of cultural blindness. We pass our blindness down from one generation to another until it becomes so firmly entrenched in daily life that nobody asks whether this or that aspect of our social belief system might simply be *wrong*.

We are stuck with the social illusions into which we are born. The emperor may wear no clothes but we learn before we are five years old to pretend he is wearing whatever our village says he is wearing, which will be whatever our parents' parents said he was wearing. In our village, truth is truth simply because it is established *as* truth, and not because we ever really see the emperor. From birth, we are imprisoned by the fact of our ancestors' investment in certain beliefs. Our ancestors would not give up, even if they had seen the truth just once, the lifetime investment they made in their favorite lies. From their graves they force us to hold onto what they invested in so heavily. If we even attempt to see how things really look, we betray not only ourselves but our parents and their parents. It takes more strength than most of us have to call a lie a lie when other people's peace of mind is at stake.

Every age has its beloved lies. In Salem, Massachusetts, in 1692 the most dynamic lie was the lie of pervasive devil-worship where it is unlikely that there was more than a little black magic going on. As fervently as we tell ourselves that there is no evil, the Puritans of three hundred years ago believed that evil was rampant. The comparison between our way of dealing with our beliefs and their way of dealing with theirs is remarkably revealing of humankind's ability to give itself over to illusion.

Salem, 1692

The series of extraordinary episodes leading to the famous Salem Witch Trials began when the children of a single family developed mysterious afflictions. The children had visions of villagers hurting them and the devil was commonly believed to be the cause of their suffering. Cotton Mather, a minister, took the children under his care and did what he could to exorcise the influences of assaulting them. His ministrations appear to have been successful. But soon after, others in the village began to see visions of the devil or other villagers hurting them. When the phenomenon spread, it became necessary for the village elders—who were also the church elders—to investigate allegations that the suffering was caused by "witchcraft," the misnomer used in those times for black magic.

It was discovered that two Salem women were indeed practicing black magic; dolls made of goat hair with pins stuck in them turned up in their homes. These two women may well have been the only people in Salem who were actually practicing invasive magic.

The phenomenon spread so fast that trials were held, and anyone who had appeared in the visions of an afflicted person was tried on the charge of witchcraft. It was the visions of the afflicted that provided virtually *all* "evidence" of guilt. These visions, which were called spectre evidence, were alleged to show the afflicted who their tormenters were. If Leah appeared in the visions of a tormented person, then Leah was guilty.

Cotton Mather had been a medical student before becoming a minister. He knew that the mind and body are not separate, that one could influence the other. Surely he knew what hysteria was, and knew that tormented people often cannot sleep, and that their nerves are frayed. He tried to make the court, of which he was not officially a part, understand that the appearance of Leah in a vision was not proof of her guilt. The question he and the judges had to answer was this: Could the devil take on the appearance of an innocent person? The village of Salem was wholly Puritan, that is, they were fundamentalist believers in the Bible as the word of the Almighty. Therefore, the answer to any question, even a legal point, had to be found in the Bible. But the Bible does not address the point of whether or not the devil can take on the appearance of someone who has not entered into a pact with him. There being no biblical answer to the question of spectre vision and its veracity, the judges had to argue the point among themselves. Cotton Mather tried to reason with them. Mather, unfairly maligned by history in regard to his participation in these trials, was the only cool head in town. He tried, in the absence of biblical authority, to promote the sensible idea that there was no reason to suppose the devil could not do pretty much what he wanted to do. Mather was firm on the point that the appearance of Leah in a vision proved nothing whatever about Leah.

The judges disagreed. They respected Mather, but on the issue of spectre evidence, they said he was wrong: The devil could take on someone's appearance only if that person had made his or her appearance "available" to the devil by signing his book and joining him in his work. Without permission, they declared, the devil cannot use the physical appearance of anyone.

So Leah was guilty of black magic every time someone suffering from spasms, terrors, twisted limbs and other extraordinary physical symptoms said he had seen a vision of Leah tormenting him. Spectre evidence, which was no evidence at all, hanged people, caused one to die the hideous death of *presseur,* and imprisoned people who died in prison.

Undeniably, something was very wrong with the afflicted. Their contortions were often beyond medical experience. One woman stiffened so rigidly that her limbs could not be moved either by her or by another person. Something was hurting people badly, but was it evil? Of course it was evil. Wherever there is pain and fear, there is evil. Evil feeds on these. Where they are made available, evil thrives. Primary evil had a banquet every time an accused "witch" was put to death.

But was evil working through the accused? It is unlikely. Primary evil works without dramatic effect. It would not have initiated the displays of physical torment that drew the elders to exorcise it—when they could—and to pray over it—which they did continually. No, primary evil would not have instigated the events at Salem.

Would secondary evil have been the cause of Salem's suffering? That seems likely, given that secondary evil often induces people to give up their energy and power, which would have occurred naturally during the physical tormenting of the afflicted and also during the mental suffering of the accused. While primary evil would have been able to achieve food from some of the deaths, the scenario as a whole indicates the presence of secondary evil.

Let us go back to the discovery of the dolls early in the Salem trials. These dolls were being used to harm people; that is why there were pins in them. It may be that, as the situation got out of hand and people were rapidly falling into one of two categories—afflicted and accused—the phenomenon drew to Salem more practitioners of black magic. It is the same phenomenon as animals gathering at a watering hole. When a place is ripe for taking energy, people make spiritual pilgrimages and ask for some of that power. Sometimes they don't ask, they just take. When a village is ripe for plucking energy from human beings, more than one or two practitioners of black magic will show up. When a few people can be so badly assaulted by psychic attack—with the possible aid of mass suggestion—that their sleep is disturbed and they cannot function, then a good start has been made on taking their life force. While there is something in this situation to draw the attention of primary evil, the situation in Salem bears, in general, the scars of assault by secondary evil.

Greed was behind the escalation in Salem. Had a couple of sorcerers been working on a very few people in order to take their energy or acquire influence within the village, the huge drama would not have happened. But too many people, none of whom is known to us, attempted to grab too much and the situation got out of hand.

The accusers and judges in Puritan Salem could not have known the difference between actual evil and the nonsense they took as "evidence" of evil, and that is where they made a horrible mistake. Their error in judgement was not in believing that there is evil, for all cultures except ours have known this, but in accepting "evidence" from exhausted people. They, like us, were to blame for having allowed the techniques of evil-detecting and exorcism to be forgotten.

Salem, Today

In reading about the Salem trials, I have found an impressive resemblance to the ways in which psychiatrists today deal with questions of sanity and mental illness. The underlying transaction, in Salem and in our society, pits an afflicted person against a self-appointed "expert" who cannot truly comprehend either the affliction or the afflicted. Despite his inability to understand the alleged aberration or the person manifesting it, he passes life-threatening judgements on both. He is inadequate to do this, but our society requires his services every time someone is violent, misaligned, or simply eccentric.

The blame here is not to be laid at the door of mental health professionals who would, in any case, have none of the priest-like status they enjoy if we did not, as a society and as individuals, passively submit to authority outside our own.

Many instances of alleged insanity are clear cases of misalignment of the astral body, as has been discussed. Many others are clearly cases of possession by one or more of the three kinds of evil. Accidental possession causes a great many cases of borderline insanity and accounts for much violence.

Also, it often happens that someone is able to see and hear activities of a realm beyond ours. This is like having your body in Australia and your mind in China. It is not medium-ship, because these situations are not under the afflicted one's control. While it is destructive, it is not insanity; rather, it is misalignment.

In dealing with the possessed or misaligned, the psychiatrist examines as far as he is able the visions and thoughts of the afflicted and, having no comprehension of either misalignment or possession, usually declares the afflicted person to be schizophrenic—when he is possessed—or psychotic—when he is misaligned.

It does not occur to us that, in these complex situations, the difficulty is not that the afflicted one is "crazy" but that our mental health professionals are woefully uneducated and thus ought not to be in charge of people whose ailments lie outside their understanding. In so-called primitive cultures, they know about people getting stuck between realms; it happens a great deal, particularly following a shock. And there is, to my knowledge, no primitive society that does *not* have experience with and understanding of possession.

Evidence that we are currently doing to ourselves what was done to the accused at Salem lies in our society's relationship with the criminally "insane." Our criminal laws are all predicated on the assumption that people have control of themselves, which is preposterous. I have never met anyone who truly had mastery of himself and I doubt that such a person exists.

In Salem, people who suffered in ways nobody could understand were believed to be under attack by an invisible being, Satan, and whatever they said was taken as truth because they were suffering. Today, we operate within a series of unprovable laws regarding what is and is not real, and these laws, or givens, are no more visible to us than Satan was visible during the Salem trials.

Mental health victims are routinely worked over by authorities armed with a set of beliefs that come down to them from three European males who may or may not have been enlightened. Surely Jung, Freud, and Adler were intriguing thinkers. That does not make them omniscient. I am sure that, with the possible exception of Freud, none of them believed himself to be omniscient. But, about forty years ago, we knelt, and we now have no other gods before them.

We have allowed ourselves just enough freedom to expand our ignorant worship of theoretitions to include others beyond the original three, Piaget, Rank, the two Reichs. The inclusion of other thinkers into the sacred circle is meant to demonstrate our ostensible power over our own choices. Hogwash. We have no power over our choices because we are always on the look-out for something man-made to worship. We cannot bear to be left alone. Indeed, spending a great deal of time alone is sometimes taken as a sign of mental imbalance. The truth is that we are so out of touch with real creation that we are forced to perpetually surround ourselves, for validation and companionship, with our own inventions-of-thought. That this company becomes first our destiny and then our imprisonment—whether or not we realize it—is not important to us. What matters is that we should never, even for an instant, be left to experience the world without prejudice, preconception, or predisposition. We pursue our passivity with fervor: surely this is a sign of cultural misalignment.

What do we truly comprehend about psychiatric beliefs and the laws that derive from them? Not much. Yet our society allows the testimony of mental health authorities to send people to jail or to mental institutions. We allow those we place in authority to induce us to foresake our personal, *valid* experiences if our perceptions displease or confound the authorities.

In Salem, Mary's affliction was proof that something *out*side Mary was harming her. In our society, Mary's affliction is proof that something *in*side her is harming her. Neither proof is any proof at all. Now, as then, nobody makes any real attempt to find out what Mary needs because the truth is that Mary does not matter. Mary is nothing more than a conduit between us and our treasured beliefs. Our lifetime investment in these is what we *really* care about; Mary is dispensable. The psychologist does not care about Mary. He cares about himself, and imposes on her the programming in which he has invested so much belief. He does this to affirm *for himself* the validity of his beliefs, and to reinforce the hold of those beliefs on the rest of us. He is enslaved to the theories he has adopted, as we are enslaved to them, and he is as unwilling to let go of his theories as a priest is to foresake his vows.

Our society's relationship with the disturbed has not changed in three hundred years. In Salem, nothing effective was done for the afflicted, and the accused were killed for unobservable behavior. Today, people are shunned or incarcerated for the "crime" of being incomprehensible to a psychiatrist. The same dynamic is at work now as was then. A possessed, attacked, or misaligned person is not diagnosed: He is dismissed because nobody is educated well enough to be able to diagnose a simple case of misalignment or comprehend the dynamics of possession.

Mary's torment and its alleviation mean nothing to us, for if they did, we would address Mary directly and make an honest search for the cause of her torment, instead we confine ourselves to theories surrounding her. Mary is incomphrehensible because nobody knows how to examine the afflicted for signs of possession, misalignment, or assault by black magic. What, then, do we achieve by turning Mary over to our uneducated, possibly uncaring, mental health "authorities"? We achieve what we truly want, which is the stability of social dictates. We don't care about Mary. We care to maintain ourselves in a state of passivity. Our freedom is lost to us—lost by our own doing.

Physics

This discipline, which may soon be even more revered than psychiatry, is at once the most innocent and the deadliest of all humankind's inventions-of-thought. Understanding how things work is a fundamental human need. But tearing life apart by viewing it with only the mind is destructive. The dynamics of life must be addressed by the whole of us: mind, emotion and spirit, if we mean to address the whole of each dynamic. We cannot comprehend the totality of anything as long as we perceive with only a partial application of our own being.

Because of the unfortunate metaphoric mix of physics and metaphysics that has become a fad, we are allowing ourselves to value most those aspects of creation that we can dissect the fastest. Knowledge is becoming just another variation of the old human contest called Who Gets What. How many theoretical physicists does it take to understand a tree? The answer, of course, is none. The reduction of life to soulless theory is desecration, not knowledge. If information is perceived *as* mere information, and not elevated from facts to wisdom, then we are safe. When we worship mere information as knowledge, we lead ourselves astray.

We must, if we wish to live worthy, vibrant lives and maintain our sanity, ask ourselves how we can avoid the intrusions of technology, psychiatry and physics. How can we find our place in the real world and find our own voice if we are surrounded by humankind's inventions-of-thought? If we can make our way into the dance of life, we will be safe. If we cannot do this, then we will, every day, lose a little bit of our spirit until we no longer honor either creation or ourselves.

Spiritual Searching for Everyone

Everyone's spirit matters as much as everyone else's spirit, and those who take the esoteric way are no more endowed with spirituality than other people. Truth to tell, some occultists follow their leaning because they have no other, while others follow occultism because they cannot begin to fathom worldly reality, and still others take up the tools of occult discipline because they believe these will bring quick excitement into their lives, or because they think the occult is the way to make money. Practitioners of the occult are as diverse as worldly people are.

Everyone at some time feels the calling of his spirit, his personal supply of that spirit which, combined with all the other spirits in this realm and others, makes up Creation. When this calling comes to us, we need only a few simple guidelines for answering the call. We do not need teachers and we do not need books.

To become enlightened is not an effort toward becoming one with the universe, as is often described. How can you become what you already are? You *are* one with creation. What must happen, in seeking enlightenment, is a moving away from illusions of separateness that make people come up with erroneous ideas like the one that we "need" to become one with the universe.

The process is one of recalling ourselves, of bringing ourselves back to ourselves. The change that takes place when we surrender to the truth of creation and move gracefully into our rightful awareness is the alignment of our astral (soul) body with our waking consciousness. This can happen only when our mental and emotional bodies are not being assailed by something outside us or something within us. Intense desire throws these out of alignment, as do anger and fear. When the mental body is sound and the emotional energies are not flaring up, then our conscious mind freely aligns with the astral body, the soul, the higher self.

Once this alignment has been affected, we can begin to perceive without delusion, feel without delusion, and know ourselves as we truly are. From this initial knowing, all else proceedes.

How can we make this alignment happen? We do it by *doing nothing*. Before we can do nothing, we must agree to set aside all the emotional and mental baggage we routinely carry around. Nearly all of this baggage is social programming. The rest is attachment and habit. We do not have to sift through this baggage in order to get rid of it, and it is detrimental to our freedom to spend much time studying it.

All we need do is to realize on a profound level that most of "us" is not us at all, but other people's perceptions and our need to match these perceptions. Once you get the hang of that, you will start on the road from imprisonment and blindness to freedom and opening all your eyes—your intuitive seeing, the seeing of your spirit, the seeing of your heart. When this begins to happen, you may find that you do not need your glasses anymore.

When you shop for food, do you buy what your body tells you it needs, or something someone has told you you ought to eat? Eating is a sacred activity—though hardly treated as such in our society. We must find our own individual way to health, and we can do so only by taking a good look at the life-forms available to us as food. Eating is a sacred transaction involving two beings, the eater and the eaten. Only you can know what is and is not good for you.

When you dress, what are you wearing? Something flattering and comfortable, something that reflects your work or beliefs, or something ugly that is currently in vogue? How much of a slave, to food fads and fashion fads, are you?

Without being harsh on yourself, ask yourself these kinds of questions throughout your day and keep it up until you see how much you do that you have never selected as a real preference.

Give yourself time for this new searching. Write out of your schedule *any*thing you do not want to do that is not a have-to. You must work, and some measure of peace must be kept within your family, so there are some activities that cannot be set aside—at least not yet. But there are many choices within everyone's scope and most of us are less than honest about our freedom of choice. If you find yourself getting anxious when you turn down parties or discontinue your participation in politics or the events of your church, let it be. You are learning what is and is not you, and this may create nervousness for a while. Live with it. Do not backslide. You need your free time for whatever you may wish to do, and how can we ever know what we wish to do if we don't give ourselves time to find out?

Spend a few minutes each day in an encounter with something that is not human. Sit at your window and look at a tree. Watch a squirrel. Notice the falling rain without thinking of it as an inconvenience. Buy a birdhouse, but only if you feel like doing so. Do not allow yourself any overpowering emotions.

A crucial crossroad for anyone making a spiritual search is the time when we find ourselves open to possibilities while telling ourselves that we need to know, beforehand, what those possibilities *are*.

Our spiritual search loses its purity and its purpose if we tell ourselves what will be involved in it. Other than the few basics, giving ourselves time every day, becoming aware of social programming and letting go of it, steering clear of passionate emotion, there must not be any predisposition toward *or* away from anything in particular. This means that we cannot check our growth with other people. It means we must not pin our hopes on anything specific, read too voraciously, or find a guru. *At all costs, we must not find a guru.* The only way to know for certain that you are on your own path is to look around and see that you are alone. If there is anybody else walking that path, it is not yours.

Presupposing is an enemy to growth. If at the start of your journey you already "know" how growth will come and what you will be able to do when you are "enlightened" then you have aborted your journey before it begins. The you that starts the journey is not going to be the same you that ends it. If the you that starts the spiritual search is in a position to dictate its progress, what do you think you will achieve? We must, in making this most magnificent journey, be willing to let go. Allow yourself to be touched by each turn in your path as it comes up.

If we study with Allen because he is psychic, then we have dictated to ourselves that psychism is important to us when it may have nothing to do with our growth and may in fact impede it. Psychism often traps people into investing far too much of their attention in phenomenological aspects of spirituality.

If we believe we ought to work with Susan because she speaks in tongues, we have decided that an occurence of dubious origin and equally dubious value is good for us. If you want to study with me because I am a medium, then you have made a great leap of faith regarding the importance of communication with the dead and discarnate spirits.

We cannot achieve growth by anticipating the results of growth. Presupposing deals a major blow to the search for truth.

Doing Nothing

In allowing our spirit and our share of the collective unconsious to become part of our waking life, there are many times in which we find ourselves doing nothing. This is difficult for Westerners because we are sure that, having created an intention to grow, there must be something we can *do* about growing. Most often, for both the beginner and the advanced seeker, doing nothing signals a process of tremendous growth. Our waking consciousness must, for periods of time, give up its demands on our bodies and our attention and simply let us be. You may find yourself wandering the house or the outdoors, sitting staring into space, or fiddling with things without quite knowing you are doing it. You may pick up an object and then set it down, wondering why you picked it up in the first place. You may decide to wash the car and, as you pick up the hose, set it down again. You may want to call a friend and then decide against it.

You are not losing your mind. You are losing your mind's grip on your life. This step is essential to the emergence of your spirit. Let it be. You may feel foolish for a while. You may wonder what is happening to your sense of resolve. Nothing bad is happening to it. Spiritual resolve creates a state of emptiness as a prerequisite to the opening of your spirit.

Doing nothing is really doing a great deal, but it cannot be planned and cannot be predicted. This kind of doing is the work of your spirit, and if you are used to busyness, as many people are, this may distress you for a while. Live with it. After the first period of doing nothing has brought forth your spirit and your spirit has led you to a wonderful new perception, you will begin to trust these periods of doing nothing as times of great inner growth and preludes to awakening.

I have included in this chapter and the next some techniques, ideas and methods for finding your way. Look at these and take from them anything that helps you. I have intended my philosophy and methodology as offerings, not dictates. Use what is right for you and leave it at that.

When We Cannot Walk Alone

When we feel a need for an authority outside our own, if we feel cast adrift without it, if we have tried for a few months to walk alone and find that we are becoming increasingly nervous instead of confident, frightened instead of peaceful about our walk, then a decision must be made regarding whether we should continue walking our Path alone or seek the company of other spiritual journeyers.

It is my view, expressed throughout this book, that, not only do we not need guides and teachers, but that these impede our growth on every front. It is my observation that free will is the foremost law of human life, and it stands to reason that if the first law is free will, then the first sin must be passivity. But if you find, after giving it a good chance, that you simply cannot handle being alone in your search, seriously consider the possibility of going back to the religious tradition in which you were raised.

The architects of this universe have provided many paths. If you believe it is not your destiny to seek alone, and if you feel there is nothing intrusive, immoral or misleading about the spiritual teachings of your past, then it is possible that you were born into the family that raised you for the specific purpose of being offered you that kind of spiritual teaching. It may be that the church of your childhood is good for you.

Examine this possibility very carefully. Give the teachings of your youth a try. I am appalled by "authority" outside my own spirit, but you are not me and what is right for me may be all wrong for you. As long as you are confident that the choice you make is not born of guilt over having left the church, then if you really want to go back to that church, go back. You are far better off making a spiritual search through an agency and philosophy you know well than forcing yourself into an alien activity you don't understand. Above all, our spiritual searching must not make us nervous, frightened or miserable.

Finding Our Voice, Singing Our Song

The first step every conscious being needs to take, if he is to create the best possible life for himself, is to divest himself of delusion. If one can realize what one is *not*, then it will become possible to find out what one is.

Delusions are dangerous because they usually come to us from agencies outside our being. Delusional, for example, are anyone's ideas regarding what is right and wrong; only our own view—our *view*, not merely our intellectual opinion—is not delusional. Other people's dictates regarding our behavior, how life should be lived, and what constitutes reality is by definition delusional because it is not our own.

Every religion and every social belief system began as somebody's personal view of life. That view was valid for him. Everyone lives within a time frame, within a place in evolutionary progress or regress. A man's view of life, evolved in his time frame and through his experiences, is valid *for him*. He is within his rights to bring his vision to others who wish to know it. But he violates others when he thrusts his views on them and invalidates his vision because no one's vision can ever be transferred, intact, to another.

When we have a powerful vision about life, its power remains with us through the changes we make and whatever events may come to us. We own that vision, and as long as we do not trade it for glory, devalue its currency by chattering about it, or bleed its energy by testing it against other people's visions, it will remain with us. The first step in keeping our personal vision alive is to let it be. In our visions, which are both symbolized and made actual by the links between us and the all-life, we may find a map of our life-to-be. But we cannot, within our unique vision, find a map for another person. If we insist on forcing our visions on others, we take the first step toward invasion of them. If we merely offer our vision to others, we may provide them with inspiration. But we may provide them with something far more insidious: we may, in telling others of our vision, become the beginning of cult and religion, major destructive powers in the world. Our vision gives people something of ours to think about when they ought to be finding their *own* way. They may invest of themselves in our beliefs or, worse, in us. This leads to another danger; they may become interpreters of our vision. Interpretation of others' visions is the beginning of delusion. Without a connection between the vision and our own spirit, that vision is delusory because it does not resonate within our portion of the collective unconscious. It takes us away from our own spirit into the arena of someone else's. This never does anybody any good. Delusion is the phenomenon of our "seeing" the clothes the emperor appears to be wearing, of following the emperor even though he may not have a shred of clothing to call his own. To see a beggar as an emperor, to believe an idea truly not our own, is self-delusion. To have an idea thrust upon us, imposed from outside our own spirit, is totalitarianism.

How can we steer clear of other people's views so that we may proceed to seek our own? How can we keep ourselves *to* ourselves, inviolate and undeluded? We can do this simply by tending our own gardens. If we insist on telling everyone what we have learned, especially when we are just starting our search, we will not be likely to learn much outside the realm of the intellect because the learning process requires quiet seeking, quiet acceptance of our experiences, and quiet accommodation of our perceptions. Each time we talk about the sacred, it is like drawing a curtain between us and the realm of Spirit. That curtain parts only when Spirit feels that we respect it, and do not mean to trade it for gain or social standing. If we trade on our "knowledge" we will be left to scrounge alone for further knowledge, because Spirit, while generous with its Powers to a true seeker, has nothing to give the man who wants only to take from it and use his stolen "wisdom" to impress others.

We can mind our own business most effectively by working alone, because when we court the teaching of another person, we tell our deepest self a terrible thing: We tell it that we do not feel adequate to learn from ourselves and from the abundant, glowing life that surrounds us. We move away from ourselves when we seek out human teachers, and move even further away by "studying," which is done with only the intellect, not the fullness of the deeper mind.

The intellect is not where the exchanges between human and Spirit take place. The intellect is there to recall and collate data; it is not there to lead us, but rather to follow our spirit and sort out what our spirit has learned.

These two ways of moving away from ourselves are subtle. The third means of losing ourselves is to acquire other people's methods of searching and assume these can work for us, when we have no idea what does and does not work for us because have never done sufficient seeking to find that out. We deny the validity of the spiritual search by pretending not to know anything about it at the onset, and by following other people's ways of seeking.

Food Blessing

A good way to begin our spiritual seeking is to start with honoring our daily bread. Without food, we die. Food is to be respected, chosen carefully, then thanked and blessed.

There are religious and spiritual traditions having to do with what is called the blessing of food. I believe that the idea behind this has been misunderstood. We must of course give thanks for what we receive, but the original intention behind blessing food was to energize our food and make it compatible with our energies, not only to thank the Creator for it.

Place your right hand over the food you are about to eat, about six inches from the food. Use your right hand whether or not you are right-handed, as the right is the giving-out side, whereas the left is the taking-in side. Say, "Bless this food." Everyone has the power to bless. You may wish to rub your hands together to start the flow of energy, as one does in beginning a healing, and then place your hand over the food. The energy generated by rubbing your hands together will add itself to the food, enlivening and purifying it in the same way a healing would enliven and purify a sick part of the body.

It is important to say your thanks directly to the food. Thank the Creator if you feel that is appropriate, but do not neglect to thank the food for making itself available to you. If you eat only yielded food, grains and vegetables and fruit, food that gives itself without psychic loss, thank the food for its yielding. If you eat fish, birds or other animals, food that does not yield itself but is sacrificed, be certain to thank the food for its sacrifice. Most animal food is kidnapped, raised to become food, or stolen from the seas or woods. The thanks you give to such food is very important. If an animal has been angered by its imprisonment and death, your humble thanks will go a long way toward assuaging that anger. Your gratitude will help the spirit of the animal to disconnect from his anger, and your honest thankfulness—one cannot fake this—will mitigate the negative energy within the food you are about to eat. In remembering to do this ritual, you will aid the animal whose life was lost and also keep yourself from having to eat his anger.

It is important to really express your feelings here and not do this by rote. Study what you are about to eat and thank every element of your meal, the grain, the beans, the generosity of the cow in giving milk for your yogurt. In doing the most you can to acknowledge and thank your daily food, you will enliven yourself, help the animals involved to forgive the intrusion on their lives, and vivify your meals. This ritual works powerfully against the pollutants in food, which include your own potential selfishness, the anger of the animal whose life was taken, and the chemical pollutants that pervade our earth, air and water.

Purifying Our Homes

In large measure, how we feel comes to us by way of reflections of ourselves found throughout our houses. I am no great housekeeper; I feel that dust, which is a natural part of our world, does not matter as much as the attention we give to our living places. While I can go for a long time without sweeping or washing floors, I do not allow paintings, artifacts, or photographs—anything into which someone has put a great deal of love—to go without dusting and polishing. I keep each item clean and honor it by placing it in whatever place feels right for that particular object.

Since light is a precious aspect of life, I keep the windows clean, to let in as much light as possible. I have managed to finagle my way out of cooking for months at a time—my goal being years at a time. My kitchen has become the house dumping ground for mail, clocks that need fixing, unused planters, and anything not important enough to go in the filing cabinet. In cleverly choosing the kitchen as my repository for ungovernable items, in littering the kitchen table with old magazines and laundry, I have managed to discourage countless guests from expecting a meal.

The point to an all-purpose messy room is that it allows us to keep the rest of our house or apartment free of clutter.

Each room, bedroom, living room, bathroom, needs to be honored by being kept free of junk. If you don't have a whole house, an apartment can be kept in good condition by assigning a corner or even a closet as your messy place.

Every room, every area of your home needs to be kept alive and energized, and this can be done by throwing away anything you don't have a good feeling about, whether old books or a couch or a vase someone gave you that doesn't reflect your taste. If the giver of the gift asks where his vase is, you can always say the cat broke it, or that your nephew knocked it off the table.

The ceilings need to be painted often because we stare at ceilings far more than we know: Ceilings are the sky of a house. We see images in them, or expanses of white, pink, gray, expanses that attune us to the vibrations of the colors we're looking at. Stains and cracks are depressing to the spirit.

If you keep plants, it's unfair to them, as living entities, to keep them in less than healthy condition. If a plant cannot be kept healthy, there's a good chance that the plant doesn't like being indoors. If you cannot find a way to move it outside or do not have a porch or windowsill, then either give it to someone who can help it or give it back to nature. I sometimes do this with plants, taking them to a woods that feels like a cheerful place, and asking nature to take the plant and create a new form for it. It may seem as though this is really just throwing a plant away, but it's not. It's giving, with love and consideration, and giving is never an inconsequential act.

Your Vibration in Your Home

We don't spend much time alone in our houses because we have been raised to think there is something wrong with us if we don't spend leisure time *doing,* instead of *being.* Doing means charging forth into the world and watching other people perform. We go to the movies or to a concert; we are fans of a football or a basketball team. Or we spend time in bars; we go to parties. All these things may be good for us but that can be true only after we have satisfied ourselves that we really want to engage in those activities. This exploration of motives will take time because it is difficult to know our wants when we've complied with other people's demands for as long as most of us do. After some thought, we may realize that we are tired of watching someone else dance and would prefer to take a ballet class or to stay home and dance, alone, to music. This can be a very powerful experience because dance, the movement of feet on the earth, generates earth energy. That's why some people can dance all night and still work the next day. They have generated so much earth energy that their bodies are enlivened and the great dose of energy they've received more than compensates for the lack of sleep.

We may find that though we hate parties, we always go wherever we're invited because we don't want to offend friends, and because we want to show off our popularity. But a real friend understands how wearing it is to be with groups of people all the time. Popularity is a worthless commodity in any case.

How can our living place reflect us if we're never there? Unless we put our energy into living there, dreaming there, puttering around the house, enjoying our quiet space, the house we live in will never be more than walls and furniture.

If we determine to stay home we will achieve two worthy new states. We will start the long process of discovering what we really like to do, and what we do only because we're used to going out; and we will make our house into a real home. Then, when we're at home, we will be able to experience our unique energy in a new way. We'll be able to feel what we are really like because our home will reflect us. The essence of our being will pervade our home. After awhile, when we come home for the evening, we'll find that we are surrounded, not by walls and furniture, but by the presence of a being—our own being.

Influences We Can Do Without

What do we invite into our home? Do we bring in flowers because we love flowers and because we like a cheerful atmosphere? Do we spend a lot of money on good furniture because we are happy living in a lovely place? Do we clean scrupulously, or pay someone to keep our houses clean for us? It's a good idea to make the very most of our home. And many of us go to great lengths to keep our homes beautiful, gracious and welcoming.

And then what do we do? Having made our homes just the way we want them, we drag into our perfect houses all the garbage, anger, negativity and confusion possible. We have television, which enlightens us a very little bit of the time and abuses us most of the time. We watch violence and degradation as hypnotic entertainment. Worse, we pick up the false notions, ideas and emotional hangups of other people by watching television. These then become the influences that pervade our homes.

We subscribe to magazines that treat the horrors of the world with the shallowest possible views, and we allow these views to become our own. How can they not become ours when we don't even know that we are being influenced?

It is impossible to shove an idea or philosophy away unless

you know it's there. The dangers in these influences, television and the popular press, lie in our easy acceptance of them. If we read them critically, read with awareness, fine, but how many of us do that?

How many of us can sit in front of a television without being hypnotized? Any screen with light behind it is an instrument for inducing trance. That's why movies and television are so popular. We may believe we are strong enough to rise above the mindlessness, casual cruelty and prejudices of television, but it is really very hard to distance ourselves from "information" introduced through an hypnotic device. The droning sound, the changing colors—these seize hold of our consciousness. It's difficult to wrench our minds away from what we are being fed, and most of us do not make much of an effort to separate ourselves from the easy, steady stream of sound and light.

If you take cocaine, there are many signals to help you realize that you are engaged in a relationship with a dangerous drug. You must buy the stuff illegally, carry it around secretly and use it furtively. With television, a hypnotic, there is virtually nothing to tell you that you are hooked on a conduit to all that is worst in humankind—shallowness, passivity, and ignorance.

If I'm Not What I Was, Then What Am I?

After we have taken the first steps away from social influences and toward becoming the real-us, learning to see our homes as ours and making them what we wish them to be, seeing our food as a partnership between us and the all-life, pushing ourselves away from other people's views, how do we maintain ourselves in the mundane world without being accosted by the habits we have left behind?

The best defense against being inundated by habits we have given up is to know that they will try to force their way back into our lives. Patterns are not alive, exactly, but they have life to them—life we gave them by repeating them so often. Do not be surprised when, as soon as you decide you love spending Friday nights alone at home, you start getting lots of invitations for Friday night activities. This is your own pattern trying to reassert itself. It is also a way of the universe; when we push something away, it feels that push and gives us an equal push in the opposite direction. Do not let this fluster you. It will subside. But you must maintain yourself by sticking to what you want to do. If you falter, if you decide it's easier on your psyche to give in to others' demands and the pull of your old habits, you are giving other people and old habits more value than you give the real-you. This is how most of us grow up: Other people's needs and views matter more than our own because they belong to a mass of people, whereas ours belong only to us. Habits are unbreakable, we believe, because we have held them close for so long. Actually, habits do not need to be broken at all. What is needed here is not the breaking of old ways but focusing on new ways.

There may come a time when you feel restless and anxious because you have given up the false supports of doing things other people's way. Those other people may stop calling you. Some may be angry with you. It is a tough time because you have given up something but have not, as yet, received anything in return. What will fill in those Friday night hours, and will it be worth all this hassle? Can you stay home all by yourself forever?

This stage has to be gotten through. It's crucial, for the anxiety you feel is not a desire to return to old patterns. It's the awakening of your deeper self to the awesome knowledge that you have made room for it. Now that you have given it space, it needs to search around and find how it wants that space to be filled. You will probably feel rocky for a little while, but remember that this feeling will pass and that you are now on your way to having a real life, not an imitation life. Do what you must to make peace with the anxiety, but do not try to overwhelm it or deny it. Let it be. Once you allow yourself to let it be, you will discover that this odd feeling is not as painful as you feared. It can even become your ally. Those quiverings from the deeper-you that cause anxiety are birth-pangs. They signal that the you long buried beneath false perceptions and false activity is about rise above falseness and take a good look around for itself. Congratulate yourself: You have given birth to your own being.

You will find what you are by experimenting with your likes and curiosities. If you feel like writing a poem, do it. The act alone will help to birth you. The quality of the poem is of secondary importance right now. Making the poem happen for no reason beyond your desire to write it is an act of self-birthing and the consequences will be powerful.

If you have no idea what you'd like to do with your time, do nothing at all. By doing nothing, you remove from your awareness all concern for action and pretense. Since mindless activity separates you from the promptings of your deep self, mindless activity is destructive. Since pretense separates you from your true desires, pretense is destructive.

Your Place in the Universe

When you have begun to clear your life of extraneous matters and taken those first steps into your new life, there will come a time when your deeper self will want to introduce you to the all-life.

The moment, if perceived correctly and not rushed, will be prompted by your spirit and not your intellect. There will simply be a time when your spirit leads you to a meeting place, and you find yourself looking with more than casual interest at the stars, a lake, the earth beneath your feet. In that moment, when enough of the real-you is available to you, when you are capable of bringing yourself to meet the universe, you will be contacted by the all-life on a profound level. There may not be any action involved. You may simply gaze at the water or stars for so long that you lose yourself in it. You won't hear voices or see visions. You will enter into a true awareness of the all-life . . . and it will become aware of you.

After that, you will never be alone again, or defenseless,

because once you come to the attention of the all-life, you will be joined to the great web of life that includes all of creation. You will be a vital entity, not floating consciousness and blocked purpose, as most people are.

The Silent Voice

The best defense any of us can have against evil or the various negative energies of this world is to have the all-life aware of us. It is the life around us—the life-forms and discarnate spirits—that warns us when we are in danger. It is not possible to receive this warning as long as we are enclosed within ourselves. But when a being who has been joined to the all-life is walking down a road and he approaches a place where a great deal of negative energy has accrued, the life around him will urge him most powerfully to walk in a direction away from the danger.

One who has not made a fundamental connection with the all-life will not receive the same treatment. The all-life will not be aware of him, and he will not be capable of receiving its signals at any rate. He is on his own. In this world, where there are lots of good energies and lots of bad ones as well, one does not wish to be on one's own.

It is the silent but powerful voice of the all-life that tells us not to buy a house if the house is haunted, not to buy an unsafe car, not to take a plane if there may be an accident. After years of looking back on dangers I passed through successfully, I have come to see, again and again, that the reason I got through those horrors was my continuing dialogue with and attention to the all-life. It was not I who saved me, but the friendship, support and guidance of the life forces I loved and which loved me.

New Ways of Seeing

We can collect ourselves and conserve our thoughts and energies if we take just a few minutes out of each day to look at familiar scenes with new eyes. I find that this technique has an astonishing effect on my moods. I may think I'm depressed and find I'm actually quite cheerful, or believe I am tired and find I am only focusing on too many concerns at once.

Find a scene outside your window, near your house or at a place where you routinely stop. Look at the familiar scene while telling yourself that you have never been there before and don't know what you are looking at.

The results can be amazing. You will see things you never saw before, despite—and because of—your familiarity with the scene. Whenever we become familiar with anything, we take its contents and appearance for granted and thus stop seeing it. Our preconceptions diminish the potential in everything we encounter; getting rid of preconceptions creates room for major change in our lives.

Addictions: Alcohol, Drugs and Excitement

Preconceptions are impediments to real seeing. Habits are detrimental to our relationship with creation. Addictions are a tragic disempowerment of ourselves because virtually all addictions are based on passivity.

Though we may hide our feelings behind alcohol or other drugs, or imprison our deeper minds by the hypnotizing effects and misinformation of television, while we may attempt to separate our consciousness from our waking minds by wrapping ourselves in loud music, these are all secondary addictions.

A prevalent secondary addiction is the addiction to excitement which prompts some people to form relationships with abusive partners. A similar addiction is that of a whole family to the moods of one member. Often women have difficulties with a lover or husband who hits them. These women live from hour to hour wondering whether their man will beat them. Sometimes they have an idea of what will set the violence off, but often they do not.

The family whose enjoyment of life depends on the mood

swings of one of the parents, or on the ability of the parent who controls the family finances to do so responsibly, is addicted to the excitement of continual daily uproar. Parents whose adolescent children engage in dangerous and illegal behavior are kept on the edge of their nerves by wondering, from day to day, whether or not their son will be arrested or their daughter will continue dating a drug-dealer.

Sometimes people make friends who engage in dangerous practices such as car-theft, shoplifting or periodic disruptive drunkenness. The person who travels with such a crowd while not engaging in any of these activities must know, in his deeper self, that he takes an awful chance of being arrested along with his friends and charged, even imprisoned, despite his innocence. People who travel with dangerous crowds are excitement-junkies.

There are women and men who neglect to oversee correct procedures for birth control. These people never know when they will find themselves faced with a pregnancy. The continual anxiety that goes with such behavior is an example of excitement-addiction.

Whenever we throw in our lot with potential trouble-makers, fail to set firm boundaries regarding the ways in which others may treat us, or indulge in other people's moods without learning how to disconnect from them, we are acting in a passive manner.

If we live with a drug addict, we live with his ups and downs because his are more dramatic than ours. If he takes drugs that excite his energies, we may be in danger of a violent outburst; if he takes soporific drugs, we may find there is no way of communicating with him.

All situations in which our well-being, our physical health and our circumstances are dictated by another person are instances of excitement-addiction. I see a good deal of this among young people, especially young women, who depend on their lovers' or husbands' permission for anything they may wish to undertake, and who suffer abuse from these situations because the man in their lives is always more powerful and in control than they are. Addiction to another person always put that other in control of our time, energy, and sometimes our physical well-being.

When the fulcrum of our lives is positioned outside ourselves, in the glass of wine we must have every day, the drug we need to get our work done, or in someone else's behavior or events we cannot control, we are addicted. Addiction to excitement is as real as substance-addiction and the consequences are equally devastating.

None of these addictions, however, is a primary one. Each of these is a secondary addiction; the primary addiction, in every instance, is to passivity.

Meditation

There are many methods of meditating, and each was evolved to create a particular state of mind necessary for a particular kind of growing. Even if we are not interested in the esoteric implications of meditation, it is nevertheless helpful in that it allows us to toss away, at least for awhile, some of the issues that crowd our waking consciousness. The more crowded our minds are, the harder it is for us to make waking connections to the collective unconscious. If we make a crowded mind a way of life, then we will, in our sleep state, have to clear out a lot of trivia before even our sleep state will allow us to connect with the collective unconscious. The better we tidy our minds, the stronger the connection between us and our astral selves.

Meditation is not a means of emptying the mind. You cannot, while awake, empty the mind entirely, and if you try to push anything out of it, a pushing in the opposite direction will occur. Everything in existence, even a passing thought of no consequence, has a sense of its own purpose. While it is we who generate our thoughts, those thoughts take on an existence of their own once we create them. If they are momentary thoughts, they will take on a momentary existence; if they preoccupy us and cause us to brood, they will take on a more emphatic existence and could, in time, become thought-forms, floating energy as discussed elsewhere in this book.

The idea behind the so-called empty mind is the surcease of all thought. Since we cannot create an empty mind by forcing out our thoughts, we do it by doing nothing at all. We make no attempt at forcing anything to happen to us, or to prevent anything from happening.

Sit in a comfortable position facing whatever cardinal point feels most familiar to you, and be sure you will not be interrupted for at least twenty minutes. The best meditation time for a beginner is not more than ten minutes twice a day, or ten-to-fifteen minutes once a day. Knowing when to stop will keep you healthy and balanced. Meditating for longer than you can handle will leave you spaced-out and vulnerable to the very feelings and thoughts you have been trying to free yourself of by doing meditation in the first place. Know when to stop. Do not become a martyr to meditation. There is nothing holy about being off-center.

The extra five-to-ten minutes of freedom from interruption is important because, after meditation, you need some time to yourself before you reenter the world. Make the entrance a gentle, gradual one.

To begin a meditation, face the direction you have chosen and regulate your breathing to an even, slow inhalation/exhalation exchange. You should take as much time to inhale as to exhale, and as much time to exhale as to inhale. We often inhale too quickly and most of us fail to exhale completely. Panic underlies uneven breathing. We rush to grab our next breath, fearing that if we don't grab it, it might not be there when we need it. Forced, tense, forward-motion underlies much of our daily activity and the reason for this is fear: a general, non-specific fear that, having no particular focus, enters our every action because it enters our every breath.

Having regulated your breathing, simply do nothing for ten minutes. Do not think. If you find yourself getting very antsy doing nothing, then give the mind a symbol to focus on such as a candle, a cloud, a splash of color. Give the mind just one symbol, not a situation. Do not give it a person, not even a religious figure.

Sit, breathing in an even inhale-exhale rhythm, and do nothing. If you find yourself getting anxious, not just a little jumpy but truly anxious, then discontinue the meditation *without blaming yourself* for stopping.

Pitfalls of Meditation

You can cause yourself harm by feeling that you have failed if the first couple of meditation sessions do not allow you to sit comfortably and calmly. For one thing, nothing worth doing usually comes easily. For another, it is a disease of Western people to attach blame to non-conformance. It is a great mystery to me that we seem to believe we can better ourselves by blaming ourselves for not being perfect. But if we *were* perfect, there would be nothing to get better *at*. It's really very odd.

Can we all eat the same foods and thrive on them? Is anyone ever allergic to medication? Do we all react to pollen in the same way? Yet, when a quasi-religious or otherwise mystical exercise is attempted, we believe we must respond to it in the same way everyone else does.

Meditation is meant to calm and center you, and to allow nonsense to leave your mind. If, after a few tries, you find it making you depressed or anxious, then meditation may not be for you. Pay attention to your feelings during and directly following meditation. You may think you like it, and ignore signals from your psyche that it does not like meditation. If you want to give it up, do. Try it again another year. But do not compound depression or anxiety with self-blame. Lots of people are not right for meditating. Meditation has taken on a certain air of correctness merely by virtue of its Eastern origins. Since it came to us from the East it seems desirable to many Westerners. In the perverse way of human beings, what comes to us from others appeals to us more strongly that what is ours.

Overinvolvement with meditation is another pitfall for

beginners. It may be as easy to remain in a meditative state as to fall asleep. Some people are thus inclined. But neither meditation nor sleep is the state we are meant to live in all the time. Too much of either can cause our spirits to drift further and further from this realm and may result, like imbalance in any occult discipline, to a sudden regrettable accident that removes us from the earth realm.

Grounding After Meditation

The time we take to ground ourselves properly after meditation can be as important as the meditation itself. We must not leave our meditation session and enter into mundane activities in a condition of spaciness that could cause an accident. This is a real possibility after meditation because meditating may prompt us to leave our bodies and we may not know that we have done so. In that case, we may take up worldly endeavors while part of our consciousness is out of our body.

To insure groundedness after engaging in any esoteric work, shamanic journeying, meditating, chanting or crystal work, sit for a moment and look at your surroundings, making sure you know where you are and feel awake. Put your head to the ground or the floor, touching your forehead to the surface for a full minute. Sit up again. Place the palms of your hands on the floor or the ground and leave them like that for a minute. The head and hands are entrance-points for earth energy in the same way that they are exit-points for spirit energy.

For the first few minutes after a meditation, pay complete attention to whatever you are doing, so as to be sure that you are truly living inside your body. This exercise is, in itself, a kind of meditation.

With meditation, as with mediumship, shamanism, or any other esoteric undertaking, we must maintain firm guidelines for the work and for the all-important transition period between that work and mundane activity.

What It Means to Give Away Energy

When we give love or hate, we give energy. If we give to someone or something—a person, an animal, an idea or dream—in a continual flow, then we actually wrap our energies around the receiver. When we love freely without meaning to force the other person into a relationship with us, or to remain in one, then we cause no harm to the other or to ourselves. If we love with intent to own or imprison another, we enclose ourselves within our need. If we love another with too much passion, our love wraps itself around him. In occult terms, this is not only a possibility but a difficulty nearly everyone deals with at some time in his life. Energy emitting from our psyche to another person, or perhaps a coveted object, moves like strands around that person or object until a part of our energy surrounds it.

If we give love freely, and if the beloved does not return our love, then no harm is done by us to ourselves or to the beloved. The all-life will, in some way, compensate us for the love-energy we have given away. Love, when offered without restriction or conditions, enriches the lover and the loved, and is never wasted.

When we give hate, we turn on ourselves. We may cause harm to the hated one by sending him negative energies with which, of course, he must deal. We hurt ourselves by enclosing our minds in obsession and preventing our psyche from the fluid movement of spirit that is essential to a good life. We create a polluted atmosphere for ourselves, and are forced to live within that enclosure until we rid ourselves of our hatred. This is easy enough to comprehend as a concept, but another matter entirely when we must handle a hate which is, we believe, entirely justified. Justifiable anger, resentment and hatred cause us more trouble than most of us realize. No matter how deeply we feel our "right" to hate, we are always better off releasing it than holding onto it. Hatred harms the hater in his mind, emotional condition, his physical and etheric bodies. Is it ever worth it to attack ourselves with hatred over a "just" cause?

The more feeling we put into the proffering of a gift, whether a book, flowers, money, the bigger the investment of our own energy in the giving. After many instances of giving to a single person, a family, or a cause, we become attached to the recipient by the strands of energy between us and them. This binds us. It is a good idea, therefore, to periodically unbind ourselves, even from those we love or causes in which we believe, by performing a ritual of releasing. It does no harm to us or to the recipient of our generosity to perform this releasing ritual because binding between any two entities can corrupt the free-flow of our spirits and theirs.

If we are on the receiving end of gifts, favors, or any transaction that joins our energy to another person or group, we should periodically perform a releasing ceremony because it is in no one's best interests to bind another or to be bound. In releasing another or being released by someone else, no love is lost and no positive energy is wasted. Freedom is achieved; nothing is rejected.

Part of any releasing ceremony involving the giving of things, services or our good wishes should include a physical severing motion. To sever yourself from anything, whether it is physical or discarnate, place your right hand at the back of your head, the palm toward the head. In a single sweeping motion, bring the hand up over your head and down past the front of your body, being certain to pass it, emphatically, all the way past your abdomen. Again, this is not a rejection. It is the withdrawing of your energies from a potentially binding situation. The good engendered by the giving or receiving between you and the other remains intact; only the binding is changed by this ritual.

Often we remain friends with someone out of habit or stay married for the same reason. If we employ this strand-cutting exercise from time to time, doing it sincerely, we will be less attached to habit than if we allow ourselves to drift closer and closer to a person or situation merely because it is familiar. In performing the cutting ceremony, we tell our deeper self that we intend to regain our freedom, and to continue the relationship by choice, not through habit.

The exorcistic value of the strand-cutting is that, if someone is trying to invade or influence us, he will make inroads through winding his energy strands around us. When we cut the strands, we effectively cut him off. It is fundamental to any black magic endeavor that the person being attacked be made available to the evil one through his energy. Everything we touch is imbued with our essence, our vibration. We can be reached, our energy touched and affected, through anything we have handled. It is only common sense that we periodically cut the strands between us and objects, doing so as a precautionary measure, not an act of fear.

When, at the end of my story about Rose, I said that I could not afford to give her anything, I was referring both to the giving of energy through making a request such as, "Please change," and also to strand-tying. Had I spoken out loud to her with the intention of changing her, or asking her to change, my desire would have thrown strands of energy from me to her. These would have been used, in turn, to reach me. It is impossible to give anything to another without creating a line of energy between you and the other. This line of energy can be a conduit between you and him, and it is safe policy to remember this.

Prayer and How It Works

Prayer, when effective, is focused thought, focused emotion, and focused purpose. Rote prayer, devoid of feeling or a sense of immediacy, is next to useless.

Prayer is the attention we give to a need, whether the need is ours or another's. In giving attention, we alert the all-life to the fact that we have a need. The more feeling we put into prayer, the more urgency that attends the announcement of need, the more effective our prayer.

As long as we pray with fervent purpose, our prayers will be heard and something will happen.

The difficulty most of us have with prayer and its aftermath is that what happens following prayer is often so subtle that we miss it. Also, what often takes place following prayer occurs inside us, and we Westerners are not used to looking within for the answers to prayer. Instead, we look for changes in fortune, a turn in events outside our control. We believe that if we ask for help in our work, help will appear as a new job or money for further education or the timely disappearance of our boss.

These things do happen in our lives but whether or not we like to admit it, tidy arrangements are not very helpful to our growth. Changes in circumstances are nice surprises but they don't teach us how to change ourselves, and it is within our psyche that the true and deep effects of prayer are to be found.

When we pray, we direct attention and feeling toward something, even if we have no conscious idea who or what that something is. We may believe in an omnipotent and omniscient god or we may not. If not, we're addressing ourselves to spiritual power per se, power greater than we are. We can not know what being or force will become the agency that responds to our prayers, but very often that agency is ourselves.

In making a prayer for something, we attune ourselves to a situation that needs altering or a concern that must be addressed, a void that needs filling or a change we want to see happen. In any case, we are praying about a situation *as we perceive* that situation in waking consciousness. Very often, what needs altering is not the situation but our view of it. When this is so, the answer to our prayer takes place in the changing of our perception.

This is an example of the law of order in the universe. What needs attending to is tended first. That is a fundamental rule here on the earth and away from here as well. If we pray for our loved ones to be more considerate of our needs, the answer to that prayer may be a new view, within ourselves, that helps us to be more aware of our own needs and how we can satisfy them and therefore be less demanding of other people.

What most needs changing, then, will be changed first. What secondarily requires help will get that help secondarily. And so on.

If we want to examine the aftermath of prayers to see how they change situations, we need to be aware of the all-life because the signals that we are given regarding prayers usually come from the life around us and not from obvious changes in situations. If we are attuned to the motion of birds, to shifts in the wind, to the atmosphere around us which changes many times during a day and night, we will bring our waking consciousness to where we want it to be. That is the key to understanding the ebb and flow of our lives and other people's lives, tuning in to the signals that are always there but can not become available to us until we move close to the all-life and become sensitive enough to read its message.

Unless we are attentive to the life forces on this planet, there is no point in hoping to understand much of anything that goes on within our own personal lives, let alone understand the laws of creation. If we are not able to receive signals from the all-life, then we are like viewers at a film who can see only one tiny corner of a screen. How much of creation can we comprehend when our vision is so limited?

If we are to enter into a full understanding of creation, we must, in prayer, direct our focus as much as we can. The more general the prayer, the less effective it can be. The more specific the prayer, the more effective it will be. This does not mean that we should tell Spirit how to do things, for we can never foresee the means through which our prayers will be answered. When I speak of directing our focus, I mean that our perception of Spirit must be altered from one kind of prayer to another, so that we can address the spirit force most appropriate to our requests.

The Six Sacred Directions and Their Meanings

Every culture, except the one we live in right now, has had beliefs regarding the four cardinal points, North, East, South, and West. These ideas vary by culture and I believe the variations are accounted for by the geographical position of each culture on the earth.

I have found that the attributes assigned by native peoples of North and South America to the four cardinal directions and to the other two sacred directions are fitting. It is their views, with some adjustments for my own experiences, that I offer here. The reader is encouraged to seek out other perspectives so as to avail himself of as much information as possible. Following that, of course, he must let his spirit decide which attributes belong, for him, to each direction. In the end, it is always our own spirits that must feel our way through the world for us.

Up

Above is generally considered the place of the Creator, the Source of all life, and most people focus their attention upward when they pray. You may find that the Source seems to lie in the Earth's realm, and if you do, then Up is not the place for your attention.

Whether we believe in God or we don't, there is in most of us a feeling of deep reverence for, well, something, and that something seems to be positioned above our heads. The power that we beseech in prayer may be our own higher self, the deepest part of our being, our all-seeing aspect. Our urge to direct our prayers upward, then, may be due in part to the existence of our higher self above our heads.

Down

Down is our focus when we address the Earth, to whom we owe a very great deal. We focus downward, also, when we address the three non-human kingdoms: mineral, plant, and animal.

North

North is first in the order of the four directions because it is in the North that everything has its spiritual beginning. We make our entrance into the world through the East, but our actual origin is in the North. North is the place of rejuvenation and healing: physical, mental, emotional or spiritual.

North is a place of mystery because it is the cardinal point hardest to explore and understand. The Northen vibration, in my experience, is most like the vibration we enter as we leave our bodies for out-of-body experiences. It is a very fast vibration and differs from most earth realm vibrations.

East

When an idea is actualized, when a dream manifests or a soul incarnates on the earth, these things occur under the guardianship of the East. East is the place of new starts. It has special qualities of exorcism because it is the place where the sun first breaks the spell of night. The energies brought to this world by the sun are quickening energies and very healthful to all life-forms.

For me, the East represents and has guardianship of the horizontal lines of the cross symbol, as the sun spreads its light across the earth horizontally.

The Earth itself represents, for me, the vertical line of the sacred cross. In my way of seeing things, the horizontal line is the only visible line; the vertical line is visible only to spirit-vision.

South

This is the place of abundance and fruition, where our dreams become fully real, our lives take off, and the rewards of our labors are made manifest, sometimes in ways we expected, sometimes not.

The human soul reverberates to the direction South because it is the place of abundance, and the harvest we most need to gather while on this realm, whether we know it or not, is a spiritual harvest.

South is the natural place of water. Without water, nothing

grows. Because it is the water-source, I rarely use South for
occult work because water power is very hard to control. I
often pray toward the South, but I rarely do occult work with
the South as my point of focus.

West

This is the magical place where human experience
transmutes itself into wisdom. It is the place we go to when we
die, and the place of endings.

Because West is where the sun travels just before its light
disappears, it is the guardian power twilight. During the dark
time, we should surround ourselves with protection sufficient to
take the sun's place. Until the sun crosses the horizon once
more, carrying to us its physical light, which is a manifestation
of the spiritual Light, we must invoke the Light for ourselves
in whatever way suits us.

Asking for help from a power you have worked with, and
know you can rely on, is a good idea during the night. A reli-
able protection is creating around ourselves a circle of white
light or rainbow light, the subtle shades of the rainbow being
preferable for protection to the more brilliant ones. If you feel
strongly in tune with one particular color and wish to use it
exclusively.

Stand facing West, where the sun last showed itself. Raise
your right forefinger and point directly upward, your arm
extended as far as it will go. Ask the power of Light to surround you and keep you safe. Having made this request,
immediately place your forefinger about seven inches above the
center of your head, pointing it directly at that place. Move the
finger down and point at your forehead, throat, and heart. Then
point ahead of you, your arm extended all the way. Moving
clockwise (to your right) make a sweeping circle around yourself with the finger pointing outward. Keep moving, your arm
extended, until you have returned to the position from which
you began.

Because West is our exit point from earth life, I usually

make a point, during daily prayers, to ask the spirit of the West to take peacefully and safely anyone who might be going to die that day.

In working with the spirits of the four directions, whether asking for help, getting acquainted with them, using a technique for cleansing or protection, bear in mind that each of the four sacred places has power over and is allied with one of the four seasons. Maintain your awareness of the seasons as you live them, and ask yourself how each season relates to the direction with which it is associated.

- East is the direction of Spring
- South is the direction of Summer
- West is the direction of Autumn
- North is the direction of Winter.

The dates for each season vary sometimes, so you will have to check them with a calendar. Usually, in the Northern hemisphere, the dates of the seasons are these:

- Spring—March 21st
- Summer—June 21st
- Autumn—September 23rd
- Winter—December 21st.

There are guardian spirits in each of the four cardinal points, above us, and in the earth. Earth-keepers are responsible for this realm and for seeing to it that humankind does not go too far in abusing the air, earth and water here.

We may not encounter the guardians of the four elements (earth, air, fire and water), as these are, I have found, a little shy about contacting human beings directly. But we may very well find ourselves talking to a guardian of one of the four directions. If we do meet a guardian of any of these, thanks are in order for favors received—the ones we know about and those we may not be aware of. You may wish to make an occasional offering to all of these directions because you get help and guidance from them throughout your life, whether or not you know this to be the case.

When I was writing this book, someone I was very close to died. During his death passage, I made many prayers to the spirit of the West. When some weeks had passed, I felt it was no longer necessary to beseech the West for help on behalf of the departed one, so I offered West a prayer of thanks. As I did, the guardian spirit of West appeared and made itself visible. I asked if there was anything I might do for it. The spirit hesitated for a moment and then replied, "Yes. *Tell* people about us. Tell them we are *real,* that each direction has a guardian and that we are as alive and as real as anything else in this world. Tell people that."

I have reported what the keeper of the West wants you to know.

Earth and Earth-Keepers

The earth is a living being. Its aliveness is not hostage to our ability to perceive it. Its realities do not change with our changing beliefs. If we all left the planet, the earth would continue to be exactly what it is: a powerful, sentient being who is able to assess its needs and the needs of the life-forms on it. While we are obligated to pay strict attention to the effect of our behavior on the earth, the planet is not as much a victim of our abuse as we might believe. The corrections that must be made in compensation for the damage we have done will be made when the earth feels they need to be made.

The earth-keepers, like the guardians of the four directions, are intelligent beings whose job is to promote order, balance, and guidance on the earth. They communicate with the plant, stone and animal kingdoms and, though we are not often aware of it, with human beings. The earth-keepers are responsible for laying down the lines of energy, sometimes called ley lines, or energy grids, and for maintaining them.

A Word to the Client About Psychic Counseling

Lay people often come to a psychic reading with set ideas about psychics, some of which get in the way of a good reading. I want to address this subject from my point of view in order to help the lay reader understand what really goes on during a psychic session.

What I say here also applies to esoteric counselling of other kinds such as shamanic counselling or spiritual healing.

Let us begin with what a psychic or clairvoyant, is not. She is not there to prove her ability or demonstrate her cleverness. If she is trying to impress you with her talent, you should be out of there as soon as you figure this out. A clairvoyant is there to help you see what she sees. That is all. She must not make decisions for you. She should not proselytize or make you uncomfortable by trying to wrench you away from your way of thinking to hers.

The word clairvoyant means seeing-clearly. A clairvoyant sees, or perceives, through extrasensory abilities. She may or may not be a medium. She may see spirits around you and these may help her by providing her with information about you. But unless she tells you otherwise, she is not getting her information from spirit guides. She gets what she knows about you directly from you. You carry with you a great resonation from your past and your present.

Deep within all of us is a past *and* a future memory. This memory is part of the collective unconscious. All a clairvoyant has to do is to read these memories. I make it sound like it is nothing. It's not nothing. But it is simple.

The major job any psychic has is to filter out any impressions of you that are not a vital part of the counselling session. You have other people's energies around you, energies of people you have been with and people at a distance who think about you. The clairvoyant must be able to discern what is part of you and what is not. This is not easy and requires much experience.

In order for the psychic to tune in on you, it is imperative that you give her permission to do so. Unless a psychic is practicing invasion, she simply cannot read you without your permission. The simple act of making an appointment for a session, or asking the psychic for help is, on an occult level, giving permission to be read. Permission is given by your soul and received by the psychic's soul. Nothing need be said about this beyond, "Will you read me?"

Once permission is given, the client's energies become open and readable to the psychic. In order to begin the flow of energy between you that allows for clarity of contact, the psychic may need to ask you a couple of questions. Sometimes a client will sit back, fold his arms across his chest, and say, "I'm not giving you any information. Tell me what you see." This attitude impedes the reading. For one thing, it clearly demonstrates that the client is not so much interested in getting some help as in "proving" to the psychic that she is not really psychic. This is a great bore to the psychic, though possibly amusing to the client.

I always need to ask one or two questions, such as the client's middle name or birthday. In asking these questions, I am tuning in on the client in the same way you have to fiddle with a radio dial to get a station to come in clearly. My asking these things is an other-world version of a handshake. A great deal of information is communicated by handshakes in mundane terms, and on an esoteric level the exchange of a little information serves the same purpose as a handshake at a business meeting or a party. It is a necessary interchange and should not be interpreted to mean that the reader is not "really" psychic. Every meeting must begin from some point of contact.

If you keep in mind that what a psychic picks up comes from the querent's being and not the psychic's own mind, you will realize that there is a practical need for the client to give permission and remain reasonably cooperative with the psychic's needs.

If you ever get a feeling that the counsellor is trying to pick up information about a subject you do not want to discuss, simply state that the subject is not up for scrutiny. If he persists, he may not have your best interests in mind. He may be new in the field and may therefore believe that anything about your being needs to be made available to him, which is not so.

When searching out a psychic, pay no attention to advertising. Ask friends for a good reader. Find out how the clairvoyant works and what kinds of readings he gives. How often do your friends consult with a psychic? A good psychic does not encourage dependency and won't see anyone more than twice a year, maybe more if the stock market or some other valid day-to-day changes are under discussion.

If you have a friend who is over-dependent on others, seeking out guidance anywhere she can get it, and if she sees a psychic every couple of months, I would steer clear of that psychic. A good reader wants to tell you all he can in one or two sessions and send you on your way. A good reader does not allow you to indulge in constant queries—what will befall you in January, February, and March? That isn't future-foretelling: it's making people nervous. In the realm of divination, there is such a thing as too much, and too much is reached when someone tells you what's in the offing for every bend in the road. A good diviner will help you to see the general thrust of your past and present, and show you how you might change your future. He won't make a nervous case of you by inspecting every little thing as though the future were a dangerous enemy to be spied on whenever possible.

The future, no matter what your circumstances or your current mood, is always to be regarded as an opportunity, not an adversary.

The Power of Names

The name given to anything should be chosen with great care, prayed about, and given in ceremony. Names carry vibrations, as all words do, and the quality of vibration carried by our name should give us the energies we need.

If you feel you have the wrong name, if you feel your name is not helping you, that you do not resonate to it and cannot identify with it, or if you want to keep the name you have while adding letters to it, giving yourself a middle name or changing the spelling of your name, do something about this situation. It is important.

When we are babies, our names are chosen for us—or imposed on us—and we can do nothing to help select our names. All we can do is hope that the namer will take a good look at us and find the right name, instead of naming us for a favorite aunt, a film actor, or one of our parents. Imposing a name on a baby to satisfy the parents' needs is cruel, for it fails to take the new baby's needs into consideration. No baby should be named until the parents have had time to live with the child for a couple of days and observe its personality.

It is important to learn the actual meanings of potential names within the cultures of origin. In naming yourself, you are declaring your independence from other people's notions about you, taking your name into your own hands and into your own personal authority. You must find the name that will give you whatever new experiences and directions you desire. Name yourself according to what you *are* and what you wish to *become*.

A name should contain some of the essence of what we already are, and a strong sense of what we wish to evolve into. Study word meanings and, if you like, study the meanings attributed to letters and names by the various systems of numerology. Do not study just one system. Find out all you can about this subject.

When planning a naming ceremony, you may wish to baptize yourself. You may wish to name yourself during the new moon, which will add a good boost of power to your new name. You may want to take your new name while you are alone, or with friends present. It may appeal to you to hold a naming-ceremony outdoors, where you can affirm your connectedness to the all-life.

It is a good idea to find out what phase the moon was in

when you were born. You may wish to schedule the naming ceremony for that phase of the moon. We are all affected by the waxing and waning of the moon and are strongly imprinted by the phase the moon was in when we left our mother's body. Do not assume that only new and full moons matter. Try to find out, not only what phase the moon was in at your birth, but also the astrological sign and degree it was in.

Try your best not to set yourself up for ridicule or disputes by letting others think your name choice is up for discussion. Having made your choice, you must let all family members and friends understand that you have decided to change your name and that you do not accept any responsibility to please them in this matter. If you were named for a still-living relative or an honored family friend, it would be polite to approach that person and explain that you are changing your name only because you feel it does not suit you, and not because you do not love and respect the one for whom you were named.

If you find people giving you a bad time about your name change, know that far more is involved here than the changing of your name: In taking authority over your name you are announcing to your deepest self and the rest of the world that you have taken charge of your life on the most fundamental level. At this time, most people in our culture are incapable of doing what you are doing. For that reason, some of your family or friends will feel threatened by your decision.

If you take a name from a culture other than your own, or one with a complicated spelling or sound, do not allow anyone to make fun of it. Tell then solemnly that your name is very important to you and that you will not tolerate joshing about it, as you would not allow anyone to poke fun at your religion or make fun of your mate. If you meet with a strongly negative attitude of hostility over this issue, consider steering clear of the hostilities until people realize they must stop behaving badly. When your friends and family realize how serious you are, they may continue to find your actions puzzling, but eventually they will shut up about it.

Releasing Other People from Our Lives

When we have decided that the presence of another person is detrimental to our lives, we may need to separate ourselves from him. Nothing is to be gained by fighting. If an honest, pacific conversation is a possibility and if you desire to talk the situation over with him, fine. If you feel like separating without discussion, there is a simple but powerfully effective releasing ceremony you can undertake any time you are centered, relaxed, and in a balanced state of spirit.

Facing West, the direction of endings, call first on the Creator, or Mother-Father God, and then on your own higher self. State aloud that you release "George Vincent" (i.e., the name of the relevant person). Say nothing beyond that. Do not say you are sorry about this rupture, or that you wish him well, because expressions of any kind are energy-giving. You want to release George, not reinforce the strands between you.

Because people are to be honored, and are not merely experiences we happen upon and then move past, it is necessary that you *do* wish him well, but you must do this wishing as a statement of general intent, and do it silently. You may want to silently phrase the thought, "May he reach the best of himself," or something else that, while entirely positive, commits you to nothing further in your relationship with George.

For the same reason that you cannot make any statements out loud, you must not put any emotion into them. Emotion is energy. Your purpose is to disconnect—kindly but firmly—from another person and you can do this only once you have centered yourself well enough that you do not feel any strong emotion about George. Any energy you give to him will result in his coming back into your life in some way. This is true whether the emotional energy you give him is positive or negative.

Everyone deserves our good will but no one's company is compulsory in our lives unless we are in prison.

After you have made the statement of releasing, thank the spirit of the West and thank your higher self and God, in that order. Having done so, forget the subject and put it and George out of your mind by doing something very grounded and involving, such as cleaning your house or working in your garden.

Generally, one of two things will happen after this ceremony: either George will get in touch with you immediately, and may seem puzzled as to why he is calling you, or else the two of you will, without prior arrangement, be brought together by circumstances neither of you have foreseen. Usually, when we release someone, the act of release brings them directly to us. The energies between you and George must be addressed by each of you before a true release can take place. This meeting is a preparation for the final separation. Perhaps if you think of this as similar to throwing away or giving away an item you have owned for some time, the dynamics will be clear. You decide to give away a book that you have enjoyed for years so that someone else may enjoy it. For several moments, or even days, before sending the book away you find yourself drawn to it. Whenever we attempt to set something in flight, it comes back to us, usually briefly. It is a natural dynamic; for every action, there is an equal reaction in the opposite direction. This is demonstrated to us often by our financial condition and our response to it: The harder we try to hold onto money, the more easily it slips from us. If we are generous and give it away, money comes to us.

When you hear from George, or actually meet with him, you may reconsider your decision. Should you decide that, after all, you do not wish to release him, then go back to the same spot where you performed the releasing ceremony, face West, call upon the Creator and your own higher self, and state simply that you want to have George Vincent in your life. Do not complicate the statement. Spirit does not respond well to complications created by the human mind. If you say, "I made a mistake about George and now I am sorry," Spirit will most likely pick up the confusion that statement reflects. What you put out is what Spirit picks up. Also, Spirit does not respond well to statements of double intent, so you do not want to say, "I released George Vincent and now I want him back again," because that statement reflects two states of being and Spirit will pick up confusion from it.

Anytime we deal with Spirit it is always best to make simple, affirming statements. The process of finding the words that best reflect our desire is a good exercise in separating the essential and non-essential aspects of any situation. If you spend time thinking about exactly what you do or do not want from George, or from Spirit, or from your job or lover, you will clarify these situations for yourself and in the process learn some interesting things about yourself and your life.

Once you have made the new statement, thank the spirit of the West, your higher self, and the Creator, in that order.

The Earth As Our Partner: Using Crystals for Divination

At this time in our evolution, when we are becoming aware of how powerfully we have assaulted the earth, air and water, and when we are beginning, as a society, to scrutinize our relationship to the other life-forms here, it is difficult for any of us to remain entirely self-encapsulated. Even people who think they are not interested in the question of our moral obligations to the planet, who think they don't care about pollution, who believe they may help themselves to meat without considering the issue of the freedom of animals, who see no reason not to destroy forests if it suits them, even these people are having an increasingly difficult time remaining out of touch with these issues. Why is that? Is something forcing consciousness on all of us? Of course something is: The Earth is awakening us, giving us every chance for complete understanding of our obligations here, before it decides whether or not to get rid of us. In the current war between humankind and the all-life, no hostages will be taken from the human race; either we all stay, or we all go.

There has been a quickening of energies between our kingdom and the stone, plant and animal kingdoms. With that an opportunity has opened for any of us who wishes to join his consciousness to that of the other three kingdoms. It is easier now for a human being to connect his consciousness with stones or plants for purposes of healing and divination than it has been for some time. With the reawakening of the human race in regard to our obligations has come a whole new set of opportunities to join with stones and plants—and sometimes with animals—for endeavors which, during the last three hundred years, were available to only a few people.

People practice divination all day long, from interpreting the state of a love affair by counting the petals on daisies to picking lottery numbers according to their children's birthdays. It is a natural human tendency—or weakness—to try to bend the future in the direction we want it to go.

For the occultist and the non-occultist, stones and particularly quartz crystals, used for thousands of years for many spiritual purposes, are excellent partners for us in techniques of divination, healing, and warding off evil.

There are many techniques for doing these things which don't involve the partnership of a stone or plant. We can delve into our clairvoyant faculty (once we have developed it) or ask for revelatory dreams or consult a psychic for answers. But these techniques, while effective, do not have the advantage of joining our energies with those of another kingdom. Divinatory methods can warn us when danger is near. Stones and plants can help us to keep our homes safe from invasion by adding their energy and power to ours.

Because the stone kingdom exists closest to the elementary powers—stones being the first form created on the earth—any chance to work with stones and learn about them is an invaluable opportunity. Stones are independent of human beings, animals and plants, and so are the least dependent of all four earth-realm kingdoms. Once a stone has been created, either by the elements within the earth's core (igneous rocks) or through the accruing of minerals on top of the earth's surface (metamorphic rocks) it does not need to be fed. It's composition will change as time goes on. It will gain or lose mineral contant, get bigger or break into smaller pieces, yet the stone is not dependent on further feeding. Stones do not need humankind, plants, or animals.

Divinatory techniques involving stones require two things of the querant; that he be honest with himself regarding the answers he receives, and that he respect the stones he uses in the process. He should at all times remember that rocks are alive and not treat them as tools belonging to him. To respect stones is not to worship them or invest belief in them. Respect means only that we consider their needs as living entities and do not view them as extensions of ourselves.

Current Crystal Consciousness

Because the partnership between quartz crystals and the human race is an ancient one, the stone kingdom is willing to put up with the current crystal fad. Crystals are making themselves available on a psychic level and are willing to let human beings examine them and perform experiments. While people can mine crystals whenever they choose, this does not assure access to the crystal spirit. If crystal spirits did not wish to be in contact with us, they would not be. We would be left with their forms but could not engage their energies. Coming forward to be used by human beings is *their* choice. If we abuse the privilege, they may decide to withdraw their favors.

Crystals are amplifiers and clarifiers of energy. They are not little people or tiny machines. They refine and expand the energies you introduce to them; they do not create energies. If you handle a crystal, the crystal will pick up all of your energy and amplify it. If you are centered and balanced, and *if* you have healing energy to give, then the crystal will indeed pick up and amplify that energy. If you are not a healer, the crystal will not make you one. You can put intention and its attendant energy into a crystal, but you cannot put a wish into one. No crystal will do what you ask it to do unless you have the necessary ingredients within yourself to make that wish happen. Crystals can help you to refine the work you are already capable of; they cannot do this work for you.

For a full understanding of crystals, their make-up, their needs and their many uses, I recommend *LIGHTSEEDS: A Compendium Of Ancient And Contemporary Crystal*

Knowledge, which I wrote with Wabun Wind.

Crystals are very sensitive. They pick up all of the energies to which they are introduced. For that reason, *no responsible crystal practitioner would ever wear or carry casually (unprotected) any crystal.* A crystal, when brought into a room filled with people, or the subway, a store, a workshop, will pick up whatever is in the room. You can not prevent this by "programming" the crystal. Such current fad ideas, resplendent with wishful thinking, are an outgrowth of human egotism. We can no more program a crystal than we can announce to a bear that we want it to become an eagle. The very notion is presumptuous.

If you bring a crystal into a room filled with people, or an empty room in which negative energies have gathered and remained, the crystal will pick up those energies and be rendered unfit for healing or any other sacred work until its etheric body has been cleansed. Also, when you wear a living thing, you are kidnapping it by subjecting it to the full spectrum of energies through which you move during your day. If everyone at work is in a foul mood and you have to live with that, so does the crystal you are wearing. Is that fair? You would not do that to your dog. Crystals are no less sensitive than animals and sometimes they are far more sensitive, physically and psychically, than any other life form.

If you do not have a crystal and wish to buy one, there is nothing wrong with doing so as long as you realize that, in buying a crystal, you are adopting a living being. If that feels right, then go ahead. Treat it well. Respect it as a living entity. Clean it when it needs to be cleaned—it is your responsibility to find out when this is necessary—and give it a place to live where it seems content. Some crystals like to be wrapped up and put away out of sight, while others do well in a potted plant or some other place that puts them in the middle of your life. Some crystals like to be near other crystals or stones, while some like to be kept apart from these.

If you honestly do not believe that crystals are alive, and if you cannot treat them as living entities, then please do not work with the stone kingdom. Find another divination aid, such as cards.

Choosing the Right Crystal for You

Ask friends where you can find a store that sells stones and crystals, someplace where the atmosphere is peaceful. If you must search without the advice of friends who have bought crystals, then take some time to shop around. The difference between the crystals of one store and another can be truly amazing. Some shopkeepers are insensitive to stones and sell them only to make money, without regard for the stones' welfare.

Two feelings will become apparent to you when you are in such a store. The first is a hurried feeling, as though nobody in the store ever takes much time with the crystals or the customers. The second feeling surrounds the stones themselves, individually and as a group: they will not feel as though they have much energy. Crystals that are kidnapped to satisfy someone's greed lose their power quickly.

If you are fortunate enough to find a store where the crystals are treated like the living beings they are, you will also find that you can take your time looking around. Nobody will hurry you to make your selection, pay and get out. In this instance, the stones will—unless they were mined in an uncaring manner or in some other way mishandled—have all their natural power and feel alive and vibrant. Even if you have not developed your psychic sense, you will be able to feel their energy because it is so powerful. All stones, when healthy and in a respectful environment, are so potent that anybody can feel their strength if given time to tune in on it.

Look at the crystals as though you were looking at prospective roommates. When a crystal connects to you, you will feel that connection. Silently, ask the stone's permission to pick it up and, if you receive permission, pick it up with your left hand, the receptive hand. Holding it with its terminal point (the place where the crystal's six sides meet in a point) upward, place it about three inches in front of your forehead, just above your eyebrows. This area is called the third-eye region, which means that your psychic "eye" is positioned there. Leave the crystal right there for a few moments. Remember to keep its terminal point up and do not turn it upside down or around so that the termination is pointed at you. The energy that leaves a crystal—focused and magnified—leaves through this terminal point, and you do not wish to receive its energy at this time because you have no idea who held the crystal last or what energies it was subjected to.

As you hold the crystal before your third eye, note the sensations it engenders. Do you feel any emotion? Do you feel like crying? Laughing? Is there a physical sensation, such as a tugging just above or below your belly button, or a warming around your heart? Do you feel suddenly hot or cold?

Any of these or comparable sensations means that you and the crystal are communicating. That does not, all by itself, mean that you and the crystal belong together.

Put the crystal back where it was, shake your hand a few times to release the energies you received from it, and walk around the store, deliberately ignoring the crystal. Try to put it out of your mind for a few minutes. If, after a little while, you feel the crystal drawing your attention, return to the crystal. Does it draw your psychic attention or just your intellect? You must not buy a crystal on intellectual prompting.

Pick up the crystal again, holding it with the terminal point up, not down or toward you, and position it at the third eye region. Do not touch your flesh with the crystal or hold it in your right hand. It's not yours yet and so you do not want to imbue it with your energy. While holding the crystal, see if a relative or friend comes to mind. The crystal may be calling out to you to buy it, but that also does not mean it's meant to be yours.

If, by now, you feel that the crystal means to live with you, you're probably right. At this juncture, inspect it. Never mind anything you may have heard during the crystal craze regarding how a crystal should look. Every crystal that is a bona fide quartz, six-sided crystal is a valid potential helper or friend. Bear in mind that for some kinds of work, particularly healing work, a crystal must have an intact, unbroken, unchipped terminal point. Look this area over carefully if you are considering this crystal for healing work. However, even a crystal whose terminal point is chipped or broken away completely has value for some endeavors. If the crystal is calling out to you, then you should very seriously consider buying it even if it seems utterly unsuitable for the purpose you originally had in mind. The stone may not be coming to you in order to work with you at all. It may simply wish to be rescued from the marketplace. Stones do not like being auctioned to the highest bidder any more than plants, animals or human beings. If you are a kind soul, it may be crying out for you to buy it and get it out of the store. If you can afford it and feel you are doing the right thing by buying it, do. Take it home.

I have bought and still buy many crystals for precisely this reason, and not because I thought at the time of purchase that the crystal and I were meant to work together. I ransom animals when I can, and ransom stones when they ask me to. Sometimes, when I felt it was the right thing to do—right for the crystal—I have given stones away. I never do this unless I am certain I'm doing the right thing. I would no sooner mistreat a crystal than I would a child or an animal.

Cleansing Crystals

When you and the crystal come together, it is your responsibility to clean the crystal when it needs to be cleaned and to give it a place to live where it will be comfortable. After acquiring any crystal, you must clean it thoroughly because there is no way of knowing what kinds of energies it came into contact with while being mined, shipped, traded, or sold. Unless there is danger of frost, put the crystal a foot down into the earth and leave it there for two days. The earth is a potent and effective cleanser.

If there is any danger of the ground freezing, you must not

put the crystal in the earth because a fast freeze may crack it.

Under no circumstances should you put it in the sun for more than two minutes because the sun can easily crack a crystal. Crystals often have bits of metal in them, called rutile. Metal always heats up faster than crystal does, and when you leave a rutilant crystal in the sun, you take a chance on the metal heating and then expanding beyond what the surrounding crystal can tolerate. This makes the crystal crack. You can not know for certain if a crystal has rutile in it because some tiny bits of metal are not visible to the naked eye.

Also, leaving a crystal in strong sunlight can easily start a fire. Crystals magnify.

Putting a crystal under the moon's light is poetic but it will not clean the crystal.

You can clean a crystal in running water by putting it in a stream for a day, but be certain to shore the crystal up somehow, safely, so that it doesn't float away or get hit by a moving rock.

Smudging, mentioned later in this book as a terrific cleanser and soother of human beings, is also an effective and easy crystal cleanser.

Build a smudge with dried sage, dried cedar, and dried sweetgrass. These must be harvested (wild), not cultivated. If you cannot obtain cedar or sweetgrass, then you can cleanse a crystal, yourself, your home or any object with just sage. This is not, strictly speaking, smudging, as that method calls for the inclusion of all three ingredients. (Sagegrass is not sage; they are two different plants.)

Placing a handful of dried sage, a sprinkling of cedar and a crumbled handful of sweetgrass in a pottery bowl or a shell, raise the bowl toward the sky and offer it to Mother-Father God, or whatever higher power you believe in. Then offer the bowl to the earth for its blessing. Following those two blessings, ask, in turn, the East, South, West and North to bless the smudge or the sage, as the case may be. Tell the powers-that-be why you are going to smudge, or cleanse: stated purpose elevates endeavor.

Light the herbs. When you have about a third of the herbs burning, put the flame out by blowing it out or waving a consecrated feather over the fire. Some people are offended by anyone blowing out a sacred fire because they feel that by doing so a human being puts himself in the place of the Creator. If you share this feeling, then use a feather or any other agreeable means of putting out the fire and fanning the embers. You will have to fan the embers every so often or else they will burn out.

Because the herbs have been offered for blessing to the six sacred directions, the smoke is now blessed, or holy smoke. Holding the bowl or shell in your left hand, use your right hand to waft the smoke over your heart, throat, shoulders and the top of your head. If you wish, put the container on the floor and hold each of your feet, in turn, over the smoke. This is a wonderful ritualistic cleansing of the part of our bodies that carries us around the world. You may desire to smudge your hands, particularly the palms. Smudge your whole body if you like.

After smudging your body and your etheric energies, smudge the crystal by holding it in the sacred smoke. Change the crystal's position as many times as necessary to ensure that the entire crystal is cleansed. The terminal point needs thorough cleansing, so hold it in the smoke for a full minute, its point directed downward into the smoke.

This ceremony is a sacred one and should be approached with honor. It is not just a cleansing but an opportunity for you to commune with the Almighty, the spirit forces of the earth and the four cardinal directions.

Finding a Place for Your Crystal

Be sure to ask the crystal where it wants to live. Don't worry that you may not have developed your psychic sense. You will know where the crystal is happy or unhappy by the feeling you get when you approach a place with the crystal in your hand. If the place is wrong for the crystal, you will not feel like leaving it there. If a good selection is made, you will feel fine about leaving your crystal there. Psychism is a natural sense and it normally comes to us quietly and gently.

If you wish to hold a ceremony celebrating the new partnership between you and the crystal, design one for yourself. As is often the case in ritual work, you will empower the ceremony by creating it. The performing of a self-created ceremony will be stronger and have a greater feeling of immediacy than a ritual designed by someone else.

If you like to drum, you may want to celebrate the advent into your life of the crystal by drumming for it. That's fine. You may wish to sing a song to your crystal, or even make one up for the welcoming ceremony. Do whatever you like that is respectful of yourself, the crystal, and Spirit. Be sure to include the crystal in the ceremony. Any activity when done with respect and intention becomes ceremony. As long as your intention is to welcome the crystal and express to it your joy in having it with you, any respectful action on your part will be legitimate ceremony. Ceremony is, by definition, neither rigid nor necessarily solemn.

Divinatory Methods

For this method you will need one crystal. I use a clear one, but any crystal will do. You cannot use a crystalline stone for this method. (Rose quartz is not a crystal but crystalline. It is a lovely stone and very comforting, but because it does not have the same atomic structure outside as inside, it does not come under the definition of crystal and it cannot be used for this technique. Rose quartz is a mass, lacking the six-sided structure essential to the definition of the term "crystal.")

Having cleansed the crystal, sit with it and face the appropriate direction for the question you want answered. Hold the crystal in both hands for a few minutes and allow your mind to touch upon all aspects of the question. Do not let your mind wander to subjects other than the one under consideration. When you feel you have a clear enough understanding of your question to synthesize all its elements into one clear question, stand up, take a deep breath, and let it out slowly. Breathe as slowly and deeply as you can and relax with each breath. Hold the crystal in your right hand, whether you are right- or left-handed, with the terminal point away from you and the base of the crystal six inches away from your solar plexus.

Holding the crystal firmly, ask your question out loud and stand there for a full half-minute without moving the crystal or touching it with your left hand. After thirty seconds, grasp the crystal—but not the terminal point—in your left hand and swiftly turn it so that the terminal point is toward you and the base is away from you. The crystal should still be positioned six inches from your solar plexus.

What impression did you receive the moment you turned the crystal? What feeling did you get? Was there a fleeting vision, a sound, even an odor? Any impression is a valid answer to the question.

Sit down again, facing the same direction, and put the crystal on the floor to your right.

If you have a flat piece of hematite, which is a good grounding stone, place the crystal on that, to your right. Do not put the crystal on your left side because the left is the entrance place for psychic impressions and other energy. If you place the crystal on your left, you will begin to pick up feelings and visions that have nothing to do with your question, thoughts generated by your neighbor to the left, or by the traffic outside your house. This won't happen as long as you place the crystal to your right.

What kind of answer did you receive? Whether you are happy or unhappy with the impressions you got, remember that this technique gives you *a* valid answer or even a few valid answers, but no technique can ever give you all the possibilities at one time. The answers you got from this method are the answers now on the horizon. Things change. People change their minds. Between the asking of the question and the actual resolution of the issue, energies will shift and the people involved will alter their perceptions of the situation under consideration. That is why we can rarely receive all the potential in any given situation at one time.

If you ask whether your cousin Joe is going to die and if Joe has decided, unconsciously, that he is ready to make his death passage, then you may get the answer, yes. If, however, Joe has not yet made his decision, then you will get possibilities, yes and no and maybe, in varying forms and visions. You may get several of the full range of possibilities, while other possibilities may not come to you at all.

All you need remember is that you are seeing *some* potential. It is highly unlikely that you will, in one session, become aware of all the possibilities unless you happen to be lucky enough to tune in on a situation that has *already been resolved.*

Be sure to cleanse your crystal after using it, even if you've left it on the piece of hematite for a while. A full cleansing is always necessary after psychic work and hematite, while an excellent grounder and partial cleanser, cannot provide full cleansing of a crystal. Also, be sure to cleanse yourself after doing psychic work.

After asking a question and receiving an answer, do not stand there for a long time waiting to see what other messages arrive from the great beyond. Without the focused energy that is provided by a specific question, the messages forthcoming will be useless to you because you will not know what they pertain to. If you have developed your seeing and feeling abilities at all, you will surely receive visions and impressions from your crystal, but these will be indecipherable and they may lead you into false assumptions. I often get free-floating movies in my head, but I have learned not to attribute these movies to anything, for to do so can be very misleading.

Psychic Self-Defense and Crystals

For this method you will need one clear and one dark crystal.

Dark crystals, called *smoky* when they are light-to-dark brown and *morion* when black, are very useful for fending off psychic attack. They absorb energy and hold it well. In choosing such a crystal, be as aware of its signals and its needs as you would be when selecting a crystal for any other purpose.

Having thoroughly cleansed the crystal of whatever energies it picked up on its journey from the mine to you, place it in a corner of your house with its terminal point facing the corner and away from you.

Surround the crystal from right to left with salt, making a counterclockwise circle with the salt. Be sure to make a whole circle. Don't leave any open spaces.

Standing behind the circle, facing the corner, raise your right hand and call upon the powers of the Light to help you. Point your right forefinger directly upward to receive the Light power, and then point your finger at the base of the crystal. Do not touch the crystal; place your finger an inch behind the base. Then, in one sweeping motion, encircle the crystal from right to left just outside the line of salt, about a quarter-inch outside the salt. Do not touch the floor, but keep your fingers a few inches above it.

The ceremony you just performed will hold any negative energy in the crystal for about twenty-four hours.

Unless I knew for certain that I was under psychic attack, and I was sure what direction the attack was coming from, I would start the crystal-absorbing process with the corner that is closest to due East. Not all streets are built North-South or East-West, so you will have to get a compass and find out where the directions are and how they fit in your house. If a corner faces East directly, fine. If East is a bit to the left or to the right of a corner, I would consider the East corner to be the one to the left of due East. The next corner would therefore be the South corner, the next one the West corner, and the fourth corner would be the North corner.

North is a difficult direction, and if you attempt this crystal-absorbing technique by beginning with North, you may not discover that other corners in your home besides North are being used for psychic attack. The reason for this is that North will nearly always pick up negativity, even negativity not created by attack, so you may find negativity in the North corner and fail to inspect the other three.

After leaving the dark crystal in the first corner for about twenty-four hours, bring a bowl of cold water into the room, along with a clear, cleansed crystal and a container (at least one cup) of sea salt. Set the bowl of water in the room at least four feet from the dark crystal and its circle of salt. Set the clear crystal down next to the water.

Invoke the Light power by facing whichever direction the sun is closest to. If it is nighttime, face West. Raise your right forefinger straight upward and ask the power of the Light to enter it. Point the finger about six-to-seven inches over your head, then immediately point it at your forehead, throat, solar plexus, and an inch below your abdomen. Without hesitation, point the finger straight out and make a sweeping circle by moving from right to left until your finger has created a full circle around your body. Make sure the circle is a full one and there are no gaps between the start and the end.

You have, with this ritual, protected yourself in your physical, etheric and astral form. Pick up the clear crystal, the water and the salt and place them not closer than two feet to the rear of the dark crystal and its circle of salt. Sit behind the water and container of salt, holding the clear crystal in your right hand at abdomen level.

Speaking out loud, say that you want to know if there is negative energy coming into your house through the corner you are facing and, if so, that you want to know who is sending that energy to you. If you need to do so, you can elaborate further by saying that you wish to know the reasons for the psychic attack.

Phrase all of this as clearly as possible. Without touching the dark crystal or the salt encircling it, and holding the clear crystal still in your right hand, bring into your mind any subject that has nothing whatever to do with psychic attack. Think of the ocean or of a sunny day or your favorite animal. Keeping your mind on the irrelevant thought, pass the clear crystal over the dark crystal three times, moving from the base of the dark crystal to its terminal point. Make the three passes one right after the other, still holding the thought which has nothing to do with the ritual you are engaged in.

Immediately place the clear crystal in the bowl of water. As soon as the crystal has settled in the bowl, remove your hand from the water. Pour into the water enough salt to cover the bottom half of the crystal and set the container of salt aside. Dismissing the irrelevant thought, look into the water—not into the crystal—and see whatever images or impressions come to you.

Continue looking into the water for a full minute or, if you like, longer. Do not look into the crystal at the bottom of the bowl or at the dark crystal unless a very powerful impulse makes you do so.

Allow whatever impressions are around you to come into your consciousness but do not force any thoughts to come.

There is a good chance that you won't receive impressions of danger. Not everybody is under psychic attack, and even when we are, the attack does not enter our homes through every one of the four corners at once.

Do not be disappointed if you receive no impressions. For one thing you may be free of attack and, for another, you have three more corners to inspect.

Above all, don't think you've failed if you do not receive impressions. There may not be anything to learn.

When your visions have ceased, or the impressions are gone, be wise enough to know that this learning session is over. Do not sit there waiting for further revelations. Seventy-five per-cent of good psychism is knowing when to stop searching.

Place the dark crystal in the bowl of salted water, being careful not to let the two crystals knock against each other. Leave them there while you sweep up the circle of salt, being mindful that it must be disposed of with prayer. Something needs to be said about the negativity collected by the salt. Make a prayer to the effect that the negativity will remain right where it is, in the salt, and be transmuted by the earth into positive energy. Pour the salt on the ground or bury it.

After the two crystals have been in the water for at least ten minutes, you can be sure that negative energies picked up by them are well on their way to being dissipated. Remove the crystals from the water. Throw the water outside onto the ground—using the same prayers you employed in disposing of the salt—and then cleanse both crystals thoroughly.

If you learned that someone is practicing invasion on you, whether or not you know his identity, you learned a lot. Invasion may come from an occultist practicing black magic, or from a non-occultist who has, in trying to take something from you, accidentally stumbled on some occult technique. He may have recalled techniques of invasion from past lifetimes. The identity of the invader is not important. You need only know that you are under attack. In time, if it is essential that you find out who the attacker is, you will.

Having investigated one corner, perform this technique on the other three corners until you find a corner that is indeed being invaded. I think you are safe in stopping the procedure once a negative corner has been found. Going beyond the necessary can make us paranoid and exhausted.

The sole exception to this would be, as I said earlier, the occasion of finding negativity in the North. I would not stop with just North because negativity often accrues there.

Once you have learned that something is trying to come into your house—which may be all you can learn with this method—do not jump to hysterical assumptions. Very often the force behind the attack is not someone we know. It would be a shame to leap from "I found negative energy coming in my West corner," to "I bet it's John who's attacking me. He never did like me." Only an amateur would waste time and energy attacking somebody out of mere personal dislike.

Do not at this early stage attempt to find out whether there is primary or secondary evil behind the human being making the attempt. Only a *trained and experienced* exorcist can learn that, and you don't need to know anyway.

You need know only that negativity is coming into your home. That alone doesn't necessarily mean you're being attacked. There may be a lot of negative energy around where you live. Surely this will be so if one of your neighbors abuses his children or sells drugs. If you live near a mental institution or a prison, there will be lots of negative energy around your home.

If there are hidden difficulties in your neighbors' homes, family troubles, a despairing man down the block or a very angry woman across the street, you may not know of these things from ordinary observation, but the dark crystal corner test will tell you if in fact there is appreciable negativity in your vicinity. Do not ascribe this energy to anyone in particular, as that is unfair and unnecessary. All you need do, once you have found negative energy around your home and been honest with yourself about whether you may be the source of that energy, is to select some appropriate protection techniques, such as the ones in Chapter 7.

Sound As a Protector and Beneficient Influence

Loud noises scare away evil spirits, which is why some cultures, including our own and the Chinese, have a tradition of creating noise as the new year comes in.

I have found it most effective to stand in the corners of each room in my house and clap my hands sharply just once. The sound is commanding and the room's atmosphere changes when I do this. In doing this exercise, I am not supposing that there is always evil around; I am shaking up the negative energies that always gather in corners. The sound disperses these energies. One could not expect this to work on the same intense level as a major exorcistic technique, but as a once-in-awhile cleanser, it's easy and effective.

Bells

Bells dispell negative energies. If the sound is deep enough and resonates for long enough, bells will also frighten away bad spirits. That is why bells are used in many religious ceremonies and why large tower bells are used to announce births and deaths. In clearing the air with sound, we permit a baby to be born without negative influences and a dying person to make his death journey free of interference.

Any bell sound will dispell negativity to some degree. If we need not only to clear the air of negativity but also to repell invasion, our bell must meet certain specifications. It must not make a light, tinkling sound. It must give a vibrant sound in the lower registers and must be made of a hard metal so that the sound does not oscillate, that is, fall away from the note it makes. The reason for this is that when we repell something, we force it away through energy. The energy of a bell-produced sound doesn't have much power if the sound oscillates.

If you are using a bell only to dispell negative energies and not to repell an invader, then you can disregard the problem of oscillation and ring any bell you like in any manner you like. Bells clear the air.

They also introduce into the atmosphere a friendly feeling, and a cheerful atmosphere goes a long way toward keeping our homes psychically clean.

Flutes

Bamboo or metal flutes, while inappropriate for exorcisms, bring wonderful spiritual vibrations into any home. You needn't be a musical genius to play a bamboo flute. Try out several of them before buying one, and select a flute with a sound that appeals to you. Never mind other people's tastes in this. Please yourself. And unless you enjoy performing, consider the flute a secret friend meant only for you. Play it for yourself when the mood strikes you. Know that any bamboo flute will play its lower sound at first and, after your breath has warmed the wood, it will play a couple of octaves higher. The shorter the piece of wood, the higher the sound. If you prefer low sounds, as I do, then you will have to find a long bamboo flute. This may require some shopping but it's worth the effort. Nothing calms and centers like music, and music we make ourselves creates a powerful spiritual vibrancy within us which extends all through our homes.

No wood flute should be exposed to extremes in temperature. Beyond remembering that fact and keeping your flute in a dark dry place out of direct sunlight, you are required to do no maintenance on a bamboo flute.

If you take a bamboo flute outside on a breezy day and hold it up in the air, the wind will play it for you. Bamboo flutes are conducive, I have found, to many such charming experiences. Once, in Hawaii, I had a bamboo flute zipped inside my backpack and was walking up a hill when I began to hear flute music. I looked around. There was no one in sight. As I walked, I heard the flute music again. It was, I realized, Spirit playing the flute inside my pack. These touches from the Creator, which happen when we least expect them, take a great deal of the sting out of life.

Helping Our Loved Ones to Die Well

An earlier chapter contains information about some of the difficulties that await us when we have a bad death journey. A good death passage is one of the greatest gifts we can give ourselves, and helping another to die gracefully and safely is a gift of immeasurable value.

If you are present during a loved one's final days or weeks, there is no reason for you to be reticent with him about his impending death unless he has made it plain that he doesn't wish to discuss the subject. If you have reason to believe he's frightened of death, then you have to make a decision: Should you force him to talk about it, thereby risk increasing his fear, or should you steer clear of the subject, which may cheat him of the chance he needs to talk about dying? You must know someone very well before you can hope to make a decision about this. Tread carefully and follow his lead. If he hints that he'd like to discuss death, either with you or with a priest or another friend, then make all the effort you need to in order to bring this about. If he lets you know that he does not want the subject broached, don't bring it up.

If your friend or relative does wish to discuss death, center yourself and remove, through meditation or, if necessary, by sheer force of will, any feelings of fear or regret you may be carrying over his dying. Your job, once you decide to befriend a dying person, is to help give him the best death possible, not to indulge your emotions.

Having focused your attention entirely on the dying one's needs, talk to him gently, unobtrusively, but firmly about the death passage. Listen when he wants to talk. When it's your turn to talk, be direct without being frightening. Make no attempt to forecast the time of his death, because the dying rarely die on cue. It will happen when it happens.

Tell him, kindly but without hedging, these truths about death: Tell him that he will leave his body gradually, and that the leaving will not be painful in any way. Tell him that the death experience is like the out-of-body experiences we routinely have during sleep. Tell him that he will be fine during his death passage, and remind him that dying is not an ending but a new beginning, a journey toward a new life.

Tell him that some people see their departed loved ones during their death passage, while others do not, and advise him not to go searching for anybody in particular when he dies, but to allow his own spirit to lead him. Above all things, tell him to place his trust in his spirit, to trust his intuition and go wherever he feels impelled to go. He may or may not encounter religious figures, such as St. Joseph or Buddha or Jesus but, again, he should not go looking for any of these because the act of searching will take him off his course.

If he is meant to see Jesus, he will. If a religious being or his mother is planning to greet him, they are perfectly capable of finding him; he should not go blundering around in search of them.

Tell him that, when he leaves his body, he may or may not see a light in the distance, a white light or pale yellow light or any other light. If he sees a light and if his spirit tugs him toward it, he should journey to that light and allow *absolutely nothing* to stand between himself and the light. He may see shapes or colors or faces in front of him and these may try to stop him from going to the light. No matter how authoritative or frightening these beings may seem, however, they have no real power and he must not let them get in his way. He may see relatives or even see himself, but he should bypass everything and keep moving unwaveringly toward the light that beckons him, trusting nothing except the urgings of his spirit.

Don't tell your friend what he ought to expect once his journey is completed because, no matter how much deathbed experience you have had, and even if you've had a near-death experience yourself, you can not possibly know what your friend's destiny will be.

If he is deeply imbued with religious or philosophical prejudice about the after-death experience, do what you can to soften his certainties without declaring war on his beliefs. Tell him that while human beings try to find out what will happen to them after their lifetime here, the truth is that nobody knows the whole story of what awaits us in the afterlife. The reason you need to bring this up is that some people create for themselves, in death, false situations which reflect their expectations. These people, unwilling to give up their beliefs, can get caught up in creating for themselves "places" that seem all too real when they are actually phantom-places. A man may create a "heaven" or, if he is fearful, a "hell" to which he expects to be assigned. Once these are created, the spirit may take up residence in a place he has created himself, which has no actual existence. While you cannot overcome someone's overwhelming need to adhere to his belief system, you may be able to mitigate some of his programming by opening his mind a little. When people face death, their minds tend to open just a bit—and sometimes more than that. You can help your friend by offering a little speculation about the afterlife, something non-confrontational, such as, "I've always doubted that we go to hell if we have done wrong. After all, everyone has done something wrong. Would a loving God expect us to be perfect?

Of course, I don't know the answer to this question . . . *and neither does anyone else.''*

If, on the other hand, it is you who hold strong religious convictions, refrain from imposing them on your friend. No dying person needs to be saddled with any rigid philosophy at a time when he is facing his departure from this earth. He needs to feel hopeful and free. He should not take his fears—or yours—with him on his journey.

It is important to talk with the dying about matters pertaining to this realm, and to discuss what will happen to his loved ones when he dies. Tell him that while there are people here who love him very much and will miss him, he is not to feel guilty over his departure, no matter how close he is to his loved ones. The same Spirit that watches over him will embrace them in their grief. He needs to be aware that there are some things we can never do for another person, and one of these is comforting the bereaved after we are gone. When we die, we must concentrate our full energies on our death journey. We cannot worry about those we leave behind.

Tell him not to be distracted by the sight or sound of grieving people, but to keep travelling toward the sky or the light or whatever his soul moves him toward.

Talk to the dying one about the life he's lived. It's unnecessary to offer him a report card, and this would be presumptuous at any rate. Tell him that he lived his life better than anyone else could have lived it. He may be envious of other people, of their success or their apparently happier lives, but remind him that we can never know another person well enough to be certain that the appearance of his life is an accurate reflection of that life. Envy is wasted energy and denigrating to our spirit. Nobody else could possibly have learned, during his life, the same things your friend learned during his. He is unique. He is a worthy being. Tell him so.

Remind him of his achievements and of the number of people who love him, including you. Try not to dwell on his worldly successes or wealth because these cannot be taken into death with us. No matter how much the world has applauded our work, worldly success does not really belong to us. The approval of others is actually a possession of those others, not ours. Accentuate, instead, your friend's character, his quirky sense of humor, his kindness, for these truly belong to him and he will take these attributes with him into eternity. Our spiritual assets, characteristics, knowledge and power are ours, and we do not separate from them in death.

If you can discuss reincarnation with him, tell your dying friend that he should take a good long look at his options before he decides to be reborn here. Nobody should reincarnate as a reaction to the lifetime he's just left. We should come back here only because we have something important to do here, and never because we have a score to settle or a regret we haven't let go of. Tell him, above all else, to take his time in making this decision, and to ask for all the spiritual guidance he can get before he decides whether or not to return to earth-realm life.

Be sure to tell your friend that his greatest need, once he has departed this realm, is to disengage himself from all this-life attachments, whether positive or negative. This doesn't mean that he can no longer love his family or be happy about his accomplishments, but it means that he must be willing to cut loose his identification with any person, place, object, or accomplishment belonging to the life he has left. If he does not discharge anger and resentment, and if he doesn't allow his attachments to drift away, he will be psychically bound to a life he no longer owns.

While your friend is dying, talk to him gently and unemotionally about your love for him. Remind him, without making things too complicated, to let his own spirit guide him through his journey and not to let himself be distracted by anything. Tell him that his spirit will know without question where he is headed, and that his one and only job is to trust himself.

If anyone close to the dying one needs to make peace with him, for his own sake or for the one who is dying, tell them that they may talk to the dying even if he's in a coma, for the spirit of a dying person hears everything. For that reason, nobody within a dying person's hearing range should ever make denigrating comments about him or his nurses and doctors, or anybody else. People must not fight where a dying person can hear them. Nobody should express a fear of dying in general or this one's death in particular. Nothing negative must be voiced within hearing of the dying, for the dying, no matter how far away they may seem or how deeply unconscious, hear everything.

If someone needs to make a confession or apology or a declaration of love for the dying one, he should sit by the deathbed and say what he needs to say without expressing anger. He should speak sincerely but briefly, and not ramble on. While we who are left behind usually have much we would like to say to a departing loved one, the fact is that the dying have an agenda that requires their full attention and we must not take up more of their time than is absolutely necessary. Dying takes work on the part of the journeyer. We must not impede his progress.

If you feel that the departing one needs physical comfort, hold his hand gently or rub his feet occasionally, but try not to touch his face—unless he needs his sweating forehead wiped—because it is important that the dying not be distracted. The touching of the face is more distracting than the touching of the body.

It is imperative that a dying person have all the painkillers and other comfort he needs, and even if you have to declare war on the hospital to obtain what he requires, do it. That is as much a part of your deathbed duty as anything else.

Once he has begun his death journey, pray for him, but do it silently. Do not tell him that he is dying, because dying is usually like dreaming; there's no reason to jolt him from his "dream" by telling him he's dying. The shock would be detrimental. Pray for peace and protection for the journeyer.

If you feel that he needs to hear your voice, talk to him gently. If you feel no impulse to talk, sit beside him quietly. If you feel that he needs to be left alone in order to make a good journey, then leave the room and tell everyone else to leave the room too. They may not like this, but the dying one's needs always supercede the needs of the living, and when you agreed to do deathbed duty, you agreed to play watchdog to your friend and attend to his needs.

If his other companions refuse to leave the room, don't fight about it, as that would be disruptive to the departing spirit. Explain to them that the journeyer needs peace and may feel constrained by their presence. If they won't go along with this, you will have to let them be. Above all, when discussing this with the others in the room, avoid the use of the word "dying," and say nothing you would not want the departing one to overhear, because he will hear and comprehend all you say. You don't want to startle the dying man by saying, "Well, I guess Charles is leaving us now."

Once your friend is dead, you may close his eyes if you wish but on no account should you attempt to close his mouth or place anything on top of his head, because the mouth and the top of the head are exit places for the spirit.

No matter how long your friend or relative has been dying and no matter how long he has been old, weak, ill or even comatose, his spirit may take a full three days to leave his body. Make arrangements for cremation or burial with this in mind, and leave the body alone for three whole days. More than three days is unnecessary. Nobody takes longer than three days to complete the removal of his spirit and energy from his body.

If the dead one was angry or rebellious about his death, maintain protection of yourself and your home for a month after he dies. He may try to hold onto this realm through you, his sympathetic friend. For appropriate methodology, see Chapter 7.

If the departed was addicted to alcohol or other drugs, throw away all bottles, drugs and drug paraphernalia as soon as he dies, so that these will not attract him back here where he doesn't belong.

If the deceased died young, try to get his family and friends to refrain from dwelling on the unfairness of the death, at least for a month after their loved one has died. This attitude may be construed by the departed as an invitation to cling to this realm. You can't control their thoughts, but try to make them understand why indulging in those thoughts could cause trouble for the departed. Explain that he needs to leave and that his journey will be harder for him if he harbors the illusion that he can come back to this realm.

Whether we die at four, twenty or a hundred years old, dead is dead, and while someone's death may seem unfair, what is, is. We must deal with death, when it comes, as a reality not subject to our approval. Continually protesting the death as unfair furthers nothing for us and may impede the dead one's progress into the next realm.

Pray for the dead. As I have said elsewhere in this book, we do not have to believe in an omnipotent God in order to pray. Prayer is energy focused on an intention or desire for ourselves or others. In order to make this intention or desire known to the universe, we need only to recognize a force, or several forces, greater than ourselves. I think the acknowledgement of *something* bigger than we are is easy for anyone to make.

You should ask the spirit of the West to help your friend, and you may feel like making an offering to West, perhaps candy or herbs or flowers or whatever seems appropriate. You may address West while your friend is still alive or after he dies or both, as suits you. Everyone who dies makes his earth-exit through the West.

If a loved one, knowing he is approaching death, asks you to help him with his death passage but you feel inadequate to comply, *say no*. It is very confusing for a dying person to have a reluctant deathbed guardian hanging around wishing he were elsewhere. If you are frightened of death, stay away from the dying. Fear does not belong in a death room, and you will do your loved one no favor by agreeing to something for which you have only dread. His death journey will be more difficult for him than it needs to be if he is saddled with your negative feelings at the very time he needs to be free to take his leave.

Know what you have agreed to when you tell someone you

will stand by him in the hospital or at home when he is dying. Some deaths are fast and some take forever. Be sure you have the stamina and heart to be a deathbed guardian before you tell anyone you'll take on that responsibility.

Having considered carefully all of these points for the purpose of helping a loved one to die well, remember them for your own sake when it is your turn to die. Dying is a great healing journey. Don't leave yours to chance.

Compassion: What Works and What Does Not Work

Because the energy fields of people, stones, animals, and trees all touch one another, it is important to learn where your compassion boundaries are. In feeling love, pity or grief for another, we can go beyond healthy caring and engage ourselves in another's troubles beyond what is good sense for us or truly useful to him. We can actually pick up another's anger, pain, or misery and we can do so much more easily than we might pick up his happiness because negative energies are often easier to engage than positive ones.

When we are aware of a friend's difficulties, the illness of a family member, or any situation belonging to another, our first task is to remind ourselves that the circumstances do indeed belong to that other person. My own tendency to fling myself into other people's troubles has taught me this, and I address the issue here because I find that most decent, caring people blur the lines between themselves and others when those others are having hard times. This can be dangerous, especially when our loved ones are ill for so long that we begin to brood about their illness, or troubled so deeply that we find ourselves feeling as though we are actually a part of those troubles. Over time, we may attract to ourselves others' pains, illnesses, and miseries. *This does not mitigate their miseries or alleviate their illnesses.* It does the sufferer no good when we suffer excessively along with them. Too much compassion merely attracts another's negative energies to our energy bodies and gives us a dose of something that does not belong to us, without removing any of the quantum of negativity from our friend. It does nobody any good when we entangle ourselves with another's woes. What is his to deal with is his.

I am not suggesting that we lose empathy, but that we learn to think of ourselves as inviolate beings. We can aid a friend without allowing his sadness, anger or physical pain to attach to our etheric bodies. During a friend's traumatic times, we must remind ourselves to establish boundaries between his miseries and our physical form, etheric body, mind and emotions.

Anyone with extensive experience as a healer knows that before he can work with or pray over another person, he must first wrap himself—in the astral, etheric and physical levels of his being—in protection. There is nothing to be gained by receiving the cast-off energies of another person's illness. The responsibility of keeping ourselves safe and inviolate is our own.

There is also the issue of respect to be considered here. Our friend has, despite any appearance to the contrary, the full opportunity and ability to solve his own problems, and the obligation not to lay his troubles on our shoulders. Everyone's woes are his to solve.

Though human miseries manifest as financial, emotional, mental and many other kinds of maladies, most are spiritual in origin or will respond to ministrations of the spirit. The tending of our spirit provides nourishment and, in times of need, guidance. There are many spiritual disciplines and many personal paths to spiritual knowing. The next chapter addresses the particulars of some of these disciplines and methods for finding our personal way.

Chapter 6

Get Out of Here and Take Those Headless People With You: Journeys in the Spirit World

I am a brother to dragons, and a companion to owls.

—King James Bible, *Job* 30:29

When we occultists are not being dragged to the stake, we are ridiculed so badly that we cannot offer our services to the society that needs them. For us, there is usually no safe haven.

It's a strange life, to say the least. Where our company is desired, it's often for cheap gain and easy answers. Where we are despised, it is without our detractors having any knowledge of what we are or what we can do. Among outsiders, nobody understands what we are about, yet everyone has an opinion about us. Our work is hostage to whether or not people "believe" in it—as though the beliefs of the ignorant had any currency in the realm of the spirit!

The treatment we often receive is a direct reflection of the separation between humankind, in its current imbalanced

224

condition, and the spirit of creation. It is hardly *our* fault that people have fallen out of step with themselves, but we are blamed for the terrible void they live in because we have managed to bridge that void for ourselves. In the eyes of the blame-worthy, the blameless are always in the wrong.

The disciplines encompassing the occult, shamanism, psychism, magic, ritual, healing, and mediumship require particulars of attention from their practitioners. The safeguards needed by each occultist vary according to the art he practices. All have a common need to stay in continual contact with the collective unconscious, and to keep themselves *to* themselves.

It is especially important today, with instant communication making the exchange of information easier than it has ever been, that everyone engaged in esoteric pursuits maintain a strict balance between spiritual work and worldly life. So much information is available that psychic-overload is almost a certainty.

Equally important is a sane approach to the truth of the occult and occultists; the plethora of schools and teachers and the easy access to information has given the study of the occult a false appearance of safety. There are no guarantees in any pursuit, and the esoteric arts have always drawn together the innocent with the ugly and venal.

If a teacher, an adviser, is corruptible, we can't change that. We can, however, discard the dangerous wishful thinking that surrounds the study of the occult today. Stamping current studies with the term "New Age" does not lessen the dangers that have always gone hand-in-glove with occultism, its study, teaching, and practice. In the arts of the esoteric, there is nothing new under the sun, or the moon. The humility and self-awareness, discipline and good sense that were vitally important to the study of occultism a thousand years ago are necessary now—perhaps more so now, because the easy availability of spiritual tools has given occultism an inappropriate and misleading appearance of ordinariness and therefore of harmlessness.

It has always been my preference to stay away from group

work because of the inevitable confusion created when a group of seekers attempt, together, what is best managed by each person alone. But I will address, in this chapter, the particulars of group endeavor as I have, despite misgivings, sometimes participated in workshops and other collective work, as student and as teacher.

Shamanism: Piercing the Sky

There is no such person as a shaman. Shamanism, the exploring of the realities behind the manifest physical world and all the universe for the purpose of healing, counseling, gathering knowledge, or expanding our horizons, can be accomplished only with the permission and full cooperation of the all-life. Any shamanic work involves partnership. To call oneself a shaman is to draw undue attention to the human element of that partnership, thus giving ourselves an importance we do not have, and slighting the spirits who aid, guide, and permit the human seeker to do his exploring. You are not the shaman: the shaman consists of you *plus* all of the surrounding, informing, protecting help you get from the universe.

Shamanic power is an agreement between you and the all-life, that is all there is to it.

Shamanism is a spiritual discipline in which one moves his consciousness out of his body for the purpose of travelling to virtually any realm in existence. In this way, the shaman explores realities, including this one, using heightened awareness and vivid perception that are unavailable during mundane consciousness. Shamanic journeys are undertaken for the benefit of the shaman or another person. The shaman may travel in order to find information, or to locate food during a famine or water during a drought. If an ailing person has become separated from his body, the shaman may attempt to locate that wandering—or entrapped—spirit and try to bring it back into its body. Shamanic journeys may be undertaken in pursuit of information about the past, present or future. Because the shaman can travel outside of time and beyond space, he can discern the causes beneath and behind situations, divine the past or future, and discover the true nature of anything or anyone by encountering its source instead of its mundane, possibly misleading appearance. Shamanic journeying is part of the tradition of many cultures and is thousands of years old. There is today a revival of interest in shamanism and there are many practitioners of this ancient discipline.

Shamanism is an attempt to cure an incurable condition—that of waking consciousness in mundane reality. There are other ways of curing this condition. Some of them are alcoholism, delusion and insanity. The final cure is death.

Traveling through all of the realms of Spirit is a healthy attempt at finding ourselves and uncovering a view of all creation. The false appearances we routinely encounter in earthly existence frustrate the seeker-after-truth. His frustration is alleviated by making disciplined journeys into the three shamanic realms—upper, middle and lower worlds—where he can find the realities behind the concrete appearances of our realm, and the false appearances created by social programming. In journeying, the searcher can find out what people, situations, energies, spirits, himself and anything else really look like, what they are made of, and learn their purpose and relationship to himself.

Shamanism is not without its dangers. There are a few fundamentals regarding the shamanic journey and these must be understood and respected each time we undertake a journey. Being well grounded between journeys is very important, for our consciousness leaves our physical form when we journey, and unless we make certain to bring it all the way back into our body, it may hover near, but not inside us. This leads to accidents. Strong, clear communication between the shaman and his spirit allies, or power allies, is imperative, for these protect and guide the shaman through all of his journeys.

Shamanic journeying can be thrilling, enlightening, funny and sometimes dangerous. Not all journeys through the universe will be peaceful because not all of the universe is peaceful. Not all of *us* are peaceful either, and we take all of our being along when we journey, not just the good stuff.

In journeying, intention is important. But intention is only part of the journey; chance is the rest of it.

When we declare our desire to find out what the universe has in store, to explore what is out there, or down there, or around the corner, we are declaring ourselves free agents, laying claim to our right to know the truth of things. The universe answers with a similar declaration: *watch your ass.*

In addressing the needs of a shaman, I am considering, most of all, the needs of the disenfranchised seeker who has no allegiance to a tribal mode of shamanic practice. The Australian aboriginal and native American who have maintained their ties with their heritage do not have the same troubles as the rest of us. We, who are not legitimately part of a tribe and its culture, who have been separated from our own African or European shamanic traditions, have to form whole new methods because we have nobody to help us except a few self-appointed guides who may be just as lost as we are.

It seems to me that we are either part of a tribe or we are not. I do not understand the contemporary popular self-induction into tribes we have no real claim to that has crept into current spiritual movements. One does not, by mere wanting, become an Apache. The question of past-life affiliations aside—because they are not legitimate claims on the here and now—it is incomprehensible to me that one can become an Aztec unless one is born into that culture.

Surely we are free to study the ways of tribes if those ways are offered to us, but we cannot adopt their culture without cheating our purpose. If I had been meant to be a Navajo in this lifetime, I would be one. If it had been meant for me to be woven among the Hopi people, I would be a Hopi. If I am unaffiliated, then I am meant to find my own way. To cheat my destiny by becoming an imitation Hopi seems spiritually uncouth.

We can find our own way by looking into the traditions of our forebears, for every culture had its shamans. We can tend our needs by looking for our spiritual ancestors instead of our genetic ones. Often, the cultures that draw our attention are not the ones our great-grandparents came from.

It takes a great deal of strength to acquire power. The all-life knows our desire, but it will not respond unless we have some moral fiber. Would you invite just *any*body into *your* home? Well, the universe will not invite you to explore its realms unless you are worthy. You may take all the classes and read all the books, but if the all-life does not believe you are a good influence, you will not get past the front portal.

How do we become worthy of help? By caring. If our motive for shamanic journeying is pure selfish greed, you may believe that we will not be invited to any party worth attending.

All you have to do is care, care about the all-life around you—daily—care about other people, care simply to know the truth behind appearances. Caring is your ticket into the universe.

Self-importance is your ticket out. Our being reverberates to the all-life, so our attitudes and true desires can never be hidden from it. The universe gives itself and its secrets by yielding; it cannot be stolen from.

It does not respond to manipulation, either. We can never be clever enough to outsmart the all-life. If we seek with caring and humility, doors open. If we try to wrench information from the universe, doors shut.

The Shamanic Journey: Purposeful Movement

Desire to see the hidden realities behind our delusional view of life leads us to a purposeful movement away from social programming and into reality. Purposeful movement is easily done. We do it in our sleep all the time. The waking self is the barrier we must get across if we are to do, while conscious, the same quality journeying we do while asleep.

Because the barrier is merely illusion, it is not hard to get across. We make the leap across by bringing our attention to an entrance place in the earth that can lead us into the universe of non-illusional reality. This entrance can be a hole in the ground we saw yesterday in the woods, the roots of a tree we remember from a childhood home, a cave we explored while on vacation. All that matters is that the choice we make should not be an intellectual one. No matter how silly our selection may seem, perhaps an old woodchuck hole in our backyard, it is a valid choice if we feel drawn to use it.

Water entrances are an unwise choice for beginners because water is impossible to control: the entrance you took into the stream will not even be there as an exit when you want to come back from your journey.

Take your phone off the hook and do whatever else must be done in order to assure yourself about an hour's privacy. Then lie down and allow your spirit to travel toward the entrance point you feel is right for you. From that entrance point, your spirit will be moving through the real universe and not the delusional one you have been raised to believe in.

Safe Journeying

There is nothing to be frightened about or brace yourself for as long as you remember two aspects of journeying: anything you encounter can be escaped from if need be, and nothing you encounter is more powerful than you are as long as you have a partner from the all-life.

When doing your first few journeys, it is important that you see, feel, hear or in some way sense the presence of an ally whom you know and can trust. The ally is a being you will find in non-ordinary reality. A friend sitting next to you while you journey cannot be a power ally. Our journey and the entities who engage in it with us exist on a level beyond the here and now. Your power ally can be an animal, a spirit force such as the sun; it may be a spirit presence, and have no discernible form at all. Everyone has help, all his life, from the spirit realm, so you have always been surrounded by help. It is therefore unnecessary to entrust yourself, while journeying, to a spirit who is unfamiliar to you. You may not recognize the form a spirit ally takes, but his character should be recognizable to you. You may not have known in waking life that your spirit ally was a horse or a bear or a mouse or a spirit-of-light, but when you first encounter the ally while journeying, he will feel familiar to you whether or not you have ever had a strong feeling of friendship for horses or bears or spirits.

If you do not feel easily familiar with or trust the ally who presents himself as you move through the entrance point, then come back through that entrance. Journey another time. Make your first full journey *only* when you have established contact with your power ally or allies. (There may be more than one.)

Feel free to travel wherever you wish to go. Have a desire in mind before you journey, however, because floating is not as revelatory as purposeful journeying. Do you want to know what this world looks like when the illusions are swept away? Do you want help with a problem? Do you want to know what Pluto looks like? Have some idea what you want before you go. The more specific your goal, the better the journey will be.

Keep in mind, as you go, the route you and your spirit ally have taken. In journeying, you will travel across barriers, down through levels, or up through levels. Remember how many levels down, up or across you went before you arrived where you wanted to be. If you fail to note the route you take, you may not be able to get back there another time. Also, you must retrace the route as faithfully as possible in order to take all of your spirit back home with you.

For this reason, you must never fail to use your entrance as your exit. Do not come back to this reality through an exit point that is any different from your original entrance, for if you do, you take a great risk of leaving some of your spirit behind.

That is another reason for staying away from water entrances and exits; water moves anything with great force and you may lose some of your spirit in the water.

If, in your journey, you encounter water in any form, a waterfall or a lake, ask yourself—and your power ally— whether it is safe for you to travel through the water. If you do not feel confident about it, find another means of getting through the water than by simply plunging in. If you must move through the water, find a way of keeping your spirit intact during the transit through the water. Wrap your spirit body in something, or ask for help from your ally. When journeying through water, a little precaution is worth a lot.

Signals from the Universe

Journeying is the safest occult discipline I know of. One reason is the ease with which you will know if there is any unfriendly force around you. Pay attention, not just to where you want to go, but to what presents itself to you unbidden and unexpected. This is one of the great joys of shamanism. Help is offered beyond what is asked for. And this seeing or sensing of things you did not expect to encounter is true psychism, not imagination.

The imagination usually contains some information from spirit, that is, true psychic intuition. At the same time, however, imagination is informed by waking consciousness. This makes imagination an unreliable conduit between our waking minds and intuition. We never know how much of our imagination is programmed by waking delusion and how much is a real tuning-in to spirit.

For that reason, some shamanic journeying will *always* be suspect because part of it will be the product of imagination. Nothing can be done about this. While we are awake, we are awake. And when we are awake, our imagination can get between us and psychic truth.

After we have had a great deal of experience in journeying, we learn how to push aside our imaginations and minimize the intrusion of imagination on journeys. This takes experience and it takes a great deal of self-teaching. We must learn to identify real intuition, and learn to identify mere imagination. This process cannot be taught. Everyone must evolve the process for himself.

While journeying, assume that some of what you expect to

encounter will be your imagination at work. But when you see or sense something unexpected, that is usually intuition at work. Intuition is to be trusted.

If you are exploring the planet Pluto and in the process of looking around, you come upon your own front door and see a shadow-being fiddling with the lock, that is an intuitive psychic message that somebody is trying to invade your territory. The trick here is to be sure to take note of these surprise appearances, and *do* something about them. Nobody should be picking your lock or fiddling with your front door. Do not just pass up this information. Take it very seriously. The universe is trying to help you protect yourself.

Warnings in the Tunnel

Not everyone who journeys will find himself in a tunnel, but many do. The tunnel is what leads from the entrance point out into the spaces beyond this realm. When you see anybody at all in that tunnel who is not a power ally, beware. Nobody should have access to your power places. Nobody except you and your spirit friends has any business in your tunnel or at your entrance place(s).

The appearance of someone in the tunnel or at the entrance does not necessarily mean that you are being attacked. Some folks are just nosy and, by nature, intrusive. Some people know no boundaries. This does not make them evil. But you do have to address this situation. For one thing, your spiritual territory is being invaded. For another, the presence of a being who does not belong in your space will pollute that space with its own energy.

Shamanic Exorcism

Because you are not the whole shaman—the universe comprising at least half of the shamanic partnership—you do not have to be the whole exorcist. When you see somebody at your door or intruding in your tunnel, stop whatever you are doing and ask your power allies for help.

Do this by stating clearly that you have seen George in your tunnel, or a stranger at your front door. Do not assume that your spirit allies have seen everything you have seen. Tell them there is somebody there and ask, immediately, for their interpretation of this situation. If your horse shrugs as if to say, "It's no big deal," then you are not under attack. You must get rid of the intruder anyway, but you have nothing to be alarmed about. Ask the horse for help. Or call out into the universe for guidance. "Somebody is messing with my front door and I want him out of my territory."

Consider very seriously whatever advice comes to you in vision or in feeling. Usually, I find, the first help offered is the best help. Do what needs doing in order to:

A) get rid of the intruder, and
B) protect your physical and psychic space.

You do not at any time have the right to harm another person. The fact that he may have harmed you or attempted to do so does not give you the right of retaliation. To fight evil with evil is to increase the quantum of evil in the universe. You never have that right no matter how angry you may be. You do have the right to remove anything alien from your tunnel and entrance, your psyche, your spirit, your house.

Mirrors

When there is something around you that you do not like, immediately envision yourself throwing a mirror, the reflecting side outward, away from you and toward the intruder. Wrap yourself in the mirror. Mirrors are magical things; a person staring at his own reflection cannot see past his own essence into someone else's essence. The mirror serves to stop the enemy and, sometimes, to show you who he is.

Call on your power ally to remove the entity. Do not expect the ally to remove him unless you ask it to. It seems, to our waking self, only common sense that a powerful ally will remove undesirable influences from around us without our having to ask him to, but that is not so. Your ally cannot interfere with your free will by taking the initiative in this—or any other—matter. You must first learn to take seriously the messages you get while journeying, then decide what to do about the messages, and then ask for help in the doing. Those are three steps. You have to move from one step to another by your own will.

Your power ally is not your servant or your master. He is a guide and an empowering force. He cannot do for you what you must do for yourself. It is your job to pay attention to what you experience while journeying and then to decide what actions to take. Only after you have exercised your free will may your ally help you. He must not make decisions for you.

Getting Our Bearings: The Three Shamanic Worlds

The levels of universal realities are usually described in shamanism as the lower world, middle world, and upper world. While any element of one may be found in another, I find the usual attributes of the three levels to be these:

The *lower world* gives a view of the truths behind what guides this world and manifests in it. Appearances change between the world we live in and the lower world. The true essence of life here will be seen in the lower world. Any activity having to do with health, illness, or conditions that threaten the mind, emotions, or body will manifest in the lower world. Work pertaining to healing or energizing will usually take place there.

The *middle world* is the world we live in during waking consciousness, but when we make a shamanic journey to this middle world we find differences between the middle world as it appears in our journeys and as it appears when we are living in ordinary reality. These differences may be just enough to make the middle world seem slightly askew in relation to "reality." The middle world, of the three shamanic worlds, is closest in appearance to actual reality.

The *upper world*, I have found, is best described as containing absolutely everything not found in the lower and middle worlds—in addition to everything that *is* found in the lower and middle worlds. I am not being facetious here. The upper world appears to hold unlimited experience and there is no end to what we can see, feel, perceive, or learn from the upper world. Many times, after journeying to the lower or middle world, I check the information I have received by journeying into the upper world. There, I generally find verification in a manner very different from what I experienced in the lower or middle world. I may also receive extensions of those middle or lower world experiences. Divination takes place in the upper world.

The upper world journey takes us to the very origins of life, to abstractions we cannot know about from our waking consciousness, theoretical truths we would never dream possible because within the limits of our waking and even our sleeping consciousness, some upper world realities do not translate into anything we can bring into human consciousness.

The lower world is the origin of realities that are manifested in the realm we live in. If the initial concept of our realities comes from the upper world, then the first concrete manifestation *of* each idea will be found in the lower world. An idea or phenomenon is born in the upper world, but shaped in the lower.

Once that concretized idea has become part of our world, it takes on attributes that vary according to who is viewing the idea. The middle world is our personal view of what began in the upper world and was made *actual* in the lower world.

Please bear in mind that these definitions reflect my journeys. They may not suit your experiences at all. If they are not useful to you, set them aside.

One reason why shamanism is the safest of all the esoteric disciplines is that, with work that relies heavily upon abstractions, such as magical work, we must deal with symbols and incantations created by other people a long time ago and used since their inception by so many people that we cannot know what vibrations have attached themselves to those symbols and incantations. The use of magical technique can be compared to wearing someone's hand-me-down clothing; you cannot control the vibrations adhering to the clothes and you would probably be better off buying new ones if you can.

While there are shamanic techniques extant from many cultures, you cannot use any of them without changing them to suit your character, and the universe will not allow you to use them without altering them to suit its needs. There is no chance that you will be able to follow any shamanic technique in precisely the same way another person used it because you don't share the same power allies. Also, the ways in which you interact with the all-life will never be exactly the same as the all-life's relationship with another journeyer.

In shamanic work there is much variation between individual journeyers, whereas in magical work there is a fundamental need to maintain formulae. To the same degree that shamanic work leaves much room for personality and character differences between shamans, ritual magic allows for no difference between operators.

The shaman is her own woman by virtue of her inability to make much use of other people's methods. She has to find her own way. She must work peacefully with the all-life, which will give her short shrift if she takes a superior attitude toward it or tries to push it around. This means that, over time, any tendency she has to manipulate other people or any aspect of the universe will be tamed because cooperation with the universe and the acknowledgement of its importance to her work is fundamental to shamanism.

Once we let ourselves journey into the spirit realms of the universe, and do so without allowing our intellect or waking prejudices to interfere with our spiritual nature, when we decide to let our spirit lead us, then we are truly on the way to the full shamanic experience. There are two decisions, however, that must be made before any journey, and these are:

(A) the selection of the realm to be visited

(B) the reason for our journey.

If we are journeying for the purpose of helping an ailing friend, we cannot allow ourselves to wander around and happen upon whatever is out there. There will always be intriguing experiences in journeying, but loose journeying is a bad idea. If we begin by telling ourselves our purpose in journeying and then select the most appropriate of the three shamanic worlds, we will have more satisfying and effective journeys than if we wander indiscriminately.

Once these two decisions are made, however, our movement can allow for no set pattern and the contents of a journey can never be anticipated. This is true no matter how many times we have journeyed to a particular place, and no matter how many times we have undertaken journeying for the same purpose. Nobody knows, when he embarks on a shamanic journey, what he will encounter. This, more than anything else, makes shamanism the most spiritually honest of all the occult paths.

Knowing that there is a universe full of help for us, knowing that our obligation is to honor that universe and approach it in a spirit of humility, we cannot go wrong. If we are attacked along the way by an unfriendly presence, there is help to tell us it is there and help to get rid of it. All we have to do is to be respectful and pay attention to everything we experience.

The magician, on the other hand, does not necessarily have any friends in the animal, mineral, or plant kingdoms. If he is approached by evil—and evil follows the work of magicians most carefully—he may not know he is in danger because he has no power allies to tell him what is going on. Not all magicians are psychic. If his intuition does not tell him he is in danger, and if he has no friends in the all-life, he may get himself into terrible trouble. Often the techniques of magic are performed in solitary. It is not possible to do shamanic work all by yourself. The shaman is a continuum made up of himself—a focused, open intelligence—combined with the permitting, protecting universe. The magician is often alone; the shaman never is.

Protection in Daily Life

The power allies we have—whether they are animal spirits, human, trees, or fantastical beings whose appearance does not conform to anything we know in earthly life—are all real beings and not figments of our imaginations. In shamanism you cannot have it both ways and expect to thrive; either the experiences we undergo and the beings we meet are real, or else they are all in our minds. If you believe that everything non-ordinary has its origins in your head, well, good luck. If you understand that the elements of the non-ordinary, the essential truths of all realities and all aspects *of* those truths are just as real as we are, then you know that the beings we encounter while journeying have needs, as you and I have needs.

The principal need that we have in relationship to our power allies, one that we must satisfy for our sake and theirs, is the need to maintain daily contact with them while we are awake, and to include in our communion with them a physical means of expressing their nature throughout our bodies. If our allies are animals, we must address their physicality through our bodies as far as we can. A bird ally must fly, so we flap our "wings" and "soar" around, as he would do if he were living in concrete reality. If our ally is a wolf, we must get down on all fours and run, jump, and be a lively wolf. If our ally is a tree, we must "become" a tree for a little while each day. This process cannot be accomplished through fantasy. It cannot be taken care of while journeying. We have to physically maintain our allies while awake and do it with as much physical motion as possible.

For obvious reasons, we do this when we are alone.

Grounding with the allies is vital to our health. We can keep in touch with our allies without physical contact, by talking to them or thinking about them. But therein lies the danger: If we keep a strong bond with our power allies and do not ground that contact, we will be drawn toward their world and away from this one. Thinking about our allies allows our consciousness to drift toward the realm the ally lives in, and away from this realm. It is only natural that both you and your ally will move toward the realm of spirit because this is where you do your journeying and it is where he lives. If you do not ground the relationship through physical activity, your soul will be attracted to the ally's realm and you can gravitate so far away from this realm that you may suddenly have a bad accident.

As long as you want to keep your soul inside your body, move that ally around as befits his physical attributes. If he is a tiger, prowl and run. If he is a being with no strongly defined physical outline, ask him what physical movements will suit him. Do not be fooled, by frequent waking contact with your power ally, into thinking that his proximity and frequent contact means that you are safe. What happens when we discontinue the *physical* expression of the ally is that our attention increasingly follows the ally into his realm. *Energy follows attention.*

At last, there is so little of our energy here in this realm that we may simply leave this world because we are no longer firmly attached. That kind of leaving is a terrible accident and not our true intention.

Our power ally will, by nature, tend to position our attention, there, instead of here, because it has its life there. We must counteract this pull by returning our attention to here, because, except for when we are journeying, here is where we live.

Insuring a continuing bond with the ally is *not* all that matters, for the bond may be so strong that it pulls us into the spirit realm. What matters most of all is maintaining the bond in a way that keeps us safely alive.

All journeying should end by securely grounding ourselves in this realm, employing whatever methods are necessary for assuring that we are fully inside our bodies. Touching our forehead and palms to the floor or the earth brings us back into the body effectively, as does eating a light meal or sipping a cup of something hot that does not contain liquor.

Mediumship; The Open Gate

Mediumship is not for the indiscriminate believer of every-thing occult and it is not for the faint-of-heart.

A medium is a living person who works as a conduit between the realm of the living and discarnate spirits or dead spirits. The difference between *discarnate* (non-incarnated) and *dead* is that dead spirits are beings, usually human ones, whose deaths were not completed successfully. Some or all of their consciousness remains here. A dead spirit, by definition, exists in an undesirable condition. Death is a journey into a new life, not an extended mode of earthly life. Dead people are not here because there is any valid need for their presence in the realm of the living, but because they are stuck here.

Discarnate beings are not dead people but spirits who parti-cipate in earth life without having a physical form. These spir-its may be part of any of the kingdoms here—stone, plant, animal or human—and may function fully within that kingdom. They desire to be here without the obligation and restrictions incumbent in taking a physical form.

Whereas discarnate beings function as whole entities, not separated from any of their spirit or consciousness, and lacking only physical form, dead people are often not whole. Some of their consciousness has remained here while the rest of their spirit and some of their consciousness has journeyed through the death passage. These dead spirits are, then, partial people. Sometimes a dead spirit is an entire spirit, meaning that none of him except his body has managed to go on the death jour-ney. Dead spirits are not, by definition, good people or bad ones. Both malevolent people and good ones can fail to make a successful death journey.

Discarnate spirits are also not, by definition, either good or bad spirits. A discarnate spirit may be one who has never incarnated in this world at all. If he was incarnated among us, then he made a successful death passage before electing to return here in order to perform a task. A discarnate spirit may be here to aid a group of people, animals, plants or stones. He may have a temporary mission or a long, on-going overseeing job. A discarnate spirit may be malevolent and come here to create trouble in our world or to continue the negative activities of a previous incarnation.

The sole difference between discarnate spirits and dead people is that a dead person has been among the living, whereas a discarnate being may never have lived among us in a physical body or, if he did, has managed his death passage successfully and then returned to our realm for a purpose.

A medium may receive impressions psychically or through the faculties of hearing, seeing, or touching. Some mediums allow their bodies to be used by discarnate spirits for brief periods during which the spirit talks, gestures, or moves around in the body of the medium. The medium may or may not recall the experience after the spirit has departed his body. Such activities are usually called trance mediumship because the medium is either in a trance or away from his body during the time the spirit works through him.

Most often, in our culture, mediums do not allow spirits to use their bodies. Rather, they receive messages and pass them from the spirit who gives those messages to the living for whom they are meant.

The spirits for whom the medium is a conduit may be beneficent spirits, evil spirits, or merely floating bits of consciousness left in this realm by a dead person who did not manage his death well. They may be mischievous spirits on the look-out for someone who will play with them. They may be dead people who have sought out the medium because they wish to say something to a living friend or relative and, being dead, cannot make themselves heard.

If a spirit is felt around us, it is the tendency of the beginner to assume that there is, in the visit, something worth exploring. Most often, this is not the case, for the realm of the dead is filled with confused spirits, and these are the ones most likely to visit us. They are not wise. They are merely dead. They haven't the ability even to handle their own needs let alone help us. Surely they will respond if we talk to them, but their presence can be of no use to us because to be dead is not to be informed, it is just to be dead.

Making *any* assumption about floating spirits is a big mistake, and when we compound the mistake by allowing the dead to create false information for us, we run the risk not only of being misled but of becoming a way-station for every misdirected spirit in the universe. If we encourage visits from someone about whom we have made erroneous assumptions, we will find ourselves receiving lots more visits—all useless, all bound to lead us down the wrong path.

Testing Spirits

The first safe means of testing a spirit is to refuse to engage its attention or let it engage yours. If we refuse to play, a mischievous spirit will leave and probably not come back.

While aware of the spirit, but refusing to talk with it or listen to what it has to say, check your feelings. What does the presence of the spirit engender in you? Does it make you feel warm? This *may* be a good sign but just as easily it may be a ruse: Spirits with trouble in mind can radiate a false warmth. It is a trick of energy control. A warmth, a charisma emanating from a spirit does not guarantee the spirit's good intentions.

Energy manipulation is not difficult to learn, and the idea that we can accurately read the intentions of another by sensing his energy is mistaken. At any rate, skill in reading spirit energy accurately, in those instances when it *can* be accomplished, requires years of practice.

The most sensible course with all spirits is to ignore them. If the spirit who desires to contact you is a beneficent one, he can come back after you have thought through the encounter with him and considered the whole question of contact with the realm of spirit.

Ignore the spirit. If he is a trouble-maker, an evil creature, or a bit of floating consciousness that seeks human interaction, he will probably give up and leave. Your sole job is to ignore him, fail to entertain him or be impressed by his attention to you.

You are perfectly safe when confronted by a spirit-being as long as you do not do what every inexperienced person does, which is jump the gun, make leaps of faith about the visit, or pressure yourself to understand everything the spirit puts out. You can make yourself a wreck by trying to accommodate what may be either a useless or a harmful encounter.

Send up a prayer to whatever higher power you believe in, making the prayer one of emotion, not intellect. Ask for protection and help. If the spirit is a bad one, the energy generated by your prayer will push him away from you and he may leave entirely. If the visitation is from a helpful spirit and it is worth your making an effort to be with him, the prayer will help make a bond between that spirit and your psychic faculty.

Hearing voices and seeing beyond the realm we live in is *not,* in itself, mediumship. People who have lost their mental balance can see and hear beyond this realm. It does not mean they are mediums. It means their psyches have no ability to filter and to discriminate. These people are not gifted. Rather, they are afflicted.

Mediumship is an evolved ability. It most often entails receiving spirit messages on a deep but conscious level. The eyes and ears of a medium are often bypassed when receiving these messages.

No medium is a trance medium unless she tells you so. The trance state, in which a conduit is aware of her surroundings but may be temporarily unable to respond to them, is, among mediums, only a sometime occurrence. Trance is not implied in the definition of mediumship, and unless a medium tells you she goes into trance as a matter of routine, you may assume that she does not.

Headless Corpses and Other Guests

I once knew an elderly woman whose many decades of experience as a medium and clairvoyant counselor had yielded up the full measure of experiences. Mrs. Allen told me about a client who consulted her periodically who always showed up surrounded by a group of ghosts. Her way of dealing with this was not to assume, as I, in the early years might have done, that if she intended to help the client then she had the same obligation to help his "friends." No. She never allowed her client past the front door until she announced that he was invited in but his friends would have to wait for him outside the house. This was not a prayer, nor was it a silently-expressed desire. She spoke out loud and very forcefully, and I am sure that if any of those spirits had tried to enter her house with their friend, she would have told her client that he could not come in. As it was, none of the ghosts ever tried to enter her house. Each time the client left the house, the ghosts would gather around him again, bobbing alongside him as he moved down the path toward his car.

An experienced medium is never enamored of the spirit world. For that reason she is safe in a way that incautious, overly-enthusiastic beginners are not safe.

Mrs. Allen told me that the one time she had to deal with undesirable spirits inside her home was an odd occurrence during which they failed to become visible to her until after the client had entered her house. She and the client, a middle-aged man she had never met before that single session, were seated at her table, talking, when suddenly there appeared a whole crowd of dead people, all missing heads. Bluntly, Mrs. Allen asked her client, "How come there are all these headless people around you? Do you know anything about what happened to them?" He turned very pale and fled from her house, the headless corpses sticking close to him as he ran off.

The fact that we offer help on a spiritual level does not mean that we are under the obligation to serve just any human being who walks in the door, or to accommodate the undesirable spirits they may bring with them. A doctor may refuse to help a patient if he feels like it, and a landlord does not rent to just anyone. That same right of refusal belongs to the medium, the shaman, the psychic healer, the counselor. Discernment is a fundamental responsibility of every practitioner of the esoteric disciplines.

The biggest problem we have in staying clear of mischievous and evil spirits is not the spirits, but ourselves. It is flattering to receive attention from spirits. Human nature predisposes us to enjoy attention, and attention from the beyond makes us feel awfully important. If someone has travelled all the way from the spirit realm just to visit with us, that says something about the advanced degree of our spirituality, doesn't it?

No, it does not. That assumption says that we are too gullible to be working with spirits. The spirit visitor may be floating without purpose. He may be disoriented. He may be setting us up for invasion or hoping to engage our attention so that he can have a playmate. He may know nothing about you—or everything there is to know. The fact that a spirit comes around tells us nothing whatever about either his purpose or our importance. This point is very hard for beginners to grasp. It is assumed, unfortunately, that *spirit* is synonymous with *spiritual*, which of course is not true. And if a spirit wants our attention, it is further assumed that we have a grand assignment, which reflects superbly on our talents and the high degree of our spiritual evolution.

All of which is nonsense. Floating dead people routinely waft through our homes. This neither makes them spiritual nor us exalted. When we are sensitive enough to feel their presence, the first thing we should do is to assume nothing about them or about our role in regard to them. In fact, we must insist that they leave, for if the contact between them and us is truly spiritual, it is best initiated when we are asleep. In our sleep state we are, unless very tired or emotionally overwhelmed, capable of discrimination by virtue of our broader awareness and greater sensitivity. When asleep, we have access to the wisdom of the collective unconscious and therefore we are much more likely to connect to the wisdom of our higher self and deeper mind, than we are during waking consciousness.

A legitimate spirit connection will be made safely in our sleep state. After that initial connection, where our safety is considered, we may continue the connection in our waking state. No spirit of good intention would ever demand that a waking person shove aside concern for his safety. No spirit of good intention would ever be demanding of a living person in any way.

The first contact made should be in the sleep state, where we are protected by the best of ourselves. When a spirit enters our waking consciousness, the only safe course—until we have learned the art of discernment and can handle such visits—is to ignore the spirit.

The Ouija Board

This is a fool's game.

Many occult objects are magnetized, that is, dedicated to a particular purpose and imbued with energy suitable to furthering that purpose. The Ouija board is such an object, and the magnetizing is all bad. The spirits who crowd around the Ouija board are always, without exception, low-level entities. They will introduce themselves as Jesus, Einstein, your brother who died in Vietnam, the spirit of a martyr who died right on the spot your house now occupies, or anything else that will make you talk to them. They are never Jesus or your brother or anybody worth bothering about. They are tricksters; sometimes they are lost souls. Anything they tell you is either wrong or injurious to you. Your first contact with them will encourage them to return to the Ouija board every time you pick it up. It will also bring them into your house. It is a lot harder to get a spirit out of your house than to dismiss it from a seance.

Relatively Safe Seances

If you must fool around with this kind of thing, the preferable way is to create your own seance table. First, write out the numbers, zero to nine, and each letter of the alphabet, plus the words "yes" and "no", and then cut each of the letters and numbers into single pieces and arrange the pieces in a circle, facing up and inward, on top of a smooth surface. Place a clear, undecorated and unbroken glass, such as a small juice glass, in the center of the circle. Have everyone present place one finger lightly on the glass. This puts energy into the glass and allows it to move around the circle, spelling out words. Do not push the glass; touch it gently.

Do not neglect to say prayers for your protection and guidance before you start the seance. If you do not ask for protection, you are unlikely to receive any.

The whole point to a seance is to contact a spirit worth talking to, not just some useless floating consciousness. The key to a successful seance is to make the spirits who come to you do *all* the work of communicating. Do not let impatience rule you and, when the spirit has spelled out "Ba," jump in with "Are you trying to spell out the name 'Barbara'?" If the spirit has anything important to tell you, he can spell the whole message out without any aid from you. Do not prompt him and do not give him any information.

When the seance is over, before the participants leave the seance table, pray aloud for the protection of each participant and ask that no spirit who attended the seance be allowed to hurt anyone there. Make it clear, out loud, that no spirit who attended the seance is permitted into the homes or the lives of any of the participants, in the physical, etheric or astral realms.

Because we human beings tend to be easily flattered by the attention of spirits, we take chances with the spirit realm that we would never take with ordinary people. Would you leave your doors and windows unlocked? If you did, how surprised would you be if you were robbed? Yet this is exactly what we do when we indiscriminately allow untested spirits to roam our homes and interact with us. Spirits who attend most seances and all Ouija board sessions are low-level beings. What do you suppose you will learn from them?

Channeling: The Grim Charade

Because no spirit of an advanced degree of spirituality, no ascended master or guardian spirit would ever stoop to abusing the writing or speaking talents of another person, living or dead, what kinds of spirits do you think are behind channelling and automatic writing?

Channelling anything other than our own higher selves is the occult version of picking up a hitch-hiker. We open ourselves to dangers on a physical level when we give a ride to a hitch-hiker; the esoteric consequences are far worse. These involve the discontinuation of our contact with our astral (soul) self, for the entity we have allowed to invade us gets between the waking self and the astral body *right away.*

Channelling of any kind other than of our own higher selves is possession or a prelude to it. The possessor may be primary evil, or he may be a sorceror practicing secondary evil. He may be dead and use the channel to increase and extend his influence in the world of the living. He may be alive and use the channel in order to increase his power. Developing power and gaining a wide range of territory is what possessing spirits achieve from channelling. What does the channeller get? He loses his ability to discern, as he is cut off from his higher self. He loses his bearings and effectively gives up his life to the possessor, following the possessor's desires and not his own. He loses etheric integrity because there is someone appropriating his energy. In the end, when his usefulness has run out or he is depleted, he will lose his life. His connection to his own soul is so weak from interference by the possessor and his etheric body so degraded and depleted that he will eventually float away from his body because it cannot accommodate him any longer. He does not lose his soul by being possessed. He loses his life so that he can reunite with the soul which, still maintaining its integrity and its energy, will call the earth–bound portion of the human being back to it.

While channelling appears, to the uneducated, to be a kind of mediumship, this is an inaccurate perception. A medium is a conduit whose faculties and integrity remain his own while he passes messages from beings to incarnate ones. The medium may allow himself to be used, *physically* by a spirit, but his astral and etheric bodies are not damaged by temporarily accommodating a spirit power. The spirit uses the medium and then leaves. He does not alter anything in the medium and his presence is not an intrusion because he leaves nothing of himself and takes nothing from the medium.

When channelling involves using only our higher self, there is no invasion going on within the channeller. His higher self has the right to speak through him; no outside party is involved. The morality of this kind of communication is questionable, to say the least. While the channeller himself is not intruded upon and is therefore in no danger of possession or depletion, he is—whether he knows it or not—fooling people if he introduces himself as anything other than himself. If he says to his audience, "I channel my own higher self," he is being scrupulously honest with them. If he presents his channel as anything except himself he is perpetrating a fraud on his audience.

There are surely many instances of channelling in which the channel really is the channeller's higher self, while the channeller himself is unaware of this. In such cases he is, strictly speaking, doing nothing immoral. He does however need some educating in the art of discernment.

In situations involving possession (assault at the onset and out-and-out possession at the culmination) when the channel believes himself to be accommodating either his own higher self or another being, the channel is in great danger.

The popularity of channelling is due to the intense passivity with which people live their lives. If we did not pursue passive roles with the gusto we bring to any endeavor in which somebody—anybody—other than ourselves tells us what to do, we would not be caught in this fad.

The lure in channelled communication is the spirit's professed love for humanity and the wonderful advice the spirit offers, which usually has to do with lofty pronouncements about the coming Earth changes and humanity's new role as spiritually-gifted beings. The hook works because we want to be told how worthy and spiritually important we are, and how rapid our ascent into divinity will be. We need to believe we are not alone in our search, that there are spiritually-advanced beings who will guide us every step of the way. Heaven forbid that we should attain our spiritual enlightenment without continual advice from mentors who are never wrong!

The package is yuppie metaphysics, spirituality-on-demand. It is offensive because the seeker bases his spiritual "education" on an egotistical need to become something wonderful, without being willing to find out, on his own, what constitutes being wonderful. The motivating force here is the searcher's personal ego, the ego of the wrong self, and his sad belief that he cannot find God except through the intervention of another being.

The truth is that all spiritual advancement is attainted in a state of solitude. Yes, we have help from the higher realm—lots of it—but we cannot lean on it, call it on the phone, or study with it in a workshop. We are built to be independent, and no higher realm teaching master would endeavor to pull us toward him, as these channelled entities pull everyone toward them that they can.

What is actually at work for the listener in channelled communication? He likes what he hears, perhaps because the contents flatter his lofty view of himself or because the content of channelled messages is often sound. When the latter is the case, we are attracted to the channelled material because it reflects our own views and our own knowledge—both of which would truly *be* ours if we searched our own psyches and found our way to waking contact with the collective unconscious. When you listen raptly to channelled messages, you are hearing what you could be finding out on your own, in partnership with the all-life, in safe situations that do *not* involve possession, the presence of evil energies, inept "mediumship", group hypnosis or plain human greed.

An essential tenet of all occult discernment is the

understanding that the display of an ability such as healing or psychism is not an indicator of intention on the part of the doer. Evil beings can heal. Healing involves two steps, removing an energy and replacing it with another. Anyone can learn to heal. It is the same with good advice—anyone can give it. The words of wisdom, healing power, insights and information coming through during a channelling session may be good but *this tells you nothing about the power behind these phenomena.* Do not confuse the singer with the song. Is a good medical doctor always a fine human being? Is a good plumber always an exemplary fellow? Do we make these assumptions about the living? No. But we make these assumptions about the unseen, when we ought to be far more vigilant than in our mundane encounters.

No higher realm being, guardian, master or good spirit would circumvent universal law by engaging in channelling. Everyone who channels is either channeling his own higher consciousness—perhaps without knowing so—or performing an act or being duped.

Malicious beings who work through human dupes first acquire energy by presenting themselves as impeccable teachers and thus achieving our respect and devotion. Devotion is energy. Their job is facilitated by our addiction to passivity. And who can resist the words of joy and brotherhood these evil ones give us? It is awfully gullible to assume that the pronouncements made by a spirit are meant sincerely! Do we suppose that an evil being will announce himself *as* evil? Of course not. He will announce himself as the messiah or an advanced being of another dimension, or someone from a hovering UFO. In lulling us into believing he is good for us, he tells us all the exalted philosophy we wish to hear until, once we are hooked, he can tear our energy from us and lead us into dangerous practices whenever possible.

These beings are *not* creatures of love. They have designs on us. Of course they begin their spiel with messages of love and trust. Would we listen if they said, "I want to abuse your energy and appropriate your mind"?

In occult work, it is imperative that we exercise discrimination. No sane occultist ever takes anything at face value. This is not a matter of paranoia. Your spiritual evolution, your sanity, and maybe your life depends on understanding a few basic truths: One of these truths is that no higher realm being ever speaks through a channel, or communicates through automatic writing.

Channels As Victims

When a channeller is not channelling his own higher mind or fabricating, then he is being possessed. In the course of this association with malevolent discarnate beings, he will lose energy and perhaps his life. It is a horrible situation. This ghastly fad encourages ignorance on the part of the channeller—to whom it may prove fatal—and also on the part of the channeller's audience, who will gain nothing but harm from their encounters with discarnate evil. No matter how secure or how well-tutored they feel at the beginning of the association, they will come out of it in need of spiritual guidance and possibly exorcism.

What lessons can we learn from the dreadful error of channelling? We must learn that manipulative beings are entirely capable of presenting themselves as warm, wonderfully-spiritual, sympathetic, advanced "masters," and that their ability to heal, psychic insights and peaceful philosophy tells us nothing *truthful* about their motives. In the realm of spirituality, discernment is everything.

In the interactions between ourselves and true spirituality, there are no guides from *UFO's,* no "knowledgeable" beings from fifty thousand years ago to invade our minds and collect crowds of unwary, vulnerable seekers. No being of good intent would participate in this horror. These are malicious entities who are harming, not helping, the human race and the faster we learn to deny them access to us, the healthier we will be.

New Age Approach to the Occult

Anyone who involves himself in the study of the esoteric needs to understand the realities of the search and to be prepared for the kinds of troubles that *inevitably* meet every seeker. There is no reason to be frightened of the occult as long as we realize that discretion and discernment are mandatory. The seeker must know how to keep himself safe from invasion by discarnate beings and living occultists who will make attempts upon his power, his talent, and possibly his life.

There is, among New Age people, an astonishing lack of good sense and a dangerous Pollyanna attitude toward the realities of the occult. New Agers like to believe they can pick and choose which elements of the occult they will deal with, and leave the rest alone. This is folly. When the door to the occult is opened, light and darkness spill out together. The idea that as long as we don't believe in evil it cannot harm us is disastrously wrong. Our beliefs have no influence on the realities behind esoteric work.

A cheerful attitude has a great impact on all aspects of our lives. But this should not be translated to mean that we *control* all the aspects of our lives by taking a positive attitude, or that we can control other people. No spiritual seeker ever attained knowledge and power by blinding himself to his own stupidity.

Counseling: Guiding Others on Spiritual Journeys

Whether we counsel through shamanism or mediumship, whether we are healers, card-readers, crystallographers, ritualists or exorcists, we need to maintain compassion for our clients while behaving toward ourselves in a sympathetic manner.

There is no reason why a lay person should have any idea what process you go through while counseling him. Unless he has had extensive experience with esotericists, he may think your talent can be easily turned on and off like a faucet, without any cost to you. It is not his fault that he does not know how much is involved.

It is our responsibility to treat outselves well without cheating the clients who come to us for help. We can do this by taking on as much work as we can handle, instead of booking as many clients as we can in one day. Counseling is not like making sandwiches or hammering crates. It is impossible to anticipate how much energy we will be required to give any single client. We must schedule ourselves with room between sessions for gathering our energies, for reflection. It is dangerous for a psychic or a medium to become depleted.

Some clients need only help for themselves, and our time with these people is not as demanding of us as is the case with clients who bring spirits with them. It is one thing to counsel and help a single client, quite another to be visited by his departed mother who died a horrible death and needs your help.

Being with a spirit whose death torments him can be a shattering experience for a medium. Finding such a soul while journeying can be just as difficult for the shaman.

Many times, while doing readings for clients, I am visited by a spirit who wants me to pass a message along to the client. I will not do that until I am satisfied that the spirit is what he says he is, and a spirit's story can be verified only after I have communicated with it for awhile. The stories of some departed spirits are terribly sad, and it is not possible for me to shut down my feelings while talking with either the client or the spirit. Of course, I have to stay as dispassionate as possible while the client is present, but sometimes when a reading is over with I get upset about the client's story or, more often, the spirit's story. While the living always know that tomorrow can be better, a spirit's life truly is over and done with, and a spirit may express heart-rending regrets about his life.

While the client is under no obligation to cater to a counselor's feelings, it might be helpful and would surely be kind if clients recognized that counselors are people too, and can be expected to respond empathetically to their stories and the stories related by visiting spirits.

Once I consulted a psychic reader whose insights about my past were very good, though she had no advice to offer.

Curious about her method of working, I asked if she would mind telling me how she got her insights. Was it through visions? Feelings? She replied that during sessions she saw a line of endless tickertape on which words were printed: she got her insights from the printed words.

I was appalled. Who needs a counselor so lacking in feeling that she gets information from a computer printout? Without empathy, there can be no true counseling because there are no insights, only cold facts.

Fears Born of Awe: How Our Clients View Us

The strange dynamic that occurs during a counselling session in which shamanism, mediumship, clairvoyance, or healing is employed involves an irony of which any counselor needs to be aware. The client wants you to be accurate in your reading of his needs, but at the same time he doesn't want you to unsettle him.

Even people who claim to treat the whole realm of psychism and the so-called supernatural as a joke usually have some desire for a bona fide non-ordinary experience. The client will become receptive to you once the reading begins. He may allow you full access to his being. But when the reading is done, he may shut the door on you without warning. Why? Because you have changed all the rules regarding what is and is not possible, and he cannot understand how you did it. Your demonstration of clairvoyance, whatever your methodology, is disturbing to him.

When he realizes that you can see beyond the sky, then he comes dangerously close to the possibility that *he* can see beyond the sky. If you breach the "reality" of the three dimensions, talk with his late grandmother, travel through space and time to find his lost power ally, or accurately recount an experience he had ten years ago without any clues from him, the client's whole view of reality is shaken. He sees that he has spent his entire life investing in a reality which may be bogus.

The average person simply cannot bear to challenge the truth of his assumptions, and when you shake his fundamental bond with reality by demonstrating that the limitations he believes in do not exist for *you,* then he has to confront the possibility that they may not exist for *him.*

This is very hard for some people, and you must be aware of how threatening the seeing-beyond process is for them. Tread gently with them, and make no direct assault on their newly-shaken view of reality. If you challenge someone when he is not ready to accept a challenge in a positive, healthy way, you may cause an emotional disturbance you are not equipped to heal.

It is our job to help and, in small doses, to offer our clients a bigger picture of the sky than they are used to. It is not our job to brow-beat anyone into seeing things as we do. If we force someone to confront what he is not ready for, we may cause a terrible disruption within him. Nobody ever achieved a cosmic view overnight—including ourselves. Remember how long you've been seeking?

Because of a client's ambivalence, wanting you to help him while being afraid of what you are able to show him, he could react to your work in positive and negative ways at the same time. Having talked warmly and openly with you during the session, he may, when the work is done, turn abruptly cold and leave in a hurry. He may become sarcastic. You may hear from him very soon or never again.

Do not confuse his response to the session with the validity of your work, or use his reaction to you as a measure of your worth or an assessment of the efficacy of the job you did. If you gave him something of value, you did your job. Our work must always meet *our* standards. Any time we view our work with the prejudices of other people, we are off-course. We cannot, in an hour or two, force another person to accept the fact of clairvoyance or traveling outside of time. We cannot force another to change his views of reality.

The client must deal with your non-ordinary talents as best he can. If you can soothe him before he leaves, do. If he insists on having a bad reaction to his new view of "reality," he may need that reaction in order to maintain his delicate psychic balance. You must leave him to sort himself out. If he is at all in touch with himself, he will.

Cherishing Our Resources

Lay people cannot know what kind of effort and preparation is required for you to heal, to journey for them, to see into their lives clairvoyantly. No one who has not trekked the medium's path can know how much experience it takes to separate wheat from chaff. No one who has not counselled others can realize the effort and agility needed for choosing the right words, for helping people instead of alarming them.

It takes a long time to get from, "Oh my God! There's a black spot in your aura!" to "Would you like to learn how to smudge? Your abdomen needs some healing, and you will like smudging. It is very cleansing and it smells great."

Because the inexperienced do not know your physical and psychic limits, it is important that you learn them and respect them. People must not be allowed to call on you at any hour of the day or night. If you do not establish boundaries, that is precisely what they will do. Why shouldn't they? To the lay person, your gifts are just that, gifts, and you neither worked to get those gifts nor require any rest from your labors. You are a mystical, and therefore unreal, being.

It is your job to make rules about calls and visits and also to make rules about encounters with spirits. Spirits live outside of time and are therefore likely to drop in whenever they feel like it. To a spirit, there is no such thing as too early or too late because there is no time-constant, as there is for us living people.

The fact that you have a talent which is unusual in our society does not mean you have been assigned the role of martyr. You are not an all-night diner to be dropped in on when people are hungry for a little spiritual nourishment.

In our culture, people are usually profligate with their own spirits; we must not allow them to be profligate with ours.

The Occultist As a Friend

In making friends with people who are not involved in esoteric studies, we occultists usually get the better bargain. People like us are not fun to be friends with. We cannot make plans far in advance because we never know when Spirit will move us to do something that forces us to cancel party plans or dinner dates. We should be grateful for the handful of citizens who are willing to put up with us at all. I have no idea why anybody puts up with me and I have not understood that for well over twenty years.

The relationship between an occultist and a non-practitioner can be touchy if rules are not laid out from the start. We must keep our schedules intact. Lay people have no idea that a quick phone call to us to find out whether it is going to be a good day at work tomorrow can be draining. We are not machines. If we explain this early on, a great deal of trouble can be avoided.

One difficulty the occultist experiences with lay people is the way in which these friends treat their own spirits. In a crisis, they know they have a spirit because it hurts so much. They call on us for help. But when the crisis passes, they may turn from us because the level of intimacy involved in their confiding in us overwhelms them. Also, they do not know why anyone would wish to live on a level of such acute awareness most of the time, as we do. It unsettles them. Expect this reaction, because sometimes it will happen.

When Our Friends Die

People in our culture ignore their own spirits whenever possible, often for years at a time. When it gets to be time to die, they panic. They may have focused their whole lives on worldly matters and now suddenly with death imminent they need to be rescued by someone who can give them an immediate plug-in to God.

Do not buy into that. Help them all you can, but if you represent yourself as a God-conduit, you are robbing the other of his chance, *perhaps the only chance he has had* in this lifetime, for a real relationship with his spirit and with Spirit. Do not, out of mistaken pity, step in and take over for him as he is dying. You would be denying him his one chance to come face-to-face with his own immortality. His destiny is his own. Leave him to it.

Be available for listening. If you know of particular techniques such as psychic healing or a homeopathic remedy that might help him, use these things. Counsel him to be at peace about death. The one thing you *must* do is tell him how to make a safe death journey, and explain to him how he can take all of his energy along with him on his journey (see Chapter 4). Ask the guardian spirit of the West to help him, making your request before your friend dies as well as after he dies. But refrain at all costs from telling him your perceptions of the Almighty or the hereafter because he will, untutored and in a panicked state, grab your ideas instead of searching for his own spirituality. Comfort him. Tell him all you can that will keep him safe, but do not dictate your view of spiritual reality and do not throw *The Tibetan Book of the Dead* at him. You cannot give a dying man a crash-course in world theology without making him frantic. Intellectual perceptions are not what he needs, anyway. Give him aid and comfort, but do not impose yourself on him.

You and Your Community

When your neighbor is up against trouble he may come to you without knowing you as a friend knows you. You may have a reputation as a spiritual being. There is often someone in any community who is known for his interest in spirituality and can be counted on for some comfort and insights during hard times, or at least a little stimulating conversation. Your neighbor may approach you for some spiritual nourishment. He may wish to take from your bank a little spirituality to help him through the difficult period. And then, when the tough times are over, he will probably revert to the same shallow behavior that resulted in his emptiness and bereavement when he needed to know Spirit. These people often turn on a spiritual contact for being disruptive—despite the fact that *they* came to *you*—as though your eccentricity has messed with their minds. Let it be. Do not take it personally. But be warned that very rarely does a person who turns to spiritual interests only when he is up against trouble ever maintain his interest in the subject. And if he feels any self-reproach after the danger has passed, he may well turn that reproach on you. It is human nature. There is not much you can do about it except to know that these things sometimes happen.

The Pitfalls of Group Work

Any group encounter is potentially dangerous. There are energy thieves at many gatherings of occultists, especially where the over-enthusiastic come together. Workshops are prime targets because participants are usually very eager to learn occultism and at this eager stage they are not equipped with any discernment. These enthusiastic beginners take one workshop after another, in any subject, without availing themselves first of techniques for self-protection. In fact, a hallmark of New Age beliefs is that everything that happens to us is brought to us *by* us and is to be looked upon as a good thing. This is a ridiculous notion because we are not omnipotent. The idea that people can be acted *upon* and not be the whole force in their own lives does not fit beliefs. This mistaken notion will be corrected as more and more people learn the wisdom of the ancients and cease to confine themselves to questionable notions perpetrated by the unknowing on the unwary. Everything is not "beautiful in its own way." This is a truth we must all learn for ourselves. It cannot be passed along from one seeker to another, although a great deal of pain would be avoided if that were possible.

What, besides the presence of potential power thieves, is the reason for staying away from group work? The major reason is that every single time you involve yourself in another person's learning, you step away from your own spirit. Do this enough times and you forget what your own spirit feels like. Keep on seeking out others for their views of spiritual truths and there will come a day when you no longer recognize the resonating of your own spirit.

Workshops

In deciding whether to take this workshop or that one, we miss a vital question: Should we participate in group work at all? We usually begin our deliberations with the notion that a workshop leader has some knowledge that will be valuable to us. In thinking along these lines, we miss a fundamental issue. While the workshop leader may know something, there is little likelihood of his being able to give you what he knows. Real knowledge is never found that way. Knowledge—as opposed to mere information—is never handed from one person to another. Knowledge is achieved as our spiritual being moves with and responds to creation. You cannot write a check for it and nobody can give it to you no matter how much he knows because knowledge is not achievable through other people.

You can't get anything from others except information; wisdom is your own unique achievement, and it cannot be gotten in tandem. Worse than the illusion of "learning" that you abuse yourself with in doing group searchings is the blow you deal your spirit when you attempt to discover truths by following another person's tracks. We want to believe that if we do not like another's teaching, we can simply forget it, but I have found that we are often vulnerable to other people's misinformation. We are vulnerable because group learning separates our spirit and our intellect. No matter how experiential a workshop may be, information is passed through speech, and speech is an intellectual entity. Being intellectual, it does not often resonate to our spirituality.

Talking About Spirit

This is the biggest pitfall to spiritual growth. Each time we yak yak yak, we siphon energy from our spirit. Each time we make a wonderful connection and then talk about it, we disconnect ourselves from the wonderful moment by letting all the attendant energy fly out of our mouths. It is disrespectful of Spirit to yammer about it. What is called "sharing" in group work is destructive to the process we and our allies in the all-life go through in moving us from ordinary to non-ordinary reality. To speak of a vision you have just seen, to tell strangers about a revelation you have been gifted with, is wasteful and disrespectful. You lose the experience before it has time to settle into your being. Also, the spirits around you see that you place little value on their aid because you are willing to chatter about it and gossip about them.

Spirit and the Intellect

I often hear people say that exposure to the greatest possible wealth of spiritual ideas is a good thing because once a mental contact has been made, one can always forget the intellectual concepts and approach the subject in a new, more valid way. This is absurd. Once you have done something for the first time, you can never do it *for the first time* again. Sometimes I am told, "But if you learn something the wrong way, you can always go back and learn it the right way," which in delicate spiritual matters is a preposterous notion. Initial revelatory learning happens once. The experience of moving the veil of ignorance away for the first time is unique. We can no more go back and remove that veil a second time than we can lose our virginity twice.

An essential aspect of spiritual learning is the free and unencumbered dialogue between our higher mind and our spirit. It is our spirit, not our intellect, that receives spiritual messages and impulses. The all-life resonates to our spirit. The intellect does not share this resonation and can only get in the way of it.

If we allow our intellect to get between us and the spirit of the all-life we can easily forget what it feels like to be free of the intellect, and there are times when that feeling of oneness with the all-life is all that stands between us and a wrong turn.

Learning about profound esoteric subjects by consulting others is like asking someone to tell us what sex is like. There are some things we must experience for ourselves. The serious seeker must first make peace with the fact that he will have to find his own way. No matter how many teachers there are, no matter how many books, how many ideas circulating, the truth is that nothing worth learning can ever be taught.

The intellectual way is good enough for the shallow seeker, the day-tripper, the dilettante. For a true seeker, learning always takes place on a far deeper level. Those deep stirrings that take place outside the level of waking consciousness and then move into consciousness are the most informing, guiding and vivifying of all spiritual encounters.

If you find yourself involved in group work, ask yourself if you are doing this work to fill a lack. If that is the case, your spirit may be trying to tell you that you *do* have a need, but the need is for depth of work, not busyness, for profound contact with creation, not talking and listening to other people's talk. Your own spirit will gladly fill this need for you once you give it a chance to do so by leaving some open time in your life.

If we decide to participate in group work, we must consider our obligations to others in the group. We owe others sufficient physical space for each to do his work, about six feet of space in every direction, or ten feet if that can be arranged. We owe everyone in the group our good will. Beyond space and our good wishes, we owe others nothing. We do not have to reveal, during a workshop, the content of our experiences and we are fools if we do.

Tread on your visions and they will retreat. Use them for currency, to impress yourself and others, and you may never get visions again.

Above all else, Spirit knows where it is welcomed and appreciated, and where it is handled ungently, abused, or taken for granted.

Protection for the Ceremonialist, Ritualist and Magician

The most important protection anyone who engages in ritual work can create for himself is a sensible approach to other people's teachings. When we depend on a book, ancient or contemporary, or on a teacher, we are leaning on someone. Leaning on others is treacherous even when those others mean well.

Any ceremony can be flawed. Ritual and ceremony and the formulae of the magician are either inspired by human beings or inspired by Spirit and translated by human beings. People are not perfect. Their work cannot, therefore, be perfect. Most occultists, like all human beings, are always becoming-occultists, becoming-healers, becoming-ceremonialists. We do not stop becoming until we are dead. There is, then, always the possibility of a flaw in our concepts and our work, a mistake in formula, a misstep in ceremony. It can happen to anyone.

You cannot afford to risk taking on other people's mistakes, because you have your own to deal with. It is therefore bad policy to take ceremony from other people. If we allow our spirits to open themselves, we will be inspired to create rituals of our own, ones that suit our needs. If we create our own ceremonies and evolve the technical aspects of our magical work, our chances of identifying mistakes will be enhanced because we are in charge. Why compound our difficulties by incorporating into our ritual work other people's errors?

If you must use a formula you have read somewhere or a ritual someone taught you, you should, at the very least, take the precaution of asking the Almighty Power you work with to show you the existence of any error in the ritual. You should adapt the ritual, if at all possible, to your own spirituality and your own perceptions of the work you are undertaking.

If we do not make our work truly ours, what good is it? We are merely acting on others' inspirations, behaving like acolytes.

If you decide to use others' work, adapt it where possible to your own being. When that is not possible because a formula must not be altered, then at least be aware that you may be using something you ought not to use, and pray for guidance about this before using the ceremony in question.

Psychic Self-Defense for the Shaman

Because journeyers concentrate so often on the lower and upper world, they sometimes forget that the best protection against invasion is found in the middle world.

A technique that helps me is to periodically address the four cardinal directions, the earth, and the Creator, and ask them for protection from invasion. I do this several times a year. The most important time is whenever I feel I ought to make the request, for this request is sometimes prompted by intuition. It is unnecessary to feel the presence of danger in order to sense the need for protection. Often, by the time we can discern threat around us, the danger has been nearby for some time.

I always ask for help from God, the four cardinal points and the earth during both the Winter and Summer solstices, during the Spring and Autumn equinoxes, and before beginning any major enterprise. This brief ceremony is not fear-inducing, for anytime we call upon the six sacred directions, we engage the attention of powerful, inspiring forces. It is *fun* to talk to them, and there is often a delightful surprise in store when we engage the attention of these forces.

Do not perform this ceremony while journeying, but do it in a state of ordinary waking consciousness.

Using a rattle or a drum or a bell, or whatever sound-making friend I might prefer, I stand facing due East and address myself upward, to Mother-Father God. I ask for protection and say I want to know if there is a problem regarding attack. If I get any feeling of confirmation that a problem exists, I simply wait and say nothing further. If there is a problem, the Creator—through the all-life in any of its manifestations—can tell me what I need to know while I remain quietly receptive.

If I feel that there is no difficulty and no message is forthcoming from the direction of Mother-Father God, I then turn my attention to the East. Again using a sound-making friend, I ask East to provide me with protection. I usually say, "Please do not let anybody use you to hurt me," which is straightforward and clear.

I make the same request, in turn, of South, West, and North.

I then address the Earth, looking downward, and make the same request I made to Mother-Father God, asking that if anyone is invading me or my work, I will know of it. I ask for protection from the earth and end this brief ceremony by working again with the drum, bell or rattle.

This exercise does not take much time but accomplishes a lot. We make a request while we affect a connection with the six directions. The more we make this connection, the better, for each incident of communication between us and the sacred six directions builds a stronger bond.

Psychic Self-Defense for the Medium

The greatest part of all psychic defense is common sense. This is at least as true for anyone who routinely works with the dead as for other occultists.

A primary need for any medium is to keep himself distanced, physically and psychically, from the dead and other spirits. There are laws regarding the invasion of the living by the dead, but a discarnate being must be fully aware of himself and capable of controlling his actions if he is to keep those laws. Panicked dead people and unconscious spirits cannot be expected to adhere to laws, so the burden of safety falls entirely on the medium.

Whenever I decide to let a spirit talk to me, I first tell him aloud that he has to keep his distance. I tell him that he is not permitted anywhere near me and I use the phrase, "You have no permission to approach me," which is bona fide occultism for creating a wall between us. The spirit, no matter how unaware of himself and his actions he may be, no matter how frenzied, must keep away from my energy field and he knows it.

Only when I have made certain that the spirit means to obey the injunction against getting too close to me, will I talk with him. If I get a feeling that he is making up words as he goes along, or worse, trying to discover what I want to talk about, I tell him he has to leave. Immediately after dismissing him, I begin a prayer of protection for myself and guidance for the spirit. For one thing, this prayer brings strong energy into the room which protects me from harm; for another, it takes my attention away from the spirit. During intense prayer it is not possible to notice anything outside prayer. This discourages the spirit from trying to make further contact with me. He knows I am not listening to him or watching him.

Often, when we ask for help for the spirit, help arrives, and the spirit is led away to the realm in which he belongs. If help for the confused or rebellious spirit does not arrive, the spirit will wander away sooner or later because he has lost his audience.

My point is this: If you do not want to be a magnet for confused or difficult spirits, then refuse to give them your attention. Once you allow them to engage you in conversation, they will return again and again. If you befriend anyone who feels like wafting into your house, you will quickly find yourself living in a Grand Central Station for the dead and discarnate.

It has been my experience that the most important part of our esoteric work is in learning discernment, and learning what is and is not ours to deal with. No single person can possibly handle every occult situation, and the thinner we spread ourselves, the greater the chance that we will become weak. This is obviously dangerous to our mental, physical and spiritual health, and it renders us worse than useless to our clients: It makes us a danger to them because, in working from a position of weakness, we make mistakes. In the realm of the occult, we cannot afford mistakes. In occult work, we inevitably affect other people, often people we do not even know, because, by definition, our work touches the unseen. It is terribly important that we keep ourselves rested, balanced, and cheerful if we engage in any esoteric work, both for our clients' sake and for our own. To that end, we must give short shrift to any living person or spirit who does not belong in our work, our homes, or our consciousness.

Chapter 7

The Wolf at the Door:
Exorcism, Cleansing and Protection

"Truth is truth, and if I tell only the truth,
I have nothing to fear!"

—Turi's Book of Lappland, Johan Turi

Johan Turi's book, dictated in the first decade of this century,
tells of the troubles the Fell-Lapp reindeer herders were
plagued with during the worst of winter, when wolves, driven
by desperate hunger, came after the precious reindeer and were
very hard to drive away. These herders had no guns. What
they used to drive the wolves away was their voices. The
tricky aspect of shouting was the danger that, if a man shouted
directly at a wolf, the wolf would capture his voice.

How do we keep the wolf away without shouting at him
directly? That is, how do we avert the disaster of a direct confrontation with evil? We do it by examining and changing our
lives and finding our unique path in life, and by using methodology that works for us. Finding these methods is an on-going
project. In this chapter I will offer some exorcism techniques

that, when used with cleansing, protection and detection techniques, ought to aid the reader in an encounter with evil.

For both the occultist and the lay reader, self-determination as a law of life and common sense approaches to daily living are more important than techniques of exorcism. Technique, no matter how well-informed and beautifully-wrought, is always subordinate to our day-to-day existence. Whether life maintains us or depletes us depends on our level of awareness and spiritual integrity.

Concerning evil, the biggest problem is not the suspension of disbelief. In seeking a safe and richly-endowed life, it is not necessary to resolve the question of whether we do or do not believe in the existence of evil: Safe living is safe living, and the attention we give to making our lives the best they can be is what really matters. If you have had an encounter with evil, then you feel an urgent need to change your life and make it safer. If you have not, and if there is nothing in your experience to make you believe in the existence of evil, you can nevertheless lose nothing by changing unsuitable aspects of your life.

We are vulnerable to true evil and unfortunate encounters with accidental evil only to the degree that we make ourselves so. Vulnerability derives from what we choose not to know about what we refuse to see about the society in which we live, and our neglect of personal spiritual integrity.

How Evil Works on Us

We open our doors to evil of all varieties when we serve ourselves badly. Attacks on us would be ineffective if we did not leave doors open. These doors open through our inability or unwillingness to know ourselves thoroughly. What we do not know about the dynamics between us, other people and creation causes the greatest trouble. Failure to curb our negativities provides opportunities for evil invasion on two counts; it gives evil a chance to get its hooks into us each time we indulge in our negativity, and the continuation of negative feelings creates, in time, life-patterns from which it can be very hard to extricate ourselves. Predisposition to anger, a desire to hurt others, especially when we feel we have the "right" to do so, overattachment to melancholy or its twin, excitement, all of these are ways in for primary, secondary and accidental evil.

The mundane realities of living and our failure to address them responsibly offer means of attack. We may habitually run out of money, ignore balding tires or overload the electrical wiring in our houses. We may let our teeth deteriorate or eat food that weakens instead of nourishes us. Attention to the facts of daily living and responsible care-taking in every aspect of our lives shuts the door on a multitude of ills. The exorcism of bad influences begins with common sense.

Any bad attitude, any shaky area in our relationship to ourselves is always a means through which we can experience the full spectrum of difficulty, from bad luck to black magic. Unless we have had experience with psychic attack, we may have a run of so-called bad luck and suppose there is nothing we can do to avoid recurrences of it. The truth—and in our deeper selves we know this—is that we have a lot more control over what happens to us than we like to admit, and that much of the bad luck that befalls us begins with our unwitting complicity. If we acknowledged our own participation in many of the bad times that befall us, we would know there are a great many things we would have to stop doing, and other things we would have to begin doing. For many of us, it is simply too much work to *live,* so we allow ourselves to drift.

Ignorance

Ignorance is second only to fear as a threat to our balance and sanity. To be ignorant is to take for granted any aspect of life by leaning on another person's experience, view or belief.

What does this mean to each of us? We must actually create our lives, not just permit them to happen. We must remember that once this lifetime is done with, we are going to have to

account to our higher selves for everything we have done and
have not done. Life is very simple when we reduce it to the
two fundamental activities of living—doing and leaving
undone.

Doing by imitation leaves us stranded in a place outside our
own lives. Doing prompted by our own wanting is real life.
Everything else is false.

Leaving things undone, except in matters of urgent practical-
ity such as keeping the rent paid and feeding ourselves is a
wise choice for most of us, most of the time. A large percen-
tage of what we human beings do would be better left undone.
We would meddle less, worry ourselves less about trivia, waste
energy less and confuse ourselves less if we stopped doing
what most of us do, which is to fill time instead of living.

We know that ignorance is on the march when people are
attacked for their color or beliefs, but do we understand that
the ignorant passivity which allows people to join angry mobs
is the same ignorance that keeps us tied to jobs, people, and
circumstances we don't care about? The first is only a vivid
extension of the second.

Fear

Fear is a potent hypnotic influence in everyone's life. Fear
has a mundane and an esoteric vibration, and every kind of
fear has a mystical and a practical component. The practical
component of a fear of fire is the truth that fire can destroy.
What can we do about that? We can be careful when handling
fire, refrain from letting our young child pour lighter fluid on
the barbeque, have our electrical wiring checked.

The esoteric aspect of fear of fire is much harder to deal
with because our fears attract us to the very experiences we are
afraid of. When we fear something, we tend to think about it a
great deal. This creates a continual stream of fear-energy
within our psyches. We feed this stream each time we engage
in fearing. The instinctual part of us will always move
toward—not away from—whatever we create for its attention.

If we are frightened of being poor and ponder poverty often enough, each time investing our musings with emotion, we will create a poverty-fear within our consciousness. Our instinctual self, the same one that drives us to eat when we are hungry, is attracted to the poverty-fear we have created. It does not know that we fear poverty, pain or loneliness because we wish to stay away from them. It believes that we fear these things because we desire them. The instinctual lower mind is always drawn to what we feed it, and if we feed it images of fear, it will draw the feared situation to us—or draw us to the fear. Over time, we begin moving closer and closer to the very experience we wish to avoid.

Energy Creates Intention. Our lower mind perceives our thoughts, our fears as intentions. It then escorts our energies toward the experience. Fears, when chewed over for a long time, appear to our instincts as intention; intention draws our energy, and our energy propells us toward what we fear.

We cannot change the lower mind. We cannot give it fearful thoughts and try to tell it that these are thoughts we wish to *avoid,* because the lower instinctual mind is not open to that kind of dialogue, nor is it open to reason. We cannot joke with the lower mind, for it takes literally whatever we feed it. The only way to avoid feeding it negative signals is to avoid indulging in negative emotion.

Instead of creating fear-energy within our minds, we can deal with particular fears by addressing the spirit being who oversees the circumstance we fear. If we are afraid of drowning, we should talk to Water, the entity, about it. If we fear fire, we should talk to Fire about it. Talk to the appropriate entity as respectfully as you would address a diety, for these beings are worthy of our respect. Any overseeing spirit is a powerful spirit, the elementary powers particularly so. Tell Fire that you realize its importance and that you wish to make a request of it. Tell it that you do not want to be harmed by it in any way. Say nothing that would draw it toward you. Words like "Fire, I want to talk to you," are inappropriate because you do not want to draw Fire, you wish to make a request of it. Phrase your request like this: "Fire, I honor you, but I am not calling you to me. I wish no harm from you." Say nothing that will draw the element or condition (fire or poverty) toward you. Make clear, simple statements of respect, and be sure to include the words "I am not calling you to me."

Some years ago I had an enlightening encounter with an overseeing spirit when, one day in the woods, I began thinking about the great difference in material wealth that exists in the world. I wondered why so many people are unable to scrape together the food they need. I considered the injustice of this long enough that I began to feel quite angry about the issue. As I walked in the woods, I looked up to see that a tall spirit being had planted himself in front of me. He had a very purposeful look, though not an angry one. He introduced himself as the Spirit of Poverty, and he told me that he was put out with me for not realizing that he had a reason for being, a purpose, just like many other overseeing spirits. I am paraphrasing here, as I cannot recall his words exactly, but he said something like, "I have a great deal more to teach people than you understand. It does not bother me that you find poverty distressing. Compassion is a fine thing. What *does* bother me is that you did not even know I exist." And he disappeared.

I guess the lesson there was that many situations in this realm have overseeing spirits and that, if such a spirit exists, it exists for a purpose. The fact that we may not be able to comprehend that purpose does not negate it.

Weapons of Evil

Fear is the greatest weapon the darkness has, for we indulge in it so often and because it admits into our lives nearly any of the many varieties of evil. Ignorance, which leads us away from where we ought to be into where we ought not to be, often leads us into fearful states of consciousness.

Once an evil being has tapped into our lives, whether or not we have the slightest inkling that we are being abused, it uses *confusion, isolation* and *self-doubt* to keep us in a condition conducive to exploitation.

Confusion

It is far easier to manipulate a mind in confusion than to
attempt manipulation on a centered, healthy one. A confused
person, one who allows himself to be thrown off-balance by
circumstances he cannot control or who routinely throws himself into a tizzy by behaving irresponsibly toward his life, is an
easy target. We cannot feel the presence of danger if we are
perpetually absorbed in crises.

Isolation

This works next to confusion as a weapon of the invader. We
begin to feel fearful. Often, we are not afraid of anything in
particular. We just feel jumpy, or have a frequent feeling of
foreboding. We may get a case of nerves or become incapable
of manifesting any joy in our lives or peace within ourselves.
We do not know why we are frightened, so we tell ourselves
falsehoods in order to create a "truth" to which we can attribute our feelings. If we are jumpy, it must be the result of
family tensions. The feeling of foreboding is coming about
because we're tired, or because there's a full moon. The more
off-balance we become, the easier it is for an invader to manipulate us into deeper and deeper isolation.

Self-Doubt

Next comes self-doubt. It helps the invader if we do not
believe in anything more powerful than ourselves, because
without an impulse to pray, we make no effort to connect our
being to God. If we go on for a long time without making the
Light connection, and if we feel cast adrift because of the fear
and isolation with which we have been living, we may forget
what it is like to feel healthy, hopeful, and balanced. People
forget feelings of well-being rather quickly after losing contact

with those feelings. Feelings of well-being do not live in our memories for very long. Feeling adrift, feeling abandoned without being able to tell ourselves what, precisely, we feel abandoned *by*, leads to misery. Misery leads to despair. Despair leads to giving up.

Giving up is how evil grabs hold of us. Just as our giving in to pain and fear under torture is a quick way for evil to feed itself, so giving up hope and turning away from the life of this realm is a start toward loosening our hold on our energies. When that hold, that psychic claim on our lives and our being, is loosened enough that we no longer have a firm connection with our etheric body, evil can enter our energy field. Once that occurs, we may become possessed. The possessor leads us to where it wants us to go, and when we have done what it wants us to do and aligned our spirit with the possessor, it will find a way to kill us—through suicide or accident, at which point it can absorb our energy.

Determining the Presence of Psychic Attack

No one signal is absolute proof that we are under attack, but certain symptoms indicate the possibility of an attack. When one or more of these is present, there is a good chance that we are being worked on by something malevolent, living or dead.

Anger, though depleting and disorienting when allowed to become excessive, can be a helpful emotion when it tells us something we did not know and should be aware of. Anger sometimes serves as a sign of emotional difficulty in the same way that fever indicates physical troubles. Anger tells us that something is out of kilter. Either a situation is treating us badly or we are treating ourselves badly.

Anger simmering beneath the surface of consciousness suggests that something is awry in our relationships, work, or attention to personal growth. Exploding anger is easier to deal with than simmering anger because exploding anger makes itself known without our having to go looking for it. Also, explosions of anger allow us to discharge a portion of negative energy while, at the same time, becoming aware that something is wrong.

Exploding anger is a psycho-physical signal from ourselves to ourselves. It is also a psycho-physical attempt to push something away from us, which is its actual biological function.

In the creation of any change within human beings, there must be a vacuum preceding the change. If we need love, a love-vacuum opens which can subsequently be filled with love. If we need to grow within our spirit, we will begin to feel restless. This restlessness signals the creation of a vacuum within us. Attention to our spiritual nature fills that vacuum. When we fight with someone, and the anger in us grows and grows, the anger is creating a vacuum into which another being can intrude itself. All new growth and all intrusion must be preceded by a vacuum.

If you feel angrier and angrier over something as the days go by, even if you know that you have a tendency to brood or to feel sorry for yourself, know that something is wrong. Set aside the subject you believe is making you angry, no matter how hard it may be to do so. Smudge yourself. Take some time in the woods. Lie by a stream. Play music. Do anything you can to calm yourself except taking alcohol or drugs.

If you can manage to dismiss your anger, all will be well. Cleanse yourself spiritually and forget the incident that sparked the anger. If you cannot close that door, and if something gets its tentacles into your being, here is how to deal with it.

Make *no* attempt to find out who is attacking you. That wild chase will lead you into all manner of wasted activity. If you tell yourself that you will be able to figure out who the culprit is, you will, in your excited state, more than likely identify the wrong person as your attacker. Most evil hides well, primary evil especially so. You need to rid yourself of danger, not play detective. Perform a spiritual cleansing on yourself, your home and any animals you have as well. Some animals like to be smudged and some don't. Some animals like to be bathed and many do not. Choose a cleansing method appropriate to each animal friend.

Having cleansed yourself, and still making every effort not to allow the blow-up situation to take over your thoughts, make a plea to the spirit-keepers of the North, East, South and West. Tell them you are under attack and ask them not to allow anyone to use their power against you. It is difficult for an attacker—alive or dead—to work on you without employing the particular aspects of at least one cardinal direction. If the directions are alerted to the emergency you are having, they will know not to allow the attacker to use them against you.

Even a dead spirit who is not bound to this realm must guide his way into your life by using the cardinal directions. The reason for this is that the directions are not symbolic *of* energies, rather they create certain energy flows. They do not stand for activities; they maintain those activities. The East is not merely symbolic of new beginnings; it helps to manifest new beginnings. The sacred directions are actual, not symbolic.

The directions and their spirit-keepers will not allow themselves to be used for non-creative purposes, but they sometimes need to be alerted to the destructive activities around them. These powers have their own particular ways of experiencing, which are not the same as human ways of experiencing. If someone is using a formula to send confusion your way, a step toward taking over your energy or inducing you into a dangerous situation, he must commandeer the forces of a direction. If you have appealed for help to the directions, you may have stopped the enemy before he made much progress.

Next, you need to ask the all-life for protection, guidance and inspiration.

The All-Life As Partner

The key to safety is your awareness of the life around you. If you were to try, all by yourself, to find out whether or not you were under attack, you would have to spend your entire life in fear, running this way and that, looking for something that usually cannot be found. You are only one person and your ability to know what is happening in the world is limited. Being only human, your ability to comprehend what you think you know is severely limited. You must turn your attention outward, away from yourself, and toward the levels of creation abounding nearby. In doing so, you accomplish two things: you avail yourself of a great deal of help from any or all of the life-forms, and you free yourself of the dreadful constraints that accompany the self-conscious state.

Should you be in danger, mundane danger such as a car accident or a danger related to black magic, the all-life will tell you. It will always aid you as long as you continue to focus on it for periods of time every day, and do not shrink back into yourself.

As you look around, you will see a bird looking at you, or perhaps a butterfly will fly over your head, turn around, and fly over your head again. To the uninitiated, these are merely animals living their lives. To the experienced and aware, they are friends contacting us. What feeling do you get from the bird, the butterfly? Do you feel a contracting sensation in the abdomen? There may be a sad event in the offing. Does your contact with these creatures make you feel expansive? This may mean that something happy is about to occur. It may mean only that you are glad to be in touch with your fellow journeyers here. Not every contact with the all-life is a telegram containing information about your circumstances. But some of these contacts do offer information and warning. Experience and time will teach you which of your encounters with the all-life contain announcements.

Once you are accustomed to receiving signals, the messages become less vague. I always know that when certain groups of flying creatures pass near my house, an event relating to illness or death is about to occur. That is one of my signals; I do not suggest it will become yours. As you put more and more attention into the life around you, all of it, stones and plants and animals, lightning and clouds and the wind, you will find out what your signals are. These signals are a gift from the all-life. Respect the gift and respect the giver. In tough situations, they may be your only help.

If you are under attack, you will always receive signals from the all-life. Your job is to understand what those signals mean. You will not learn these overnight, and you cannot learn how to interpret your personal signals by studying someone else's signals. You will never learn this through your intellect. The ability comes to you day by day and night by night as you invest yourself—through attention and giving respect—in the world around you. The manner in which signs and signals are communicated will never be the same for any two people.

You can make a strong leap forward into the world of psychic signals and signs by learning and practicing the essential technique for shamanic journeying. After you have begun making journeys, you will find that animals or plants, rock formations or insects, will appear in your mind while you are in a state of ordinary waking consciousness. These are psychic signals and they come to you through your spirit, whereas butterflies swooping over your head come to you through the physical world. One is not better than the other. If you learn journeying techniques and practice these respectfully, you will increase your contact with the all-life by being able to relate to it psychically as well as physically.

Concerning visions, only experience can teach us how to know whether our visions are self-created, and therefore belong to the faculty of imagination, or whether they are born of energy outside ourselves, which makes them bona fide psychic communication. The difference is important because imagination is an enclosed faculty; we create and receive a vision without reference to anything outside ourselves. In psychic seeing, we are contacted by something beyond us. While the communication may be shaped and interpreted by us, it is not we who create the communication.

If I am walking in the woods and I have a vision of a cat playing the violin, how do I know whether the vision is a psychic one, and therefore initiated by something outside me, or my own imagination, which means that I birthed it? I can know the difference only after I have had sufficient experience with psychism, to feel my consciousness being touched from outside myself. Usually, a vision that flashes through my mind is a creation of my imagination, whereas a tree-stump in the physical world that looks like a cat playing the violin is a message born of something outside me. The message may intend to communicate "Fun is coming into your life," in which case it will have been received by my deeper mind and fashioned into the cat/violin image by my imagination. On the other hand, there may actually be a musical cat-spirit in the woods. In any case, it is a psychic contact only if it originated from something outside me. If I gave the vision to myself, it is a product of my imagination.

Honor your friends in the all-life by thanking them for their attention to you, whether or not that attention occurs during a time of high drama in your life. What should matter to us most is daily communion with our companions in the world of form, the trees and mice and rocks, and the joy of that communion. The ability of our friends to warn us of danger, guide us through difficult times or even predict the future is not their paramount value. We need them for spiritual nourishment. Looking to the all-life only for what it may accomplish for us is a mechanistic way of encountering creation. It limits the scope of our experience and relegates creation to the role of servant.

You may wish to honor your friends in stone, plant and animal form, the elements and directions by making occasional gifts such as candy, herbs or anything that strikes you as fitting. You may wish to acknowledge them by simply saying hello several times throughout your day. Above all, honor these companions by refusing to drag them from the realm of the sacred—which is where they belong—to the realm of idiotic chatter.

Never speak of spiritual occurences unless you are sure that you are talking to a serious spiritual seeker. This applies to experiences of journeying and of ordinary waking consciousness. Never tell anybody who your spirit allies are or what you do when journeying. Never commit the unpardonable breach of good manners by asking anyone who his power allies are. When our spirit friends feel that we disrespect them, they may leave us until such time as we are ready to treat them with respect and realize that they need their privacy at least as much as we need ours.

There is no reason to be obsequious with our power allies or other friends, but we must not devalue their importance to us and others by stooping to gossip about them. What is sacred is sacred; what is mundane is mundane. Nobody can afford to confuse the two.

Protection for the Corners of Your House

The corners are not all that matters, of course, and protection for the walls and the rest of the house will be offered later. But corners are particularly important because both ordinary and extraordinary negative energies can gather there. If you are in a bad mood and give off negative energy, that energy will find its way into the corners of whatever room you are in. Negative energies entering the house from outside will come in through the corners, especially through the northernmost corners. The tendency of negative energies to gather in corners is one reason why some cultures avoid square or rectangular structures when building their houses, and live in circular or eliptical-shaped dwellings.

Unless you feel certain that you are under a major attack, the following technique can be limited to one room—the bedroom—because it is usually in sleep or just prior to it that we are attacked.

For this method of protection you will need a pen with black ink that makes a bold mark (not a ballpoint pen) and white unlined paper, such as typing paper. It is important that the paper be white and have no designs or markings other than the ones you place there. You will need one piece of paper for each corner of the room.

When you have achieved a centered state—not excessively emotional, nervous or depressed—take a pen into the room you wish to work on and as many pieces of paper as there are corners.

Say a prayer for your protection and the protection of the house. Make up a prayer of your own and take that prayer seriously. You don't have to think of yourself as a mystic in order to affect a good strong prayer. Just be sincere and talk to whatever higher power you believe in. If you don't believe there is a higher power, then talk to the guardian spirits of this world, beseeching their help and protection.

Sit on the floor facing a corner, starting with any corner that suits you, and draw the following symbol on a piece of paper:

Draw it from upper left to lower right and then from upper right to lower left, like this (don't actually write out the numbers):

Then draw a square around the X to encompass it, drawing from the top left straight across, then down the right side of the X, then from right to left across the bottom of the X, and finally from bottom to top at the left side. Be sure that, in making this square, you touch every one of the four points of the X, and be sure that you never take your pen off the paper while making the square. If you inadvertently bring the pen off the paper, throw away what you have done and start another symbol. It's important that the square surrounding the X be created in one unbroken line.

When you are finished drawing, the symbol you have created will look like this:

Place the symbol in the corner, with the symbol facing the outside of the room. Tape the paper to the wall or prop it up. It must stand flush with the corner. Be certain not to block the symbol with the tape or impede in any way the visibility of the symbol from outside.

Create a symbol for each corner, making each one while sitting facing the corner for which the symbol is intended. Do not make them all at once and then place them around the room.

This fundamental exorcist's symbol will last for five days in each corner without its energy having to be replaced. Just make certain that each symbol is positioned straight up so that the symbols can be seen from outside. This matters whether or not the room contains outer walls. Even a room where some or all of the corners are interior and where none of the corners actually face the outside must be designed as I have described.

If you believe you are under attack, do this in one room of each floor in your house. If you are truly beleaguered, do it in every room. The room second in importance to the bedroom is the bathroom because that is where we clip our nails and wash ourselves, and we often leave bits of our bodies around, strands of hair or nail clippings. These are filled with our essence and for that reason, an attacking entity may try to enter our bathroom and contact us through our physical essence.

Protection of Your House With Mirrors

Mirrors—psychic ones—are wonderful helpers because they repell attack and sometimes show you who is attacking you. But mirrors have to be established with energy. A mirror, mentally imaged, evoked with energy and placed around your house, lasts no more than twenty-four hours.

The creation of psychic mirrors requires that you take this technique seriously and do it carefully. If you think all psychism is nonsense, then you won't be able to invest this method with enough of your psychic energy to manifest a powerful mirror. If that's the case, skip this and find another protection technique.

Center yourself and quiet your mind. Wait to perform this technique until you are in a good mood. Do not attempt it while trying to find out whether or not someone is invading your house, because you can't do two things at once.

Go outside and look at your house or apartment from every angle. Starting with the front, place a mirror large enough to cover the whole front area, the reflecting surface facing outward.

You must do this placing by energetically *making* the mirror and not by an act of mere visualization. Visualizing has a tentative impact on the visualizer but is not an act of creation because it does not establish anything in the etheric, the physical level of reality, or the astral realm. You cannot make a mirror by the simple intellectual remembering of what mirrors look like and then pretending to see one. For this protection—and for any occult technique where something must be *evoked*—visualization is useless because it makes no actual change in anything, but is only a communication between the visualizer and himself.

Asking your higher self for help, breathe evenly and deeply, while concentrating your whole mind on your abdomen and stomach. Can you feel pulsing energy around the area of your solar plexus? Think of a mirror and while thinking, draw energy from your solar plexus. Pull it, by an act of will and concentration, from your body to the outside of the house. Think of the mirror while simultaneously pulling energy out of yourself. Bring the energy to the mirror. Having done these things, you have created a mirror that has an actual existence in the astral realm. If you had merely visualized the mirror, it would have had no impact in reality—physical, etheric, or astral reality—but would have remained only a personal communication, thus affecting you and only you. Visualizations may, over time, create changes within the visualizer, but that is the only life they have. In the moment they are visualized, they do not make a change in any level of actual reality.

After you have established the mirror by mating the thought of it with some of your energy, extend the mirror to cover the entire area to be protected. Moving in a counterclockwise direction (right to left) go to the side of the house or apartment and create another mirror over that corner. Do this by simultaneously thinking of the mirror and gathering energy from yourself. Be sure that you move the energy from your body to the place where you envision the mirror. Do the whole process and do it thoroughly.

Be certain to join the second mirror to the first. Create the mirror for the third side and be sure to join it to the previous mirror. Be sure that each section of mirror is joined to the preceding section.

Having done this and arrived at the front again, extend the mirror to the top of the building and cover the roof. The roof is very important. Then go around to the left side of the house, still moving counterclockwise, and join the established mirror to the roof over the left side. Go to the back and join the established mirror to the roof covering the back. Go to the right side of the building and create a mirror there to join with the other three mirrors and cover the right side. Be sure to cover any chimneys or water towers or aerials so that the entire structure is covered seamlessly. Stand for a moment where you've established the final roof mirror and make sure that you can see the mirror in its entirety, covering the sides and top of the house. Be sure the mirror's reflecting surface faces outward, not in toward your house.

You need not protect the earth beneath the building unless you know there has been some physical trouble in the basement such as flooding. If there has been, then create a mirror that reflects from the bottom of the building to the ground, being careful to join this one seamlessly to the other mirrors.

Did you create mirrors that reflect outward, not inward? Did you perform this technique by moving in a right-to-left, counterclockwise direction?

The mirror will repell invasive force. It lasts for one day, remember, and no more.

After you have mastered this mirror technique you may feel confident that you are able to create the seamless mirror without going outside. If you feel you can do this, you most likely can. But when establishing the mirror for the first few times, do it by moving around outside your house. You may forget a chimney or an aerial unless you can see it as you move along.

I have found the instances wherein I could see the face of an invader by looking at the mirror to be very, very rare ones. It is enough that the mirror repels. We don't always need to know who it is repelling. Most often, we would not recognize the face of the invader if we saw it.

The Cross As Protection for Your House

The cross, as I have mentioned elsewhere in this book, does not belong to any one religion or philosophy. Everyone has the right to use the cross.

The cross is so complex a symbol and subject that a whole book could be devoted just to its meanings, past and present, esoteric and exoteric. It symbolizes, besides many others ideas, the square, the circle, and the number four. You may have noticed that nature tends to create in fours. There are four cardinal directions, four elements, and four kingdoms on this earth.

Go to any room in the top floor of your house and stand facing a wall, not a corner, that is closest to North. Using your right forefinger, draw a line from the ceiling down the wall and straight through the floor. Then draw a horizontal line starting from the wall to your left—including the corner between that wall and the one you are facing. Continue the line across the wall you are facing and on through the corner to your right. You have drawn a cross from top to bottom and side to side that includes both corners adjacent to the wall facing you. Draw this protective cross from left to right.

Turn to face the wall to your right and draw the same cross on it, including the corners to its left and right. In turn, do the remaining walls.

Always draw from left to right, and always begin with the

vertical line and go on to the horizontal line. By drawing each cross to include two corners per cross, you are insuring that the corners of the room will all be protected.

Do this procedure in one room of each floor of your house. It does not matter whether you do an interior room or one that includes an exterior wall.

Draw the cross, from inside your house, on every exterior door, including front and back doors, and entrances to cellars and attics. When drawing the cross, be sure to include the top door lintel, the floor beneath the door, and the sides.

This protection lasts for twenty-four hours.

The Cross and Reflecting Surfaces

When you are protecting your house from invasion, it is important to consider the reflecting surfaces throughout the house and place a cross on each. I find this observance especially important during times of personal transition and times during which transition for all of us is implied, such as the Winter and Summer solstices, the Spring and Autumn equinoxes, and all other spiritually-derived days of observance, as opposed to calendar holidays.

Because of the peculiar nature of mirrors they should be regarded as magical objects. They have an existence beyond the mundane use for which they are intended, acting as both entrance and exit points for spirits.

Windows are entrance and exit points as well, as they admit light during the day and reflect at night. How many times do we speak of "mirroring our thoughts" or "windows on the world" or similar metaphors? Both of these are inter-realm objects, and have esoteric and exoteric implications.

The most effective protection that I know of for windows is to mark each one with a plain unadorned cross. The cross, in its nondenominational form has so much power that it is not necessary for us to energize it as we must energize the mirror. We cannot however, merely visualize or think of a cross and expect it to attach its power to a window or mirror. We must mark a cross by actually drawing one, and we use the right forefinger—or the entire right hand—to do this. Make the cross from top to bottom and then from left to right. In marking the cross on a window, mirror or other object, be sure to cover the entire object.

If you believe you are under attack, draw a cross on the doors of your house, including any exterior doors and all the interior ones. Cover the door from top to bottom and left to right, including in the cross the lintel over the door, the floor beneath it and the sides. The point here is to ascertain that all of a door is covered by the cross.

The drawn cross must be replaced every twenty-four hours. If you feel beleaguered and need maximum protection, make the sign of the cross over all doors, windows and reflecting surfaces once during the daylight hours *and* once at night.

Salt And Vinegar: All-Purpose Purifiers

Salt, while not a repelling protector such as the X-protection or the cross, helps us by its unique ability to attract and hold negative energies. Vinegar cleanses quickly. Salt and vinegar are to spiritual cleanliness what soap and water are to physical cleanliness.

There are many uses for sea salt, and after you have worked with it for awhile, you will probably find uses for it that I have never experienced. We create new ways of using the help we are given as we become familiar with our helpers.

Sea salt is the salt you will want to use because it does not contain anything that would harm the water or land. The sole danger in using sea salt is its inherent ability to hold negative energy. For this reason, you must offer prayers when you dispose of negative-bonded sea salt.

Salt cannot stave off attack or repell a force, but if negativity has entered our homes, we may deal with it by cleansing with sea salt.

If you have an object that needs some cleansing and time won't allow for smudging or a water cleansing, sprinkle salt on and around the object and leave it there for at least ten minutes.

If you feel you have been under attack, place a pile of salt an inch high in each corner of the room you sleep in, as well as any room you use for spiritual work. Leave these piles where they are for a night and a day, but be sure to sweep them up after one night and one day and dispose of them in a paper bag, praying that the negative energies bonded to the salt will not adversely affect the earth or water. The piles of salt in corners will become negatively charged, so you are obligated to make prayers to counteract that negativity before disposing of the negatively–bonded salt.

Since sprinkling salt on objects does not allow for a buildup of negativity, no mitigating prayer is required unless you leave the salt on the object for an hour or more.

If you feel beleaguered, attacked, or just tired and frazzled, put a handful of sea salt in bathwater and soak for half an hour. If you are in need of grounding as well as cleansing, use a handful of sea salt and a quarter-cup of white vinegar in the water. It is all right to add perfume or water conditioner to this bath, but do not add bath salts.

If you are just very tired, add four drops of Bach Remedy *olive*. If you feel, or have felt, the presence of something unclean or threatening around you, add four drops of Bach *crab apple*. If you are frightened and know what you're fearful of, add four drops of Bach *mimulus*. If you have the jitters, add four drops of Bach *aspen*. In any situation where evil is even a possibility, add four drops of Bach *walnut* to the bathwater and, later, sip slowly an eight-ounce glass of water to which you have added two drops of *walnut*, two drops of *white chestnut*, and two drops of *cherry plum*. If you have been under a powerful attack and are suffering because of it, add two drops of Bach *sweet chestnut* to your glass of water and four drops of it to your bathwater. The general exorcist's dosage, in times of exorcism and during its aftermath, is *white chestnut, walnut, crab apple* and *elm;* two drops of each in a glass of water, once in the morning and once at night. Sip the mixture slowly.

These homeopathic rememdies will not interfere with any other
meditation you may be taking. The Bach Remedies work on
the etheric body and help to bring your own balancing and
healing powers into play. They cannot hurt you.

Vinegar cleanses without harming. Use it in bathwater
unless you have an open sore or wound. If you have frequently
been in crowds or in situations that have left you feeling
drained or jumpy or contaminated, put a drop of white vinegar
in an eight-ounce glass of water and rinse out your mouth. Do
not swallow the mixture; spit it out.

When doing your housecleaning, place a bowl of water containing a few drops of white vinegar in any room that has just
been cleaned. Vinegar cleanses the atmosphere. Leave the
bowl of water and vinegar there for two hours.

Preparing Our Homes Before We Move In

Because ghost energy can remain attached to land for hundreds of years, and because we have no means of finding out
what took place on the ground beneath our house prior to a
few years ago, it is important that we clean out our new house
spiritually as well as give it a good scrubbing.

We may be living in a new house that was built after the
previous one burned down and we may know that much, but
what if we don't know that the fire was deliberately set,
because nobody ever found that out? What if there was a mental institution on the site of our house two hundred years ago,
and what if it was peopled by deeply unhappy people who may
have stayed behind after their deaths or perhaps left an appreciable dose of negative energy behind when they died?

After the institution is torn down and the pieces carted away,
after the foundation is dug up and removed, and after five
houses in succession have been built on that site . . . the same
ghosts or ghost-energy may very well remain.

Smudging is a wonderfully effective spiritual cleanser. Sage
alone can be counted on to remove negativity. If you are able
to obtain sweetgrass and cedar, all the better, because a proper

smudge, which is made up of all three ingredients, will not only remove negative energy but also evoke positive energy.

I would not move into an apartment or house until I had smudged all of it, paying particular attention to the corners. Life is difficult enough without our having to live with other people's negative energies.

I smudge the inside and outside of my car once in awhile, especially after driving in heavy traffic. I rub dried sage on the outside of my car every three or four days, starting at the front and moving around the car in a counterclockwise direction, covering the car in a complete circle. While I generally work in a clockwise direction for bringing forth, I find that the protection of a vehicle that will always operate near other vehicles requires attending to in a counterclockwise manner because one is asking the sage-protector to repell negative situations.

If I buy an antique or a work of art, particularly art of a spiritual nature, I always smudge it. Smudging items is not an act of warfare against other people's vibes but a way of smoothing our lives.

Understanding Exorcism

Exorcism is energy-displacement. When we banish invasive energy from a location, object or person, we both expel those energies and send them to a particular place. Exorcism is similar to healing but not exactly like it: In healing, we remove invasive energy, either by excising tissue or ridding the body of disease; in exorcism we remove the invasive energy and send it to its place of origin.

An example of exorcism as energy-displacement is found in a ceremony performed by Tibetan monks of the Gyuto Tantric University. In this ceremony, which is accomplished through chanting and will, a universe like ours is established, energized by an act of will, created as a viable entity in the astral realm. This universe is invested with energy to banish evil. Because the newly-created universe has an actual existence and because this existence is situated in the same soul-place our world

exists, in the astral realm, it has a powerful effect on our physical world. This operation is something like creating a drawing
of a person who is diseased, and then removing the disease
from the drawing. In the Tibetan chanting ritual I am referring
to, the drawing is not made on a piece of paper but impressed
in actual astral reality. What is done to that world within the
astral realm must affect the physical world, because the intentions with which the world of the astral is invested are
empowered by real energy. The ritual is then a creation of
actuality and not an imagining or a visualization.

To affect the astral is to affect the physical. To affect the physical is to affect the astral. The key to all of this is intention
and real energy. Unless we invest our rituals with energy and
move energy from one point to another, we are not engaged in
an act of true creation.

In the mirror-protection mentioned earlier, we created a mirror that has a real existence in astral reality by moving energy
from our bodies to the mirror. Always, when an actual change
is to be affected, energy must be moved from one place and
invested in another.

Anything willed into existence by energy transference is
valid creation. Anything displaced from one realm of existence
to another is exorcism.

In order to banish from our lives anything intrusive, invasive
or undesirable and do this morally, we need to bear in mind
that everything, not just ourselves, is meant to enjoy freedom
of being and freedom of movement. This right includes the
"right" of primary evil to exist despite its having no claim to
creation. The "right" involved here is not actually primary
evil's right to remain extant, but *our obligation not to destroy
anything*—even primary evil. It is the job of the Creator to
expunge that which It is moved to expunge. We do not have
the right to do this.

We are within our rights to remove anything we wish to
remove from our lives but we may not destroy anything. Exorcism, then, is the removal of energy to a place apart from us
and not the destruction of that energy.

We cannot send evil back to its source multiplied either, as I have sometimes known occultists to do. Their excuse for this terrible act is the erroneous notion that in doing to others, tenfold or a hundredfold, what has been attempted on them, the defender is "helping" his attacker by teaching him a lesson. The teaching of such lessons is the job of the Almighty and Its overseeing, guiding spirits, and we must not presume to elevate ourselves to their status by taking on their roles. We may never create a ceremony that increases evil, for if we do, no matter what our motive may be, we are violating the laws of right action. If we manipulate evil, and increasing it *is* manipulation, we create for ourselves powerful repercussions.

In exorcism, the path to take is the Light path.

Bring yourself to the attention of whichever cardinal direction is right for your needs, keeping in mind the attributes of each of them, and then state clearly, aloud, what is wrong as you perceive the situation. Never mind arranging your words to sound elegant. Be plain-spoken; the message will get there faster and more clearly than if you tried to speak like a preacher.

Having alerted the direction—or all four cardinal directions, if that feels right to you—talk to the spirits of Air, Earth, Fire and Water. Speak to the Earth and the Earth-keepers, and to Mother-Father God.

In nearly all the methodology in this book, I have begun with the Creator, gone next to focussing on the Earth and Earth-keepers, and progressed from there to the four directions. In this situation, reverse that order and begin with the cardinal points because you need the help of the spirits closest to this realm and you need it fast. Once you have alerted the directions to your need, you can relax a bit, knowing that powerful forces are aware of your need and are protecting you.

Keep yourself centered and eschew anger, using all the will-power you have if need be, as the messages you will receive from the forces of the directions may be overt or subtle. *Do not go looking for signs and messages.*

If you look for signs, you will always see them and they will be bogus products of your imagination or mere reflections of the situation. Any powerful circumstance touches territory around it; you may see a signal that pertains to the circumstances, not because you are receiving a psychic impression, but because the circumstance has impressed itself on life and life-forms surrounding it.

If you wonder, for example, whether your friend is going to get the new car she wants, and if you go looking for signs so that you can predict the answer, you will see—I guarantee it—at least one "car for sale" sign on the way to work. Soon thereafter a friend will tell you that he is thinking of selling his car, and you will think, "Aha! That's it!" and a few hours later, four other bogus "signs" will pop out at you and you will think you have the answer to your question. Such is not the case. Real spiritual signs come only when they approach *us*, not when we go looking for *them*. It is not possible ever to manipulate their coming, only to be aware of them when they appear. Most of all, by refraining from trying to create signs, you will allow them to create themselves when they wish to.

Cleansing As Preparation for Exorcism

Now that you have the directions on your side and have spoken with the elementary powers and with Mother-Father God and the Earth and Earth-keepers, your job is to go home and do a cleansing on yourself and your home. It need not be an elaborate, exhausting ritual. Smudging is fine. A sprinkling of cold water in the corners of every room in your house and in your car will do a good deal toward removing negative energy. This is not an extensive enough cleansing for you, however. To cleanse yourself with water, you must stand under a stream of cold water—the shower will do fine—and ask blessings of Water, the power, on yourself. Ask that your physical body be cleansed of any negativity and also that your astral, soul body be cleansed. Ask the same for your etheric (energy) body and for your mental and emotional bodies.

If you like, you can cleanse yourself by lying on the ground on your front for ten minutes and on your back for the same time. This will not, however, cleanse your other bodies, such as your astral bodies, whereas smudging or water cleansing will work on all of you.

The Importance of Safe Focusing

When we sit in a dark room and someone lights a candle, we see the candlelight immediately. In the realm of the spirit, it works the other way around. As long as we concentrate on Light, if there is darkness, that darkness will become apparent. But if we search around in the darkness looking for Light, we won't find the Light because, in the realm of Spirit, darkness can overwhelm.

My point is that we can never help ourselves by looking for evil. If we search around in dark places, we get disoriented, even lost. All we can do, if we want to determine the presence of evil, is to stay focused on the Light.

Surround yourself with prayer and remain centered and unemotional. Know that you have the help of the directions, the elementary powers, God, and the Earth as long as you ask for it. Speaking aloud, say that you wish removed from your life any assault, any attack, any evil that may be present.

Do not try to find out who is attacking you because evil is capable of taking on any appearance it wants to, and when it knows you are seeking a culprit, it may appear to you disguised as a perfectly innocent person. This causes bad blood between you and the innocent one whose appearance was used to fool you. You can be thrown off-balance and sent on a fruitless chase to track down something you cannot find unless you are a trained *and experienced* exorcist.

Ask aloud for the complete and thorough removal of any evil in your life. This request will cause changes in your being and in your life, because while evil comes from outside us, the potential for evil invasion comes from our circumstances, our fears, our refusal to see things as they are, our willingness to accommodate social programming and bow to other's will and our emotional weaknesses.

Do not, therefore, undertake lightly the above request. The potential for evil invasion lies within us, and when we ask to be made safe, we are embarking on a long project requiring our full cooperation, and ending in the resolution of many personal difficulties.

Exorcist's Declaration

When you believe there is evil around anything over which you have authority, your house, work, animals, or anything involving your family, and if you are certain that, in using your authority to exorcise, you are not intruding on anyone's free will, follow this procedure:

Having decided where you think the trouble is centered, take a handful of sea salt and, positioning yourself where you will stand during the exorcism, sprinkle the sea salt around your feet in a circle. Be sure that the circle is entirely closed, that is, that there are no gaps in it. Should you find that you haven't enough salt to accomplish this, it is perfectly all right to go fetch more salt. You need not hold yourself inside the circle until you have begun speaking the exorcist's declaration.

Raise your arms to form V-shaped angles to your shoulders and head. Concentrating your mind on the infinite and all-encompassing power of Light, and refusing to let yourself think about the dark force, say these words:

> By the power of Light—I, (use your name here), am Light—I send out of here, out of the physical, etheric and astral component of this place, and to its point of origin, anything and all that is not Light.

Those words are both an invocation and a dismissal. You are invoking the Light and dismissing the darkness.

When you use your name, use the name you feel truly belongs to you. You may use a name you have given yourself, a sacred name, one that you feel you had in another incarnation, or a secret name you believe suits you. You may, for example, feel that your true name is a sound you would not dare utter in the presence of others, an empowering sound with a hidden meaning. You may believe your true name is Raphael, or Soaring Eagle. If you feel that your everyday name suits you, use it. So-called ordinary names are not necessarily less powerful than ceremonial ones.

In stating "I, (name), am Light," you are aligning your many bodies, etheric, astral, physical, emotional and mental with the Light Power and affirming your right to work with the Light. You are, in stating that you are Light, placing yourself within the protection of the Light Power.

Anyone who states that he is Light when, in fact, he is not will feel a most interesting reverberation within himself as he says the words. If you are, in fact, making a false declaration when you claim the Light, you will feel the falseness of it.

If you have investigated the situation and feel there may be more than one object, person or place in need of exorcism, then elaborate the invocation-and-dismissal this way:

> By the Power of Light—I, (name), am Light—I send out of (fill in anything you need to fill in) in their physical, etheric and astral components, and to its place of origin, anything and all that is not Light.

Speak the invocation-and-dismissal aloud unless you have a reason to believe that doing so would be harmful to the person or animal you are exorcising. If you feel that speaking these words aloud would cause a shock, then say them silently. If you feel that the sight of you towering over the victim would be unsettling, then you may perform the declaration without creating the V with your arms. You cannot, however, do without the salt. If you feel that drawing the circle of salt at your feet would have a disquieting effect on the animal or person to be exorcised, then, instead of making the circle, get a piece of cotton—only pure cotton will do—and place a tablespoon of sea salt within it, being careful to bind the material tightly so that none of the salt can spill from it. Place this package in your right pants pocket or in a right-hand pocket of your overcoat. Do not place it in any pocket above your hip area. If need be, put it in your shoe. Do not place the package of salt anywhere on your left side. No matter whether we favor the left or right, we receive from the left and give out from the right. You do not wish to receive the vibrations of evil which the salt will attract and hold. Because of this, you must not place the salt on your left. Do not place it before or behind you. Find a way of placing the salt on your right. You must not tamper with this instruction.

In order to exorcise, you *must* use the words "and to its place of origin." If you neglect to use those words, you will succeed only in "sending out." That will call the evil being or energies out of the victim . . . and place them right where they can get you or reenter the victim once you have finished making your declaration.

Some exorcist's declarations include the enjoining of a spirit to "come out." *Do not use this phrase.* You do not want the evil to come out, you want it to leave, and you want it to return to its origin. In ordering it to return to its place of origin, the coming out of the spirit is implied and need not be spoken.

You can use the exorcist's declaration on yourself by saying,

By the Power of Light—I, (your name), am Light—I send out of my physical, etheric and astral bodies, and to its point of origin, anything and all that is not Light."

When performing this exorcism on yourself, you must say the words aloud. You may eschew the V-shaped position. You may not neglect the use of salt in a circle around your feet or in a right-hand pocket or in your shoe. Do not leave the salt on the floor or on your person once the exorcism is finished. Bury the salt in the ground. Wash the cotton in cold water.

Before doing any exorcism, memorize the essential words and *do not substitute* other words for the ones given here. The reason you must memorize the invocation-and-dismissal declaration is that, once you begin the ritual, there may be distracting energies around you. You cannot afford to be distracted from the words and you must say all of them. Further, when you begin the declaration, you may suddenly feel a need to include among the objects, places or beings to be exorcised, one or more additional entities. If, in the midst of the exorcism, you suddenly feel a need to include a bed, a tree outside your window, or a crystal, you must know the words so thoroughly that including additional entities does not throw you off. You cannot really know, before beginning an exorcism, all of what needs to be exorcised. You need to be prepared for the declaration because there may be information forthcoming during it, and you will have to be centered and balanced and aware in order to receive that information. *Memorize the declaration.*

Do not refer to a piece of paper with the words on it because if you are reading you will not be receptive if and when Spirit makes new information known to you.

The reason the declaration is phrased "anything and all" instead of "all and anything" is that the most effective procedure is to name the specific first and then the general. In doing so, we attach our authority to the particular evil spirit we are displacing, instead of weakening our effort by naming evil generally. In performing an exorcism, we cannot afford loose phrasing or blurred objectives.

Exorcising Through the Power of Jesus Christ

Should you feel that Jesus Christ's power is greater than the power implicit in Light, or should the Light Power be new to you and therefore fall short of inspiring your total trust, then substitute the words "Jesus Christ" for the word Light. Do not use *only* Jesus or *only* Christ; use them both. There are many Christed beings but they may not all be empowered to exorcise. There are many people named Jesus who are not necessarily Christs. If you invoke Jesus Christ as the power, then omit the words, "I, (name), am." It would be awkward to say, "I, (name), am Christ" because, while within the widest metaphysical interpretation, you may be Christ, there is always the possibility that you are not. At any rate, while you may be *a* Christ, you are not Jesus Christ.

In invoking the power of Jesus Christ for this declaration, the words are phrased this way:

> I call upon the power of Jesus Christ. In the name of Jesus Christ, I send out of here (name person or place or object) in its physical, etheric and astral bodies, and to its place of origin, anything and all that is not God's Light.

Power and Authority to Exorcise

Why do you have the power and authority to invoke and dismiss? You have the power to invoke because the Light offers itself to you as long as you are engaged in right action. You have the authority because you are a human being, created by God, and your right to live and function freely on this planet is a God-given one. Because evil does not have rights—primary evil has no legitimate rights and secondary evil beings have abnegated their rights by operating outside the laws of right action—you have complete authority over primary and secondary evil as long as you place yourself within the Light.

Why You Cannot Exorcise Accidental Evil With the Exorcist's Declaration

As has been discussed, accidental evil is not true evil. You do not necessarily have authority over ghosts or possessing dead spirits. You have the right to deal with them gently, if you use methods *other than* the exorcist's declaration. But you must not use this invocation-and-dismissal on accidental evil because to do so would most likely traumatize the dead spirit and cause more harm than good. Also, since the dead do not fall within the definition of true evil, the exorcist's declaration will not work on them anyway.

Exorcisms You Should or Should Not Perform

What do you do when an animal, person, or situation that does not belong to you is in need of exorcism? We must always consider not merely the question of whether evil truly is involved in a difficult situation, but whether we are within our rights to address the situation at all.

Your first step is to pray for guidance, calling upon the Creator or, if you do not believe there is an omnipotent Creator, then on the Source of Life. Call on your own higher self as well, but also be certain to call on a power greater than just you. Next, call on the powers of the four directions, naming each of them. You may wish to call on an elemental power if, for example, you are contemplating exorcising the ground or the atmosphere around a disturbed place. In those instances you would call on, respectively, Earth and Air. Whether or not you feel it is necessary to invoke the elemental guardian powers, you must call upon the guardians of the four sacred directions.

State, aloud if possible and in the simplest, plainest terms, the situation as you perceive it. Ask the Powers and God and your higher self for guidance. Having done so, forget the subject and go do something grounded. Guidance will come to you most easily and clearly if you do not try to force it by waiting for it. Even if you feel that the situation you are facing demands immediate attention, leave the subject and do something enjoyable that engages your attention and allows you to think about something other than the exorcism. Only when you are rested and grounded will you be ready and able to receive messages of guidance from Spirit. Never approach an exorcism in an hysterical or worried state of mind. If you do you will surely miss Spirit's signals and you may even forget to say all of the words you must say.

In waking life, we see only some of *any* situation. The whole truth is never known to us. That is why we must never act alone and unguided in any dangerous undertaking. Spirit may not agree with your assessment of the situation. There may be evil present, but this may not be the time to deal with it. Always let Spirit lead. He who does not follow Spirit causes major trouble for himself and others.

If you perform the exorcist's declaration on an object or a place, such as a woods, you cannot cause harm to the exorcised entity. But when you are dealing with another human being, you are obligated to be careful not to scare the wits out of him. He may already be in a misaligned state. He may be a nervous wreck, suffering from whatever is assaulting him. If you show up at his door, raise your arms, and speak the invocation-and-dismissal over him, you may cause irreparable harm. You never have the "right" to behave irresponsibly.

If Spirit has led you to help the person you are concerned about, consider whether you might gently and unobtrusively speak to him about the subject of invasion, approaching the subject as though you were speaking theoretically, and did not mean your remarks to concern him personally. Think this through. Is there any way you can broach the subject without alarming him? If so, and remembering that this discussion must begin as an exploration of a theory, pick a quiet time and a place free of interruption and distractions. Talk to him gently. Say nothing like, "I think you might be possessed," as it would be unforgivably cruel to be so confrontational with a disturbed person, not to mention irresponsible if you are wrong.

Observe his reactions to this discussion carefully without looking as though you are scrutinizing him. You will have to be on your toes during this conversation. If he does not seem disturbed by the discussion, tell him quietly that you think there might be some kind of difficult force *near* him, or that he *might perhaps be under attack*. Say nothing alarming or accusatory. If he listens to what you have to say and seems neither upset nor belligerent, ask his permission to make the exorcist's declaration. Tell him the words you will use. Do not make a big deal out of this. If he gives you permission to perform the declaration, then do. Use the salt and make the V-shape with your arms. Speak aloud, not silently.

When you approach someone about a situation which you have assessed as evil, you should speak to him only about the problem as it affects him. If you sense that he is beleaguered but that his wife is actually possessed, talk to him about his association with the difficulties, but do not tell him you think his wife is possessed. If you feel that you cannot speak directly to her about this, then Spirit is probably telling you to steer clear of her.

You may not take permission for an exorcism from anyone except the one on whom you are going to perform it. Even if Robert asks you to exorcise his wife Edna, you may not do so without consulting Edna. Approach her with the same degree of caution you maintained in approaching Robert. Be gentle with her and watch for signs of upset.

If you are inconsiderate to an afflicted person, and especially if your desire to "mend" him subordinates the beleaguered one's needs, you will probably make things worse for everyone than they already are. Keep your ego in check. A possession or invasion situation is no time for showing off our prowess.

If the one you approach does not give you permission, or if you feel that performing the exorcist's invocation-and-dismissal would alarm him or whoever you believe needs it, then write the words of the declaration down and ask your friend to read the words when he feels like it. Reading the words will give his own spirit a healing resonance and this may, later on, encourage him to seek some kind of help, possibly from you, possibly not. What he really needs is not your services but the help and guidance of his own spirit, and when the words of the declaration reverberate within his psyche, something within his own powers will help him.

Do not do an exorcism for which you do not have express permission unless you have prayed about this and are certain you have the right. Never, however, perform an exorcism on someone who has told you that he does not wish it. No matter how dire his circumstances and no matter how badly he may need exorcising, you may never interfere with another's will.

Do not perform an exorcism on a child. The spoken declaration would upset a child and is unnecessary. Prayer for a child always evokes help from Spirit. Babies and children have more spiritual protection than adults. Performing an exorcism on a child would be intrusive and is unnecessary.

Cleansing After an Exorcism

Having made the declaration, use a cleansing detailed later in this chapter, on yourself and all participants. Be sure to smudge the room or rooms involved and bury the salt in the earth.

Smudging is an effective means of removing any attendant negative energies, created by or preceding an exorcism ceremony, from rooms, people or objects. If you can build a large bowl of smudge or use a smudge stick, you can leave it in an area and allow it to do its work without having to stand there and watch. This is, I find, a good idea when smudging a room where there are a lot of items or where there are animals. The smudge will cleanse without disturbing the animals and without necessitating your having to pick up every item in the room.

If you've exorcised a place where there are a lot of crystals or special power objects, however, you do have to carefully smudge each of these.

Of course, it is not necessary that the exorcist do the cleansing. He ought to see to his own cleansing, but the other people involved are capable, after cleansing themselves, of building and using the smudge and of cleansing their own crystals and other important helpers.

It might be a good idea to suggest this, because it's always important to help people without allowing them to lean on us. You are the exorcist; that doesn't make you the maid-of-all-work.

Protection After an Exorcism

An evil being, when exorcised in the correct manner, using the aforementioned declaration, must return to its point of origin. But in doing an exorcism, there's a chance that you may make someone mad at you, so you must protect and cleanse yourself and your house for a few days afterward, and pray for protection.

If you have exorcised primary evil, the likelihood is that it will just go. It probably will not bother you afterward. Primary evil has no energy to waste on revenge. Only an experienced exorcist should expect primary evil to make an assault on him, because only an experienced exorcist is "worth" getting rid of. If exorcism is a rare endeavor for you, primary evil probably won't bother you.

On the other hand, secondary evil may come looking for you after you have exorcised it—and it's hard to know whether the evil you exorcised was primary or secondary. Secondary evil most often involves a live human being and this person has probably worked for a long time in order to get himself into someone's house, become part of her work, or insinuate himself into her consciousness. This is particularly true if the person you helped does any occult work or is influential in society.

A living human being does have the energy to waste in going after you, to punish you for your bold interference or to scare you away from him. He may wish to learn how much you know about the situation. He may think that, in disconnecting him from your friend, you are aware of him—whether or not this is so. He may want to scare you away from exorcism, so that you don't mess with any more of his plans. Or he may simply come looking for you to find out who you are.

If you have exorcised secondary evil, and you may have, then you may feel a pressure around yourself. This pressure is a frequent signal, though not guaranteed to occur. It feels as though a wall is closing around you. (This signal may appear in instances other than the aftermath of an exorcism.)

Protect yourself and your home and above all, keep in close touch with common sense. Common sense is one of humankind's best friends and counts, at times, for more than ritual and more than knowledge.

Ceremony for Protection

The wall you feel is the presence of energy seeking you out. And indeed someone is doing just that. When the feeling of pressure from this surrounding wall increases, you have been found and are being surrounded with intention. Break that intention with ceremony. Don't think this invasion will go away just because you pray for its removal. You must do something concrete and empathic. The ceremony may involve the use of rattles and drums, water or fire, crystals, dancing, chanting, anything that you have found works for you. Open this ceremony with an offering to the six directions and a prayer for aid and protection. Make this prayer to God, the Earth and Earth-keepers, and the four directions. It would be a good idea to include in this prayer for aid and protection the four elements and the three non-human kingdoms. One can never have too much help.

I would consider whether you find dawn or twilight to be the more powerful of the two times, and choose that time for this ceremony. Smudge yourself or cleanse yourself with water if you want to approach the powers that be in a cleansed condition.

Speak up. Talk to the six directions, starting with Up and what Up means to you, then address the Earth and Earth-keepers, and then speaking to East, South, West, and North in that order. Talk then to the elements and kingdoms, if you wish to include them in this ceremony. You may make offerings to the elements and the kingdoms, as well as to the six sacred directions. Talk plainly. Do not do this ceremony silently. Speak aloud and be blunt. Say that you have exorcised someone or something and feel the need of help, such as guidance and protection. If you believe in angels, ask for angelic protection.

If you are wondering why you have to ask for help, why the

universe doesn't already know you are in need, the answer is that while the universe does know, free will is a fundamental law of our lives, and it would be a violation of your free will for protection to be given to you without your asking for it. Wishing or expecting won't do it; you have to *ask*. In the universe we live in, you must ask or you don't get.

Cleansing of Haunted Areas

We do best with getting rid of ghosts' energy when we remember that only very rarely is a ghost a personality. It's usually just energy, leftover feeling from a trauma. In that way, it is real but not human.

The rare exception makes itself plain by moving objects around in your house, pulling your hair, crying, or in other ways demonstrating that it is a person. If it is a person and not just energy that's attached itself to the area around your home, you must seek the help of an expert exorcist, not just for your protection, but for the sake of the ghost. A ghost with a lot of its personality still with it can easily be damaged. You must never say the word *dead* to a ghost. More than likely, if he really comprehended his state, he would have left this realm. Telling a dead person he's dead can cause a terrible shock. A ghost is a bad enough shape without having to hear an abrupt announcement that he's dead.

If all you have around is energy, you will know this because there won't be any manifestations of a real person, only a feeling of coldness, a feeling of unhappiness, a feeling that makes you want to stay away from a particular area. If this is what you are dealing with, have no qualms about getting rid of it.

The first line of defense is prayer. You don't have to decide, on the spot, whether or not you believe in an omnipotent being or, if you do, how to address the deity. All you need is to know that there is a power beyond your individual power. If you don't believe in an omniscient overseeing god, then look around at the world you live in and see if you can find its beginning and its end. That is as much god as anyone needs.

Look carefully at the area you think is haunted. How big a space are you going to exorcise? You'll need to know that before you start gathering equipment.

Obtain enough sea salt to sprinkle over all of the land you're working on. If the haunted area is inside a house, you will have to sprinkle it there and leave it for ten hours, allowing nobody to walk on it or otherwise disturb it.

Get one black and one white candle, each one long enough to burn for at least two hours.

Your first line of defense being prayer, which is supplication to something bigger than we are, pray to what you believe in, even if you are praying to a concept such as energy. Be sure to hold the black candle and maintain your full concentration while praying. Ask the power to help you remove negative energy without causing any harm. Ask for protection for yourself and, in case there is more in the haunted area than just left over energy from a trauma, ask for protection for the ghost whose energy is attached to the area.

Speaking aloud toward the earth, tell the spirit of Earth that you need its help. Say there is sad or angry or confused energy here and tell the earth that you want this energy removed. The earth is very powerful and it will, given a little boost, begin to transmute the negative force.

If the energy you're concerned with is in a wall or on the ceiling, you nevertheless want to talk directly down to the floor and, thus, to the earth because the negative energy, no matter how high up it is, will be transmuted primarily through the earth. So even if the haunted place is on or inside a wall, your focus should be on the floor.

Having asked for help, wait a moment and do nothing. Feel whatever response your prayer may receive from the haunted place. Do you sense a stirring there, an awakening? Fine. *Don't talk directly to the haunted energy.* Continue talking to the power you were praying to, knowing that the energy is aware of what you are doing and knows there is a change on the way.

Sprinkle sea salt all over the affected area. If a wall or

ceiling is affected, throw some at the place involved and let the salt touch it for a moment before it slides down onto the floor. Once the salt has been sprinkled, leave it alone. Do not touch it and don't let anyone else touch it.

Salt attracts energy to itself. It binds energy. If you are to remove the haunted energy, then you must gather it together in one place. If it is able to move around, you won't be able to control what happens to it.

Light the black candle and set it as close to the center of the haunted place as you can. If the negative energy is in the wall or on the ceiling, set the candle down on the floor—not near the wall, or you could cause a fire. The black candle and salt will draw all negative energy in the room toward them and will aid the earth in drawing it down into the ground.

Let the black candle burn down. Do not blow it out. If it begins to flicker and you need to trim the wick, put the flame out by waving something at it but do not blow it out. The candle, is a powerful drawing agent now, because of your prayers: We are not trying to remove *you*. Your breath is as much an imprint of your essence as fingerprints are an imprint of your body.

When the candle has burned all the way down, you can wave it out for good. Let it burn for at least an hour; two hours is better.

Leave the black candle right where it is and, without disturbing the salt, leave the area for ten hours. Be sure the candle is no longer burning. Cleanse yourself by using any of the methods detailed later in this chapter under the heading "Cleansing Ourselves." Stay out of the room for the full ten hours and keep others out, including animals.

When the ten hours are up (it can be a longer period of time if ten hours isn't convenient for you) go back to the ground or room, bringing with you the white candle, a broom and dustpan (not a vacuum cleaner or other electronic appliance), and a paper bag big enough to contain the salt. Bring with you a cup of cold water or, if the area is bigger than twenty feet, more. You will need approximately one cup of water to twenty feet of space.

With as much speed as you can produce without becoming nervous, sweep up all of the salt and dump it into the paper bag. Do not use a plastic bag.

Pick up the black candle and place it in the paper bag. If it's convenient to pick up the candle before sweeping the salt, do so.

Leave the white candle, unlit, in the room or on the ground while you take the bag, now containing salt and black candle, to a place where you can bury them a foot deep without interfering with your garden. If you have no ground in which to bury the bag, you can put it in the trash but this must be accomplished with sincere prayer: state that this bag is filled with the means through which powerful negativity was removed from your house or your yard. Place the bag in your trash can and make a firm cutting motion from the back of your head across the top, and then all the way down your front, past the abdomen. This will remove any negative energy that might have attached itself to you during the removal of the haunted energy from the house or grounds. It is unlikely that any of this energy has touched you, but safety is always a good policy.

Go back to the area and light the white candle, being prepared to stay with it for at least two hours. You can blow this one out if need be, because the negative energy is gone now and you can't hurt yourself by implicating your essence in the room any more. Place the water container near the candle.

Do not leave a lit candle unguarded.

After the candle is lit, make prayers for the cleansing you have done and ask that the higher power bring positive energy to the recently-cleansed place. Sit on the floor or ground while you pray because you are a conduit and your body on the earth or floor will help to conduct positive energy to the place.

After the white candle has burned for at least ten minutes, place your right hand palm down over the water container and your left hand palm up above your shoulder but not over your head. Ask the higher power for blessing and energy to manifest positive energy in this place. Leave your hands as they are for a full minute. The energy you asked for will be received into your left hand and channeled into the water by your right hand.

Having finished the water blessing, use your hands to sprinkle the water all around and through the previously-haunted area. Water is a powerful energy-giver and the blessing will have imbued it with good energy, which will sink into the earth or touch the floor, carpeted or not, long enough to attach that good energy to the area. The blessed energy will follow the negative energy down into the ground or onto the floor and will prevent the negative energy from rising again, like putting a cap on a bottle.

Let the white candle burn for as long as you can, though two hours will do. Sit with the candle and say whatever prayers come to you.

The candles and salt and water are helpers, but the vitalizing force in the room is you. It was your personal desire to heal negative energy that made this exorcism happen.

After the candle has been removed from the room or the grounds, blow it out and, if you can, bury it in the earth with prayers for the area that was cleansed. Pray for the salt, water and candles, since these must be honored for their work as you are honored for your participation. At last, be sure to say prayers for the earth.

Cleansing Ourselves With Water

In the course of our daily lives we come near to other people's sadness, cruelty, hopelessness, anger, frustration, and confusion. Each of these energies affects us and, at the end of a day, weighs on us collectively. Rather than be burdened by other people's negative feelings, we can live free of these unnecessary intrusions by incorporating a few cleansing methods into our daily or weekly routine. They're not hard to make use of and the benefits we receive from taking the time to use them will soon become apparent.

Bathing and Other Water Cleansings

A quick way to ground negative energies—our own or other people's—from our physical and etheric bodies is to fill a tub with tepid water, adding to the water a handful of sea salt and a quarter cup of white vinegar. Add the salt and vinegar while the water is running, so these are distributed all through the bath water. If you don't like to bathe without perfume or skin softener, these may be added after the salt and vinegar, but not before.

Sit in that water for a full half hour. Every once in a while, splash some water on your chest, if the water level doesn't reach that far, and onto your throat. Have a clean washcloth handy, one you don't use for soaping your body. Dip the cloth into the water several times while you sit there and apply the wet cloth to your forehead.

This bath will disperse and ground the negative energies you've picked up during the day or the week. The regular baths or showers you may take each day will not do the same dispersing and grounding that the salt and vinegar do, though surrounding your body with water is always soothing and water will always help disperse some negativity from your body and your psychic energy.

During the day, when you can't get to a bathtub, it will help keep your psychic energies clean if you occasionally get to a bathroom and flick drops of cold water around your head, especially the top of the head, and around your heart area and wrists.

Some people spray their faces periodically during the day with deionized or other water so as to keep their skin from drying out. People who work in offices which are too hot during the winter and too heavily air conditioned throughout the spring and summer benefit from this several-times-a-day attention to their faces. If you do this, why not put a drop or two of white vinegar in your spray bottle? It will help cleanse your energy body and a couple of drops won't leave a vinegar odor on you for more than a moment.

Water Blessings for You and Others

When you are in a pool, natural or chlorinated, you may wish to try the following blessing and see how it suits you. I do it every chance I get. I find it soothing and energizing at once.

Remember that water is a powerful disperser and magnifier. This is where the legend comes from that magicians can't cross water. When a magician has been making invocations, he knows he must maintain the most delicate balances in order to keep his esoteric work completely under his control. Because water magnifies everything, he takes a chance, when his body is positioned over water, that his carefully wrought formulae will change when the energies of these are touched by water's great power.

The power of water to magnify energy can be used in prayer and blessings. Taking a deep breath while holding in your mind the ones you love—including yourself—and saying whatever blessing upon these you feel suits you and them, plunge into the water, being sure to cover your whole head. Come up again and say a similar blessing on the rest of life on this planet, and then plunge yourself into the water again. Be sure to cover your whole head when you submerge. For the third and final blessing, create a prayer for the whole universe, or for all the universes, and then plunge in one more time, making sure to cover your whole head.

It isn't necessary, of course, to limit yourself to three blessings. You may feel it's appropriate to plunge in once for every family member, or for everything you perceive as needing healing . . . the four kingdoms of the planet, the water and air and earth of the planet. You may wish to say a prayer for an endeavor of yours or a friend's.

The first few times you do this blessing, try it the way I have described the process because it is too easy for us human beings to pray only for what we are currently engaged in, and to forget the existence of the rest of the world, the all-life, the planet as a living entity, and the universe beyond the Earth. After you've performed this blessing ceremony a few times, you can trust yourself to depart from the way I have described it and to recreate the ceremony to suit you.

Water Blessing for the All-Life

When you feel the time is right—and the time may be during the full or the new moon, because moon cycles affect water— take a glass of water outside and put it on the ground. Think first about drought, about how much we all need water. Consider how the plant life and animals need it, how the birds and fish need water. The Earth is composed mostly of water, not of land masses.

Then, without employing your intellect, allow your spirit to compose a prayer to the effect that all life on this realm shall have as much water as it requires, always. Honor Water as the living entity it is. Tell it how much you honor it. Send up a prayer to the Creator asking that there be sufficient water for all living beings, including human beings but not excluding anyone else.

Hold your right hand over the water, palm down, while holding your left hand, palm up, between your left shoulder and your head. Ask blessings of the Creator on this water and on Water, the entity. Hold the position for a moment so as to receive the blessing in your left hand and pass it through your right hand into the glass of water. Then pour the water onto the roots of a favorite tree or around a plant. If you like, you can pour it into a dish for the animals who live around your house. Drink a little of it yourself.

If you live in a densely-populated area and feel it would cause you trouble to be seen performing this ritual outside, then do it inside. After you have swallowed some of it, pour the water into a plant, a window box, or even down the sink as long as you make it clear that you want this blessed water to return to its source and energize the water it came from, whether that water is a reservoir a mile away, the Hudson river, or the Pacific ocean.

By performing this ritual on a regular basis you will bring blessings to Water and to the wish that all living beings will have as much water as each needs. At the same time, you will extend your respect and good wishes to Water and to the all-life, thus making a powerful connection between you and all of creation.

As is always the case, a blessing given outward brings some blessing back to us. This must not, of course, be our motive for praying, but why shouldn't we, as legitimate dwellers in this realm, be blessed as we offer our blessings to our companions?

Cleansing With Fire

Fire cleanses completely. Burning something negative works without any effort on your part. But you do have to prepare the item to be burned in such a way as to collect all the negativity first, so the prayers that go with a fire cleansing are important.

Fire has an obvious physical effect. It changes things from form to formless, or nearly formless. The spiritual characteristic of fire-cleansing is more powerful even than its physical counterpart. The changes created by burning are so far-reaching that we must always say prayers for the protection of all involved in a situation before we light a fire.

If you have a photo and believe there is negative energy in the photo, you are within your rights to burn the picture but not before you say *aloud* prayers for the protection of the people in that picture. We can never know for certain that someone is evil, not ever. And what becomes of evil is entirely the business of the Almighty, not ours.

Place the photo or letter or other burnable item in a fire grate or, if you have no fireplace, then in a sink or tub. Sprinkle sea salt all over and around the object. The salt will attract and hold all negative energies to itself. Don't pile on so much salt that you can't get a fire going.

Speaking aloud, ask for protection for any beings associated with the burnings. In this, you must hold nothing back. Think of anyone who might be connected with the picture or letter or whatever, and even if you are sure that someone involved meant to cause you harm, you do not ever have the right to retaliate by trying to cause him harm in any way. Pray for the welfare of anyone connected with the burning and state that you wish to cause harm to none, including yourself. State that the burning is meant as a purification *and nothing else.*

Having left the salt on and around the item for at least five minutes, and after making your prayers, light the fire. Either stand there and watch it or turn away from it. Let the fire burn itself out; do not put it out.

If you are of a mind to, look at the charred remains of the item and see if there is a face, a shape, or any interesting configuration there. It may or may not tell you something about the situation you and the fire have just purified.

Dispose of the remains with final prayers for the protection and blessing of all concerned, and thank Fire, the entity, for its help.

Earth: The Greatest Power

While minerals have their role to play in protection and cleansing, and while we would have a hard time creating good energy and dismissing bad without ceremony, the elements and the sacred directions, there is one element of exorcism, cleansing and healing that is the most powerful single entity available to us and that is earth. Dirt.

The ground that changes our bodies into compost and eventually into tomato plants, that cleanses any item buried in it for a day or more, that draws our spirit back into our body safely when we are off-balance, this is the most powerful force in our realm.

If you are troubled by an attack that won't be stopped and have not as yet figured out what your next step should be, sit on the floor or ground and place your hands, palm-down, flat on the surface. Place your upper forehead, near the hairline, on the surface and rest it there. Anyone who has had experience with healing by transferring energy knows that the hands and head are channels for healing force. These places also attract earth-energy and pull it into your body.

While writing this book, I was assaulted by one of the most gruesome and vicious attacks I have ever experienced. I was asleep and, I suppose, had wandered out of the body in a tired state when I ought to have been resting, not travelling. I was accosted by a being who had the appearance of a white, brown-haired female, and who told me she was a Christian minister. While talking to me she wove a blanket of energy around me and managed to paralyze me completely. I found myself utterly terrified, unable to move any part of my body. She bent over me and smiled, showing that her central front teeth were missing. All I could see were her enraptured eyes and her cuspid, or fang, teeth. As she moved toward the flesh beneath my ear, I screamed to the higher powers for protection from this vampire. A force intruding on my physical body, at the lymph area near the armpit, began to pull me awake. I knew that the attack on the lymph was far more dangerous than the vampire's fangs on my astral body. I forced myself into wakefulness and jumped out of bed as soon as I was able to move at all, which was not immediately.

I felt a venom-like substance begin to surge through my body and, invoking all the powers of Light, I began an attempt to heal myself and stop the movement of the venom. I was unable to stop its course, and I worked for two hours, feeling every change in the direction the venom moved. I know I am sensitive to alien energies in the bloodstream because I have always been able to track the effects of insect and spider bites through the upper and lower body, the deep tissue organs, the fingers and toes, all of it. More than one friend has scoffed at this, but I am certain I can feel the movement of venom, and I felt, without let-up for two hours, the progress of this substance through my body.

I first used a morion (black-smoky) crystal in the armpit, holding it so the terminal point was directed at the floor and the base of the crystal was as tight against my skin as I could make it. I rubbed both the armpit and the place beneath my ear, where the teeth had touched my astral body, with white vinegar. I used salt on both places to contain the substance, and a piece of hematite to hold the blood still. I called for help, again and again, from every powerful being I have ever called on.

I had had only an hour's sleep after a long work day. It was only when my mind cleared enough for real concentration that I thought to sit on the floor, place my palms face-down, and rest my head on the floor. The relief was instantaneous. The venom-like substance continued its progress, because it was well into the bloodstream and could not be stopped, but I felt much stronger for that contact with the earth, and I clearly remember that the moment I placed my hands and head on the floor, the earth energy rose up to meet them.

All of the exorcist's helpers have their place, but I offer this incident as illustration of the power of the ground, the earth we walk on every day and whom some people barely notice. After I had employed several remedies and after each had, I know, affected some help, it was the earth that gave the fastest relief and felt the most powerful.

The earth is a highly intelligent, very powerful being. It can be a friend and adviser. All we need do is consider it a living, *aware* being, and we will be on the right track in our relationship with it.

Cleansing With Earth

When we have had a difficult day or are tired or have been depleted by spending time in crowds, a good way to balance our psychic energy and bring energy into our bodies is to lie face down on the ground for about fifteen minutes. The earth, which transmutes energy so powerfully, will absorb our anxiety, or at least the energies produced by the anxiety, and take our negative energies. It will revive us, replacing the negative energies with positive.

If you have an object that needs to be cleansed, bury it in the earth for a full day and night, knowing that the earth will transmute the energies surrounding the object as efficiently as it transmutes our negative energies.

If, however, someone has magnetized an object for a purpose, the earth's energy will remove some of the negativity but cannot remove all of it. This is because the magnetizing of an object is affected on the physical *and* the astral realms. To dedicate an object to a purpose or use it to influence someone, the occult work done on that object has to be done on its physical being and the astral counterpart of the object. If we suspect that someone has set negative energies within a crystal, for example, or imprinted a purpose on a book before it was published, stamped an angry intention on a letter or placed a harm-intention on an object, we must do a ceremony to remove these before we can put the object in the earth for cleansing. Once the intention has been removed through ceremony, it ceases to exist in the astral realm. All that remains to do, then, is cleanse the object. This can of course be done through smudging or other cleansing techniques; the earth-cleansing is not the only technique available to us.

If the concept of setting an intention on a concrete object is puzzling to you, think of it as the black magic version of a priest blessing a religious medal. Negative intention is the opposite of a blessing. Intentional blessing includes imbueing an object with energy, doing so with a particular effect in mind. A mild version of intentional blessing is the act of giving a birthday present to a friend. If you hand an object to someone and there is a real suggestion of good will in the act, this is a kind of blessing.

If you wish to cleanse an object that may have been negatively magnetized, first pile sea salt all over it to gather some of the negative energy in the object. Leave the salt there for an hour. Lighting a blue or white candle and leaving the candle beside the object will invoke good spirit, as long as you ask the help of God as you light the candle. Unless you ask, silently or aloud, for power or energizing, and unless you make this request of a higher power, the candle will be just a candle. Candles, like other objects, are not magical unless they are made magical.

Having left the salt on the object for at least an hour, with or without a burning candle (do not leave a flame unattended) then remove the salt by pouring it into a paper bag. Holding the item aloft or, if it is too heavy for that, placing both your hands on it, your palms down, beseech the aid of God and if you like, the guardian powers of the sacred directions. Ask that the imprinting on the object be removed entirely. Concentrating all of your consciousness on God, or whatever is the highest authority and power in which you believe, take a long, slow deep breath and then blow directly at the object as though blowing out a flame. Be sure to exhale completely.

Bury the object in the ground for a week. If there is a possibility of frost, consider that some items such as quartz crystal may break during a frost and refrain from burying the object until the danger of freezing is over. In this situation, you must not allow the object to be gazed at or touched by anyone, including yourself, while you wait for a safe burial time. Wrap the object in a black cloth—pure cotton is best but not mandatory—and place it out of sight for the time being.

After you have buried the object and retrieved it, take care to replace the earth in the position you found it before you dug it up. Respect earth: you owe it a great deal.

Healing Our Lives: The Age of True Remembering

Whether we have been attacked by evil, preyed on by sorcerers, let down by a friend or simply dealt ourselves a bad blow, we always need to attend to our own healing with at least as much dedication and as strong an intention as we bring to helping others.

Healing comes from within and without us, for when we reach a profound level of awareness and create within our being a state receptive to healing, our needs reverberate to the all-life. When we look within, as long as we do our looking honestly, we will attract help from creation. Once we have embarked on a course of spiritual searching, we will always find, in the realm of spirit, sympathetic responses to our endeavors and our needs. It helps immeasurably if we ask for help and guidance, but even when we forget to do this there is always an empathetic link between the *awakened* human spirit and the realms of the all-life and of Spirit. As long as we maintain, on a daily basis, an appreciation and respectful awareness of the joyous, powerful creation of which we are a part, we will thrive.

Our continual thriving is life-enhancing for us and provides healing between us and the all-life. That healing is essential to the future of our existence in this realm. The rift we created between us and the spiritual life of everything else in this realm must be healed before the human race can move into its next evolutionary cycle. The breaking of the sacred circle of creation was our doing; it is we who must mend the break. Each time any member of the human race experiences himself as a part of Spirit, he creates a healing vibration between himself and creation. When all of humankind is ready to see the rift between our species and creation, and everyone moves to heal that rift, then we will enter the Age of True Remembering, and know what we are *for,* what we are meant to *do,* and who we really *are.*

There are people alive now who have retrieved enough of their real selves that they can partake of some of this Remembering. These people recall what it feels like to fly in their spirit, to travel the earth and all the realms away from here, and to bring into waking consciousness everything they encounter during spirit-flight. Every day, one, two, thirty or a hundred people take the first step toward True Remembering. The time is coming when many people will take those first holy steps. But until every human being turns away from his wrong self, no one will be allowed the fullest expression of his true self. Until everyone remembers what it is like to fly, his spirit soaring without restriction or limitation, none of us will fly as high as we might. The awakening to spirit-flight is not a process of learning but of Remembering, for all of us have flown. *We have taught ourselves to forget.*

It is a law of the Creator Spirit that all must wait for the last sister and brother to begin Remembering. Only when everyone is prepared may we enter fully into our next evolutionary stage, the Age of True Remembering.

The End and the Beginning of the Circle

Many mystical traditions would have us believe that when we incarnate into earth life, we strand ourselves in a bleak, unforgiving realm, a place from which we can expect experience but no joy, and from which we are best parted as soon as we have finished learning the lessons we came here to learn. It is only, we are told, when we leave here and ascend to a far better place that we will be able to repair our battered souls and become whole again.

But it is here on the earth that we must repair ourselves, for it is here where we lost our way. We cannot find our lost way in another realm because we did not lose our way elsewhere. It is on the earth, where all things are possible, that we must recover the spiritual purpose with which we were created. Each of us agreed to carry this purpose; our agreement is part of our ancient, sacred vow. Here is where we must rediscover and live with the integrity-of-being we brought with us when humankind first arrived in this world. Here is where we will heal the rift between ourselves and the sacred circle of creation. We still possess *and are bound by* our integrity-of-being, but most of us have lost touch with it. We will find it again in our personal share of the collective unconscious, and we will find that sacred reservoir when we begin again to honor creation and our own spirit.

It is in this world that we will find the heaven and nirvana of mystical tradition. The earth, the sacred directions, the elementary powers and the three kingdoms we live among are the way, for us, to heaven. It must be, for if we do not find the God-in-all while we are here, how *will* we find it? If we lose our communion with the God-force while we inhabit this realm, we will lose our communication with the Creator.

We human beings are not going to destroy this planet, for it is a wiser spirit than we know, and will not permit us to destroy it. If we betray the sacred vow that still lives *and functions* within us, if we lose ourselves to our delusional separateness, then we will lose the human race.

As mentioned earlier, no hostages will be taken from the human race in the final encounter between the all-life and we who declared war on it. Either all of us will go, or all of us will stay.

What awaits us? The crossroad we approach now will show us our Way, our individual and collective Way. When each of us agrees to forsake the path of delusion, to step away from the common road and make our own Way in the world without permission from others and guidance from his wrong self, then we and all the life of this realm will dance together again, as was meant to be.

What is at risk now is not "the environment," which is infinitely more complex and powerful than humankind is yet capable of understanding. What is at stake as we approach the ultimate crossroad is us. We set ourselves against ourselves when we stepped away from creation. It is ourselves with whom we do daily battle, not just the all-life and our host, the earth. If we do not reclaim our true selves and know, once more, our purpose and our reason for being, then it is we, and not the earth, who will perish.

Whatever your path in life, I wish you good journeys.

The Light is always with us

ACKNOWLEDGMENTS

For insights and help, thanks to DL, KM, CJP, WW, DW, JD, MK, JFM and especially JC.

The author is grateful to the University of Pennsylvania, Swarthmore College and the Helen Kate Furness Library for the use of their resources.

Thanks to the *aloha* spirit and the ancient powers for aid and illumination.

Thanks for permission to quote from *The Seed and the Sower,* by Laurens Van Der Post, to William Morrow and Company, New York.

Made in the USA
Columbia, SC
30 December 2019